RALPH WALDO EMERSON

RALPH WALDO EMERSON

THE MAJOR POETRY

Edited, with Introduction and Commentary, by
ALBERT J. VON FRANK

THE BELKNAP PRESS
OF HARVARD UNIVERSITY PRESS
Cambridge, Massachusetts
London, England | 2015

First Printing

Additional copyright notices appear on pages 307–309, which constitute an extension
of the copyright page.

Library of Congress Cataloging-in-Publication Data
Emerson, Ralph Waldo, 1803–1882.
[Poems. Selections]
   Ralph Waldo Emerson : the major poetry / edited, with introduction and
commentary by Albert J. von Frank.
      pages cm
   Includes bibliographical references and index.
   ISBN 978-0-674-04959-8 (alk. paper)
   I. von Frank, Albert J., editor. II. Title.
PS1624.A1 2015
811′.3—dc22   2014043588

CONTENTS

From *May-Day and Other Pieces* (1867)

From *Selected Poems* (1876)

Uncollected Poems

ABBREVIATIONS

CEC   *The Correspondence of Emerson and Carlyle.* Edited by Joseph
       Slater. New York: Columbia University Press, 1964.

CS   *The Complete Sermons of Ralph Waldo Emerson.* Edited by Albert
       J. von Frank, general editor; Ronald A. Bosco, Andrew H. Del-
       banco, Wesley T. Mott, and Teresa Toulouse, editors. 4 vols. Co-
       lumbia: University of Missouri, 1989–1992.

CW   *The Collected Works of Ralph Waldo Emerson.* Edited by Alfred R.
       Ferguson, Robert E. Spiller, Joseph Slater, Douglas Emory Wil-
       son, and Ronald A. Bosco, general editors; Robert E. Burkholder,
       Jean Ferguson Carr, Joel Myerson, Philip Nicoloff, Barbara L.
       Packer, Albert J. von Frank, Wallace E. Williams, and Thomas
       Wortham, editors. 10 vols. Cambridge, Mass.: The Belknap Press
       of Harvard University Press, 1971–2013.

EL   *The Early Lectures of Ralph Waldo Emerson, 1833–1842.* Edited by
       Stephen E. Whicher, Robert E. Spiller, and Wallace E. Williams. 3
       vols. Cambridge, Mass.: The Belknap Press of Harvard University
       Press, 1959–1972.

ETE   *The Letters of Ellen Tucker Emerson.* Edited by Edith E. W. Gregg.
       2 vols. Kent, Ohio: Kent State University Press, 1982.

FuL   *The Letters of Margaret Fuller.* Edited by Robert N. Hudspeth. 6
       vols. Ithaca: Cornell University Press, 1983–1999.

JMN   *The Journals and Miscellaneous Notebooks of Ralph Waldo Emer-
       son.* Edited by William H. Gilman and Ralph H. Orth, chief edi-
       tors; Linda Allardt, Ronald A. Bosco, George P. Clark, Merrell R.
       Davis, Harrison Hayford, David W. Hill, Glen M. Johnson, J. E.
       Parsons, A. W. Plumstead, Merton M. Sealts, Jr., and Susan Sutton
       Smith, editors; Ruth H. Bennett, associate editor. 16 vols. Cam-
       bridge, Mass.: The Belknap Press of Harvard University Press,
       1960–1982.

L   *The Letters of Ralph Waldo Emerson.* Edited by Ralph L. Rusk and
            Eleanor M. Tilton. 10 vols. New York: Columbia University Press,
            1939–1995.

LL   *The Later Lectures of Ralph Waldo Emerson, 1843–1871.* Edited by
            Ronald A. Bosco and Joel Myerson. 2 vols. Athens: University of
            Georgia Press, 2001.

OED   *The Oxford English Dictionary.* (All references are to the current
            [2008] on-line edition.)

OFL   *One First Love: The Letters of Ellen Louisa Tucker to Ralph Waldo
            Emerson.* Edited by Edith W. Gregg. Cambridge, Mass.: The
            Belknap Press of Harvard University Press, 1962.

PN   *The Poetry Notebooks of Ralph Waldo Emerson.* Edited by Ralph
            H. Orth, Albert J. von Frank, Linda Allardt, and David W. Hill.
            Columbia: University of Missouri Press, 1986.

Strauch,   Carl F. Strauch. "A Critical and Variorum Edition of the Poems of
Diss.   Ralph Waldo Emerson." PhD diss., Yale University, 1946.

TN   *The Topical Notebooks of Ralph Waldo Emerson.* Edited by Ralph
            H. Orth, chief editor; Ronald A. Bosco, Glen M. Johnson, and Su-
            san Sutton Smith, editors. 3 vols. Columbia: University of Mis-
            souri Press, 1990–1994.

W   *The Complete Works of Ralph Waldo Emerson.* Edited by Edward
            Waldo Emerson. Centenary Edition. 12 vols. Boston and New
            York: Houghton, Mifflin, 1903–1904.

INTRODUCTION

*Why should not we have a poetry and philosophy of
insight and not of tradition?*

—Ralph Waldo Emerson, *Nature, CW* 1:7

EMERSON'S readers know him best as an artist in prose.
From 1833 to 1873 he earned his living as a lecturer, persisting through
early controversies to emerge later in life as the country's most revered
public intellectual. Today he survives to us as a master of the essay
form, a philosopher of self-reliance, and the central figure in the "tran-
scendentalist," or idealist, strain of American romanticism. It may be
that none of his many claims on our attention has been more generally
slighted than the commanding position he achieved as a theoretician
and practitioner of poetry. It is still very much a minority view that
David Porter advanced in calling Emerson "a poetry theorist of pro-
found reach, a revolutionary committed to the introduction of a radical
aesthetics."[1] With the evidence newly available in the recent editions
of Emerson's poems and poetry notebooks, it is time to look again,
with fresh eyes, at his accomplishments under this important heading.[2]
What makes Emerson's innovative view of the function of poetry so
entirely distinctive and so consequential is his belief that poetry and
philosophy comprise in fact a single pursuit. In 1834, just as he discov-
ered his mature poetic voice in such works as "The Rhodora," "Each
and All" and "The Snow-Storm," he endorsed the view of the German
writer Novalis that "the division of Philosopher and Poet is only ap-
parent, and to the disadvantage of both" (*JMN* 4:302).[3] Emerson was
schooling himself just then in the writer's cardinal virtue of sincerity,

becoming practically convinced that in order to be authentic the language of ideas could not be conventional, that no true mode of expression could ever be prior to or independent of the thought to be conveyed, but was inevitably and organically a coeval birth. "What is poetry," he asked, "but the truest expression?" (*EL* 3:361). Emerson discovered early that poetic language is not a common inheritance but rather an innovation caught in the nick of time, belonging always to a radically creative spirit—and offering a way, as Ezra Pound would later say, of making it new. Thus the first step toward a "poetry and philosophy of insight and not of tradition" was to clear one's personal field of vision of artificialities and all second-handedness, and especially of such prior constraints as were implied by the classical rhetoric and poetic diction of contemporary "fine writing." Emerson would insist on "life" (or, in his many synonyms, "change," "metamorphosis," "flowing," "ascension," or "evolution") in place of the forms as already given.

In November 1834, when he moved permanently to "the quiet fields of my fathers" in Concord, relinquishing at last all thought of a career in the ministry (*L* 1:420–21), he turned, emancipated, to literature, declaring in his journal, "Henceforth I design not to utter any speech, poem, or book that is not entirely & peculiarly my work" (*JMN* 4:335). This intellectual declaration of independence—anticipating the clarion call of the American Scholar Address of 1837—led in December 1834 to the commencement of his first major poetry notebook (called "P"). Before the month was out he had written one of his finest poems, "The Snow-Storm." While there is something rather deliberate-seeming in this embrace of the poet's vocation, his newfound sense of purpose was in fact a kind of negotiation between inspiration (as Emerson understood the concept) and the painstaking private labor of making, the latter always in service to the former. Acknowledging what was ineffable in the act of literary creation, he once defined the Muse as *"supervoluntary ends effected by supervoluntary means"* (*LL* 1:179). The practical validity of the proposition was most strikingly illustrated to him in 1851 in the writing of "Days," which seemed as effortless as dreaming.[4] Nevertheless, over the course of his career he filled 1,700 pages in the poetry notebooks with rough drafts, fair copies, and fragments (long or short, abandoned or developed), precisely because he was a craftsman, one who revised extensively, submitting the inarticulate inspiration, as it were, to his judgment and knowledge of the world.[5] Always he would insist on a synergy of passivity and activity in his philosophy of composition.

Among the various influences that turned Emerson into a poet at the age of thirty-two was the example of Ellen Louisa Tucker, his first wife. Their brief time together (she died of consumption in 1831, at the age of 19) was a particularly intense unfolding of the themes of love and death (instilling, in consequence, an appreciation for the fleeting comedy of presence and the enduring tragedy of absence), especially as mediated through the verses that each addressed to the other. The poems that Ellen contributed were of the period, perhaps, in the way they dealt with sentiment, but they were also lucid revelations of her character and situation, simple, direct, and with a minimum of flourish or adornment. Years later Emerson recalled these poems as "very sweet, & on the way to all high merits" (*JMN* 10:188).[6] One might infer that they taught him something at a crucial moment in his emotional history about writing sincerely from one's experience and not for effect. For all of Emerson's life after Ellen's death, the Muse would be a decidedly feminine presence.[7]

In "The Poet," the long lead article in *Essays: Second Series* (1844), Emerson dealt harshly with certain unnamed popular poets, who, being "contented with a civil and conformed manner of living," lacked "vision"—that is to say, had no unmediated access to the world—and so were condemned to "write poems from the fancy, at a safe distance from their own experience" (*CW* 3:3). For Emerson, the "truth" that poetry had permanently to be concerned with was that to which personal knowledge or experience gave access. Here indeed was the key to the advancing "high merits" of Ellen's verse—its constant dependence on experience that, refashioned and clearly expressed as a private insight of hers, could not be contradicted, denied, or rendered false. Such originality, neither "civil" nor "conformed," must necessarily have a perfect authenticity and deep effect. Whether Emerson dealt in his own poems with "natural facts" (a rhodora, a humble-bee, a river, or a mountain) or with the "spiritual facts" they signified to him (*CW* 1:17), this was the kind of reportorial truth, grounded in self-reliance and firsthand experience, that his philosophical poetry enshrined. It followed that the holder of such a view would reject "stock-poetry," in which "the rhythm is given, and the sense is adapted to it" (*JMN* 8:97), or that he might doubt the credentials of the more overtly melodious

poets, like Tennyson or Poe—as, for example, when he famously re-
ferred to the latter as "the jingle-man."[8] For Emerson, appropriate tune-
fulness arose organically from the subject and could not be artificially
helped along: "It is not metres," he said, "but a meter-making argument,
that makes a poem,—a thought so passionate and alive, that, like the
spirit of a plant or an animal, it has an architecture of its own, and
adorns nature with a new thing" (*CW* 3:6). Poe was deeply instructed
in the rules of prosody; Emerson was antinomian: "Leaving rule and
pale forethought," he declared in "Merlin I," the poet "shall aye climb /
For his rhyme" (ll. 32–33). In this respect as well, Emerson bid defiance
to popular expectation. Some judged from the result that he had a defi-
cient ear for music, but those who luckily had the poems from his own
lips were left with no such impression.

Emerson's work was in some part about promoting the intellectual
possibilities of poetry to some equality with the easier requirements for
tunefulness or feeling. Poe, for example, had found nothing legitimate
in a poet's concern for truth and explicitly rejected it as "the heresy of
The Didactic."[9] Also laboring under the Victorian belief that poetry
was an affair of the heart and not of the head, Matthew Arnold would
concede that if, indeed, Emerson "makes one think," still he fails fatally
as a poet ever to be "simple, sensuous, or impassioned."[10] But the in-
tellectual side of things could not be fenced out; it was, rather, how-
ever much denied, the special province of expression in verse. "You
shall not speak truth in prose," Emerson once said: "You *may* in verse"
(*EL* 3:359). Good Platonist that he was, Emerson understood that form
in nature or in art was the necessary enactment of or sequel to some
thought, so that all of creation became representative and meaning-
ful; all was symbol. How much this came as a surprise to readers in the
1840s is evidenced by the initially incredulous reviewers, both those
who recognized Emerson's originality and those whose expectations
about how poetry was meant to work were stressed and tested.

The unaccustomed glimpses of philosophy—or indeed of mere
thinking—felt like invitations to struggle and so led to charges of "diffi-
culty," abstraction, aloofness, and coolness of temperament. Certainly,
Emerson taunted his audience with interesting versions of unavailabil-
ity, with exotic allusions to Greek fable, with German mysticism, and
eventually with Muslim, Hindu, and Confucian hints of an ultimate

Orient. In placing "The Sphinx" at the very entryway to his first collection (*Poems,* 1847), Emerson made it clear that he was trying to do something extraordinary in challenging his audience to engage with poetry in a new way.

⟪⟫

Emerson published two major collections of verse during his lifetime, each summing up a distinct phase of his work as a poet. The first—*Poems* (1847)—gathered what he had written since the breakout year of 1834, including the four poems he had published in James Freeman Clarke's *Western Messenger,* and twenty-one of the twenty-four he had published in the *Dial* between 1840 and 1844.[11] Also included were some seventeen works composed or brought to completion during his intensely creative period (1844–1846) immediately prior to the book's publication. This last group included some of Emerson's best known poems, such as "Uriel," an appraisal of the writer's critical "heresy" in the 1838 Divinity School Address; the "Ode, Inscribed to W. H. Channing," his fascinating response, as a poet, to the antislavery movement; the two Merlin poems and "Bacchus," which declared his aims and methods as a poet; "Hamatreya," which memorably brought the thought of India home to the familiar Concord landscape; and "Threnody," the brilliant and moving elegy for Waldo, the poet's son, who had died at the age of five in 1842. Between the cessation of the *Dial* in 1844 and the publication of *Poems* on Christmas Day 1846 (dated 1847 on the title page), Emerson was at the peak of his powers, and if he felt a need to fill out his projected collection with a supply of new matter, clearly there was nothing forced in the performance. The older matter, poems republished from the *Dial* together with a few from other sources, were no less challenging and innovative. Perhaps the most rewarding of these is "Woodnotes II," a work often overlooked yet full of surprises, not least for the narrative role that Emerson gave to a pine tree. One of the charms of Emerson's poetry is the writer's unflagging delight in conversing with nature—that is, with the distributed versions of the human spirit that he found and acknowledged throughout the natural world ("They nod to me and I to them," as he said in *Nature* [*CW* 1:10]).

The second collection, *May-Day and Other Pieces* (1867), came two decades after the first, and had the feel of a valedictory performance. The title poem, an extended paean to springtime in New England, celebrated the return of life after a long and debilitating season (at the time the poem was written) of strife and civil war. Spring had always been Emerson's favored time for composing verses, when at last cordial breezes came from the "bland warm wise poetic South whispering odes choruses cadences & wonderful caesuras from his lyrical wings" (*L* 2:282). It may be that Emerson projected an ambitiously scaled poem on this rich theme earlier in his career, but in fact it was nearly all written during the sustained mutual slaughter of American armies from 1861 to 1865, a context nowhere directly evoked. That winter was now over and the poem meant to be hopeful about the season to come.

The valedictory mood of *May-Day* is surely captured best in "Terminus," a confession of mortality that shocked the poet's son Edward Waldo when his father first read it to him in 1866 (though it seems in the main to have been written much earlier). This poem, along with "The Past" (an uncharacteristic expression of satisfaction with endings) served to introduce Emerson's second elegy, this to his younger brother Edward Bliss Emerson, who had died in 1834. "In Memoriam. E. B. E." assimilates the brother's memory with the memory of the dead at the battle of Concord and relates the waste of death to qualities of character and the idea of the heroic. That connection (redefined by the war) is in turn the main burden of "Voluntaries," a stately memorial for Robert Gould Shaw, a young friend of the Emerson family and commander of the Massachusetts Fifty-Fourth, who died with a great many of his black troops in the assault on Fort Wagner. The valedictory mood is sustained in a different but related way in "The Titmouse," Emerson's "indirect tribute to Thoreau,"[12] who lay on his deathbed as the poem was being written in the first months of 1862.

As a collection, *May-Day* would seem to have had, from the start, fewer admirers than *Poems* for all the shadow and letting go that it contains. But these qualities, which might be reckoned worthy natural aspects of aging, are counterbalanced by surprise and defiance and humor in ways that recurrently bring the younger Emerson to mind. The titmouse is himself a particle of defiance, showing how death by freezing is to be avoided—and what traits of character make him a savior.

"The Adirondacs," the next longest poem after "May-Day," is an experiment in the mock heroic, whereby romantic pieties about man's place in nature (including some that Emerson had fostered) are serially undermined. And "Brahma," which elicited such widespread bafflement and skepticism on its first appearance in the *Atlantic Monthly* in 1857, may be one of the best instances in American literature of an author's capacity to surprise.

A NOTE ON THE TEXT

The poems selected for this edition, with the exception of those included in the Appendix, are drawn from volume IX of *The Collected Works of Ralph Waldo Emerson: Poems, A Variorum Edition*, edited by Albert J. von Frank and Thomas Wortham (Cambridge: The Belknap Press of Harvard University Press, 2011). In establishing the text of each poem, the editors determined the appropriate copy-text ("the earliest feasible form of the text," such as, in many instances, manuscript printer's copy in the author's hand [*CW* 9:cxviii]) and then emended based on evidence about the author's subsequent revisions. The order in which the poems appear, both in the *Collected Works* edition and in the present selection, follows that given them by Emerson in his several collections, *Poems* (Boston: James Munroe, 1847), *May-Day and Other Pieces* (Boston: Ticknor and Fields, 1867), and *Selected Poems* (Boston: James R. Osgood, 1876). A few poems published but not collected by Emerson (such as "Grace" and "Nature") are added at the end. Following the text of each poem, a date of composition, when known, is given to the left of a pair of vertical lines, and a date of first publication to the right. Readers interested in additional information about the poems are referred to *The Poetry Notebooks* (*PN*) for the history of their composition, and to the ninth volume of the *Collected Works* (*CW* 9) for the history of their publication.

The poems and fragments gathered in the Appendix under the general title "The Ellen Poems, 1828–1831" are drawn from various sources, as indicated at that location. Three of these items were published by Emerson ("To Eva," "To Ellen, at the South," and "Thine Eyes Still Shined") and are therefore reproduced from *CW* 9. The remaining texts have unique sources in Emerson's manuscripts and are quoted from *JMN, PN, One First Love,* and, in two instances, from unpublished manuscripts at the Houghton Library. These important biographical documents have never before been brought together.

NOTES

1. David Porter, *Emerson and Literary Change* (Cambridge, Mass.: Harvard University Press, 1978), p. 1.

2. *The Collected Works of Ralph Waldo Emerson, Volume IX: Poems, A Variorum Edition,* ed. Albert J. von Frank and Thomas Wortham (Cambridge, Mass.: The Belknap Press of Harvard University Press, 2011), and *The Poetry Notebooks of Ralph Waldo Emerson,* ed. Ralph H. Orth, Albert J. von Frank, David W. Hill, and Linda Allardt (Columbia: University of Missouri Press, 1986).

3. Admirers of Emerson's poetry have always appreciated this relation. For example, Julian Hawthorne asserted that "Emerson the poet is Emerson the philosopher transfigured. Here his strength is at its maximum, and his weakness seldom appears" (Hawthorne and Leonard Lemmon, *American Literature: A Text-Book for the Use of Schools and Colleges* [Boston: D. C. Heath, 1891], p. 128).

4. See the headnote to that poem, below.

5. *The Poetry Notebooks of Ralph Waldo Emerson* makes possible the study of the evolution and composition of nearly all of Emerson's poems, each of which is analyzed in an appendix to that volume (pp. 720–979). For no other American poet of the nineteenth century is evidence of this kind so complete.

6. Also quoted in Edith W. Gregg, ed., *One First Love: The Letters of Ellen Louisa Tucker to Ralph Waldo Emerson* (Cambridge, Mass.: The Belknap Press of Harvard University Press, 1962), p. 147. Gregg's collection includes a sampling of Ellen's poetry. Emerson's poems to Ellen have for the first time been gathered together, in the appendix to the present volume.

7. The central portion of *Poems* (1847) is given over to verses inspired by or in various ways related to important women in Emerson's life, beginning with the "Ode to Beauty" ("Beauty" was one of his affectionate names for Ellen), and continuing with "Give All to Love," "To Ellen at the South," "To Eva," "The Amulet," "Thine Eyes Still Shined," "Eros," "Hermione," and the "Initial, Dæmonic, and Celestial Love." In the careful architecture of Emerson's first book of poems, here was concentrated its informing eroticism.

8. Quoted in William Dean Howells, *Literary Friends and Acquaintance* (New York: Harper, 1900), p. 63. Emerson often praised Tennyson but also complained of his "superfineness," noting that his lyrics lacked the strength and rude truthfulness of Ben Jonson's verses (*CW* 10:250). The objection, in both cases, seems not to have been to the musicality, but to its displacement of recognizable experience.

9. "The Poetic Principle," in *Edgar Allan Poe: Essays and Reviews* (New York: Library of America, 1984), p. 75.

10. "Emerson," in *Discourses in America* (London: Macmillan, 1885), pp. 153–154.

11. "Good-Bye," composed in 1824 and never a favorite with Emerson, was one of the few early poems admitted to this collection. For the significance of 1834 as a turning point, see Carl F. Strauch's seminal article, "The Year of Emerson's Poetic Maturity: 1834," *Philological Quarterly* 34 (October 1955): 343–377.

12. So called by R. A. Yoder in *Emerson and the Orphic Poet in America* (Berkeley: University of California Press, 1978), p. 157.

FROM

Poems

(1847)

THE SPHINX

Emerson placed this poem at the very portal of his first collection, *Poems* (1847), where the experience of reading it made for a formidable initiation into his poetic method. "Knock and it shall be opened unto you," the poem seemed to say, though readers have often found the key missing and the door shut to them. That it should function as a "threshold poem," as Saundra Morris has called it (p. 778), may have something to do with the brass Sphinx-head knocker on the door of Concord's "Old Manse," where Emerson lived in 1834–35. All his visitors literally gained access by dealing first with this suggestive icon. Emerson's attention was otherwise drawn to the Sphinx by Thomas Carlyle's allusion in *Sartor Resartus:* "The secret of man's being is still like the Sphinx's secret: a riddle that he cannot rede; and for ignorance of which he suffers death, the worse death, a spiritual" (p. 53). Still another and greater influence was the chapter called "The Sphinx; or Science" in Francis Bacon's *De Sapientia Veterum* (*Wisdom of the Ancients*), which explained the myth's allegory. In this account, the Sphinx's riddles about Nature and the nature of Man point to a parallelism of knowledge and self-knowledge. The relevance of this source is finely developed by Walls (pp. 28–32).

Emerson interpreted his own poem in 1859: "I have often been asked the meaning of the 'Sphinx.' It is this,—The perception of identity unites all things and explains one by another, and the most rare and strange is equally facile as the most common. But if the mind live only in particulars, and see only differences (wanting the power to see the whole—all in each), then the world addresses to the mind a question it cannot answer, and each new fact tears it in pieces, and it is vanquished by the distracting variety" (Unpublished notebook BL, Houghton Library, Harvard University, p. 241; see also the article by Smith).

Thoreau wrote a lengthy analysis of the poem on its first appearance in the *Dial* for January 1841. The Sphinx, he argued, was not some external challenger but the alternately quiescent and active human capacity for wonder, and the consequent need to understand the world and the self. After several journal pages of convoluted observations, Thoreau concluded that the poem mirrored the mystery it spoke of, rendering his own analysis "as enigmatical as the Sphinx's riddle—Indeed I doubt if she could solve it herself" (*CW* 9:677–682).

THE SPHINX

The Sphinx is drowsy,
 Her wings are furled;
Her ear is heavy,
 She broods on the world.
"Who'll tell me my secret,   5
 The ages have kept?—
I awaited the seer,
 While they slumbered and slept;—

"The fate of the man-child;
 The meaning of man;   10
Known fruit of the unknown;
 Dædalian plan;
Out of sleeping a waking,
 Out of waking a sleep;
Life death overtaking;   15
 Deep underneath deep?

"Erect as a sunbeam,
 Upspringeth the palm;
The elephant browses,
 Undaunted and calm;   20
In beautiful motion
 The thrush plies his wings;
Kind leaves of his covert,
 Your silence he sings.

"The waves, unashamed,   25
 In difference sweet,
Play glad with the breezes,
 Old playfellows meet;
The journeying atoms,
 Primordial wholes,   30
Firmly draw, firmly drive,
 By their animate poles.

"Sea, earth, air, sound, silence,
 Plant, quadruped, bird,

By one music enchanted,   35
   One deity stirred,—
Each the other adorning,
   Accompany still;
Night veileth the morning,
   The vapor the hill.   40

"The babe by its mother
   Lies bathed in joy;
Glide its hours uncounted,—
   The sun is its toy;
Shines the peace of all being,   45
   Without cloud, in its eyes;
And the sum of the world
   In soft miniature lies.

"But man crouches and blushes,
   Absconds and conceals;   50
He creepeth and peepeth,
   He palters and steals;
Infirm, melancholy,
   Jealous glancing around,
An oaf, an accomplice,   55
   He poisons the ground.

"Out spoke the great mother,
   Beholding his fear;—
At the sound of her accents
   Cold shuddered the sphere:—   60
'Who has drugged my boy's cup?
   Who has mixed my boy's bread?
Who, with sadness and madness,
   Has turned my child's head?'"

I heard a poet answer,   65
   Aloud and cheerfully,
"Say on, sweet Sphinx! thy dirges
   Are pleasant songs to me.
Deep love lieth under
   These pictures of time;   70

They fade in the light of
    Their meaning sublime.

"The fiend that man harries
    Is love of the Best;
Yawns the pit of the Dragon,   75
    Lit by rays from the Blest.
The Lethe of nature
    Can't trance him again,
Whose soul sees the perfect,
    Which his eyes seek in vain.   80

"Profounder, profounder,
    Man's spirit must dive;
To his aye-rolling orbit
    No goal will arrive;
The heavens that now draw him   85
    With sweetness untold,
Once found,—for new heavens
    He spurneth the old.

"Pride ruined the angels,
    Their shame them restores;   90
And the joy that is sweetest
    Lurks in stings of remorse.
Have I a lover
    Who is noble and free?—
I would he were nobler   95
    Than to love me.

"Eterne alternation
    Now follows, now flies;
And under pain, pleasure,—
    Under pleasure, pain lies.   100
Love works at the centre,
    Heart-heaving alway;
Forth speed the strong pulses
    To the borders of day.

"Dull Sphinx, Jove keep thy five wits!   105
    Thy sight is growing blear;

Rue, myrrh, and cummin for the Sphinx—
    Her muddy eyes to clear!"—
The old Sphinx bit her thick lip,—
    Said, "Who taught thee me to name?   110
I am thy spirit, yoke-fellow,
    Of thine eye I am eyebeam.

"Thou art the unanswered question;
    Couldst see thy proper eye,
Alway it asketh, asketh;   115
    And each answer is a lie.
So take thy quest through nature,
    It through thousand natures ply;
Ask on, thou clothed eternity;
    Time is the false reply."   120

Uprose the merry Sphinx,
    And crouched no more in stone;
She melted into purple cloud,
    She silvered in the moon;
She spired into a yellow flame;   125
    She flowered in blossoms red;
She flowed into a foaming wave;
    She stood Monadnoc's head.

Thorough a thousand voices
    Spoke the universal dame: 130
"Who telleth one of my meanings,
    Is master of all I am."

1840 || 1841

EACH AND ALL

This poem was published in the *Western Messenger* in February 1839 with the title "Each in All." As both "The Sphinx" and "Each and All" attest, Emerson's interest in science in the 1830s centered on the role of human subjectivity in the interpretation of nature. Even as the science of Emerson's day characteristically developed by objective analysis or the separation of particulars (of each from the other and each from all), as in the system of Linnaeus, for example, or in the identification of chemical elements, Emerson relied on hints from Coleridge and Goethe that physical facts represented spiritual facts (i.e., meanings), to be sought in the mind of the observer. "The Classification of all Nat. Science is arbitrary I believe," Emerson wrote on May 3, 1834, "no Method philosophical in any one. And yet in all the permutations & combinations supposable, might not a Cabinet of shells or a Flora be thrown into one which should flash on us the very thought? We take them out of composition & so lose their greatest beauty. The moon is an unsatisfactory sight if the eye be exclusively directed to it & a shell retains but a small part of its beauty when examined separately" (*JMN* 4:288). The meaning or spiritual significance of nature, in other words, is inseparable from the affects of perception, in how a thing in the perfection of its relatedness strikes a fully receptive human consciousness. Thus, "Every particular in nature, a leaf, a drop, a crystal, a moment of time is related to the whole, and partakes of the perfection of the whole. Each particle is a microcosm, and faithfully renders the likeness of the world" (*CW* 1:27).

EACH AND ALL

Little thinks, in the field, yon red-cloaked clown
Of thee from the hill-top looking down;
The heifer that lows in the upland farm,
Far-heard, lows not thine ear to charm;
The sexton, tolling his bell at noon, 5
Deems not that great Napoleon
Stops his horse, and lists with delight,
Whilst his files sweep round yon Alpine height;
Nor knowest thou what argument
Thy life to thy neighbor's creed has lent. 10
All are needed by each one;
Nothing is fair or good alone.
I thought the sparrow's note from heaven,
Singing at dawn on the alder bough;

I brought him home, in his nest, at even;   15
He sings the song, but it pleases not now,
For I did not bring home the river and sky;—
He sang to my ear,—they sang to my eye.
The delicate shells lay on the shore;
The bubbles of the latest wave   20
Fresh pearls to their enamel gave;
And the bellowing of the savage sea
Greeted their safe escape to me.
I wiped away the weeds and foam,
I fetched my sea-born treasures home;   25
But the poor, unsightly, noisome things
Had left their beauty on the shore,
With the sun, and the sand, and the wild uproar.
The lover watched his graceful maid,
As 'mid the virgin train she strayed,   30
Nor knew her beauty's best attire
Was woven still by the snow-white choir.
At last she came to his hermitage,
Like the bird from the woodlands to the cage;—
The gay enchantment was undone,   35
A gentle wife, but fairy none.
Then I said, 'I covet truth;
Beauty is unripe childhood's cheat;
I leave it behind with the games of youth.'—
As I spoke, beneath my feet   40
The ground-pine curled its pretty wreath,
Running over the club-moss burrs;
I inhaled the violet's breath;
Around me stood the oaks and firs;
Pine-cones and acorns lay on the ground;   45
Over me soared the eternal sky,
Full of light and of deity;
Again I saw, again I heard,
The rolling river, the morning bird;—
Beauty through my senses stole;   50
I yielded myself to the perfect whole.

1834–1836? || 1839

THE PROBLEM

On August 28, 1838, just one week after Emerson delivered the Divinity School Address and one day after he was attacked for that performance by Andrews Norton in a Boston newspaper, he wrote in his journal:

> It is very grateful to my feelings to go into a Roman [Catholic] Cathedral, yet I look as my countrymen do at the Roman priesthood. It is very grateful to me to go into an English [Anglican or Episcopal] Church & hear the liturgy read. Yet nothing would induce me to be the English priest. I find an unpleasant dilemma in this, nearer home. I dislike to be a clergyman & refuse to be one. Yet how rich a music would be to me a holy clergyman in my town. It seems to me he cannot be a man, quite & whole. Yet how plain is the need of one, & how high, yes highest, is the function. Here is a Division of labor that I like not. A man must sacrifice his manhood for the social good. Something is wrong, I see not what. (*JMN* 7:60)

The following January Emerson preached for the last time at the church in Concord. On the tenth of November following, while seated in his pew listening to Concord minister Barzillai Frost, he composed this poem.

THE PROBLEM

I like a church; I like a cowl;
I love a prophet of the soul;
And on my heart monastic aisles
Fall like sweet strains, or pensive smiles;
Yet not for all his faith can see   5
Would I that cowled churchman be.

Why should the vest on him allure,
Which I could not on me endure?

Not from a vain or shallow thought
His awful Jove young Phidias brought;   10
Never from lips of cunning fell
The thrilling Delphic oracle;
Out from the heart of nature rolled
The burdens of the Bible old;
The litanies of nations came,   15

Like the volcano's tongue of flame,
Up from the burning core below,—
The canticles of love and woe;
The hand that rounded Peter's dome,
And groined the aisles of Christian Rome,   20
Wrought in a sad sincerity;
Himself from God he could not free;
He builded better than he knew;—
The conscious stone to beauty grew.

Know'st thou what wove yon woodbird's nest   25
Of leaves, and feathers from her breast?
Or how the fish outbuilt her shell,
Painting with morn each annual cell?
Or how the sacred pine-tree adds
To her old leaves new myriads?   30
Such and so grew these holy piles,
Whilst love and terror laid the tiles.
Earth proudly wears the Parthenon,
As the best gem upon her zone;
And Morning opes with haste her lids,   35
To gaze upon the Pyramids;
O'er England's abbeys bends the sky,
As on its friends, with kindred eye;
For, out of Thought's interior sphere
These wonders rose to upper air;   40
And Nature gladly gave them place,
Adopted them into her race,
And granted them an equal date
With Andes and with Ararat.

These temples grew as grows the grass;   45
Art might obey, but not surpass.
The passive Master lent his hand
To the vast soul that o'er him planned;
And the same power that reared the shrine,
Bestrode the tribes that knelt within.   50
Ever the fiery Pentecost
Girds with one flame the countless host,

Trances the heart through chanting choirs,
And through the priest the mind inspires.
The word unto the prophet spoken   55
Was writ on tables yet unbroken;
The word by seers or sibyls told,
In groves of oak, or fanes of gold,
Still floats upon the morning wind,
Still whispers to the willing mind.   60
One accent of the Holy Ghost
The heedless world hath never lost.
I know what say the fathers wise,—
The Book itself before me lies,
Old *Chrysostom*, best Augustine,   65
And he who blent both in his line,
The younger *Golden Lips* or mines,
Taylor, the Shakspeare of divines.
His words are music in my ear,
I see his cowled portrait dear;   70
And yet, for all his faith could see,
I would not the good bishop be.

1839 || 1840

THE VISIT

Emerson wrote this poem during a weeklong visit from Caroline Sturgis, between August 28 and September 4, 1843. Sturgis (1818–1888), a contributor of poems to the *Dial*, had become an important friend, a frequent correspondent, and an occasional guest at Concord following her introduction to Emerson by Margaret Fuller in 1838. His accounts of this visit (*L* 3:203; *JMN* 9:16, 19–20) seem entirely cordial, though visitors, never in short supply at the Emerson home, often proved distracting. Emerson's son Edward saw the poem as an instance of the comedy of the antisocial host, which his father had invoked in an 1842 journal entry about a certain Professor Fortinbras, whose patience with visitors regularly shut down at nine o'clock, and who noted that "if they cannot see the clock, [they] should find the time in my face" (*W* 9:407).

THE VISIT

Askest, 'How long thou shalt stay?'
Devastator of the day!
Know, each substance, and relation,
Thorough nature's operation,
Hath its unit, bound, and metre; 5
And every new compound
Is some product and repeater,—
Product of the earlier found.
But the unit of the visit,
The encounter of the wise,— 10
Say, what other metre is it
Than the meeting of the eyes?
Nature poureth into nature
Through the channels of that feature.
Riding on the ray of sight, 15
Fleeter far than whirlwinds go,
Or for service, or delight,
Hearts to hearts their meaning show,
Sum their long experience,
And import intelligence. 20
Single look has drained the breast;
Single moment years confessed.

The duration of a glance
Is the term of convenance,
And, though thy rede be church or state,   25
Frugal multiples of that.
Speeding Saturn cannot halt;
Linger,—thou shalt rue the fault;
If Love his moment overstay,
Hatred's swift repulsions play.   30

1843 || 1844

URIEL

In sending a manuscript copy of "Uriel" to Caroline Sturgis in 1845 or 1846, Emerson added a note: "You have heard news from Saadi, that the most baleful heresy has been broached in heaven at some Epoch not fixed. It seems some body said words like these, that Geometers might say what they pleased, but in Uranometry there was no right line" (*PN*, pp. 711–712). In this parable, then, what appears straight, or "right," from an earth-bound perspective is actually, from an absolute, or heavenly, perspective, curved. To declare the difference, as Uriel does, is to distinguish "what subsisteth" from "what seems" (l. 14), while to speak the Uranometrical truth to an establishment of Geometrical fabulists is to invite the charge of heresy. This is what Emerson famously did in the Divinity School Address of July 15, 1838, and the choir of School patrons, led by Andrews Norton, did not fail to bring just that charge against Emerson. That the poem is a comment on this celebrated controversy has been long and widely acknowledged (see *W* 9:409).

Commenting on the matter in October 1838, Emerson wrote, "At the first entering ray of light, society is shaken with fear & anger from side to side. Who opened that shutter? they cry, Wo to him! They belie it, they call it darkness that comes in, affirming that they were in light before. Before the man who has spoken to them the dread word, they tremble & flee" (*JMN* 7:126). At this time Emerson took notice of several instances of calmly heroic adversarial truth-telling, which may have helped him to see his experience not only as part of the ongoing "miracles controversy" between young Transcendentalists and older conservatives at the Divinity School but also as part of the general history of heresy. On October 28, Emerson had been impressed by the way the poet Jones Very had opposed the conservative dogmatizing of Concord pastor Ezra Ripley (Emerson's step-grandfather) during a meeting at Emerson's home (*JMN* 7:127–128; *L* 2:171). Likewise, he saw how the truth of antislavery protesters was discomfiting aristocratic slaveholders (*JMN* 7:125–126). The astronomical references in the poem forcibly imply the model heresies of Galileo and Copernicus—as Edward also noted (*W* 9:408). On July 1, 1838, Emerson wrote, "Do let the new generation speak the truth, & let our grandfathers die" (*JMN* 7:39).

URIEL

It fell in the ancient periods
　　Which the brooding soul surveys,
Or ever the wild Time coined itself
　　Into calendar months and days.

This was the lapse of Uriel, 5
Which in Paradise befell.
Once, among the Pleiads walking,
SAID overheard the young gods talking;
And the treason, too long pent,
To his ears was evident. 10
The young deities discussed
Laws of form, and metre just,
Orb, quintessence, and sunbeams,
What subsisteth, and what seems.
One, with low tones that decide, 15
And doubt and reverend use defied,
With a look that solved the sphere,
And stirred the devils everywhere,
Gave his sentiment divine
Against the being of a line. 20
'Line in nature is not found;
Unit and universe are round;
In vain produced, all rays return;
Evil will bless, and ice will burn.'
As Uriel spoke with piercing eye, 25
A shudder ran around the sky;
The stern old war-gods shook their heads;
The seraphs frowned from myrtle-beds;
Seemed to the holy festival
The rash word boded ill to all; 30
The balance-beam of Fate was bent;
The bounds of good and ill were rent;
Strong Hades could not keep his own,
But all slid to confusion.

A sad self-knowledge, withering, fell 35
On the beauty of Uriel;
In heaven once eminent, the god
Withdrew, that hour, into his cloud;
Whether doomed to long gyration
In the sea of generation, 40
Or by knowledge grown too bright

To hit the nerve of feebler sight.
Straightway, a forgetting wind
Stole over the celestial kind,
And their lips the secret kept,   45
If in ashes the fire-seed slept.
But now and then, truth-speaking things
Shamed the angels' veiling wings;
And, shrilling from the solar course,
Or from fruit of chemic force,   50
Procession of a soul in matter,
Or the speeding change of water,
Or out of the good of evil born,
Came Uriel's voice of cherub scorn,
And a blush tinged the upper sky,   55
And the gods shook, they knew not why.

1845? || 1846

ALPHONSO OF CASTILE

Alphonso X, king of Castile, León, and Galicia (1221–1284), was a prodigiously gifted scholar in various fields, literary, scientific, and legal. According to legend, Alphonso criticized the desperately complicated mathematics by which Ptolemaic astronomers sought to patch and save their theory, saying that if he (Alphonso) had been present at the creation, he would have recommended a simpler, more elegant plan. It has recently been shown that the story was a deliberate libel, concocted posthumously, in order to magnify the king's arrogance into blasphemy if not, indeed, into the kind of heresy with which Galileo would later be charged. Medieval and Renaissance accounts cite the remark as the cause of the king's downfall and death. Later versions, including those that Emerson knew from Bernard de Fontenelle's *Discourse on the Plurality of Worlds* (1686), Pierre Bayle's *Dictionary* (1697–1702), and Voltaire's *Essai sur les moeurs* (1756), tend to regard Alphonso's observation as a witty pleasantry (Goldstein). To whatever extent the hint of blasphemy operates as a trace in Emerson's poem, the effect would be to align it with "Uriel."

A passage from "Montaigne" in *Representative Men* offers another useful context:

> Charles Fourier announced that "the attractions of man are proportioned to his destinies;" in other words, that every desire predicts its own satisfaction. Yet all experience exhibits the reverse of this; the incompetency of power is the universal grief of young and ardent minds. They accuse the divine Providence of a certain parsimony. It has shown the heaven and earth to every child, and filled him with a desire for the whole; a desire raging, infinite, a hunger as of space to be filled with planets. . . . Then for the satisfaction;— to each man is administered a single drop, a bead of dew of vital power, *per day,*—a cup as large as space, and one drop of the water of life in it. Each man woke in the morning with an appetite that could eat the solar system like a cake; . . . but on the first motion to prove his strength, hands, feet, senses, gave way, and would not serve him. He was an emperor deserted by his states, and left to whistle by himself or thrust into a mob of emperors all whistling: and still the sirens sung, "The attractions are proportioned to the destinies." In every house, in the heart of each maiden and of each boy, in the soul of the soaring saint, this chasm is found,—between the largest promise of ideal power, and the shabby experience. (*CW* 4:103–104)

The journal entry on which this passage is based (*JMN* 7:474–476; December 1842) responds to theories of communal living then being discussed by

Bronson Alcott (1799–1888) and his Fruitlands colleague Charles Lane (1800–1870) and to Fourierist ideas simultaneously under debate at Brook Farm. The premise—no doubt alluding to the economic difficulties following the Panic of 1837—was that "the parsimony which for a long time had characterized the government of Olympus, could not be sufficiently reprobated. It was stingy, it was shabby, it deserved worse names." Further along in this entry Emerson quoted a couplet of fit summary—later erroneously attributed to Thoreau, but actually by Caroline Sturgis: "Ask! must I ask? The gods above should give; / They have enough, & we do poorly live" (cf. Caroline Sturgis Tappan Papers, Houghton MS Am 1221.268].)

ALPHONSO OF CASTILLE

I, Alphonso, live and learn,
Seeing Nature go astern.
Things deteriorate in kind;
Lemons run to leaves and rind;
Meagre crop of figs and limes;   5
Shorter days and harder times.
Flowering April cools and dies
In the insufficient skies.
Imps, at high midsummer, blot
Half the sun's disk with a spot: 10
'Twill not now avail to tan
Orange cheek or skin of man.
Roses bleach, the goats are dry,
Lisbon quakes, the people cry.
Yon pale, scrawny fisher fools,   15
Gaunt as bitterns in the pools,
Are no brothers of my blood;—
They discredit Adamhood.
Eyes of gods! ye must have seen,
O'er your ramparts as ye lean,   20
The general debility;
Of genius the sterility;
Mighty projects countermanded;
Rash ambition, brokenhanded;
Puny man and scentless rose   25

Tormenting Pan to double the dose.
Rebuild or ruin: either fill
Of vital force the wasted rill,
Or tumble all again in heap
To weltering chaos and to sleep.   30

Say, Seigniors, are the old Niles dry,
Which fed the veins of earth and sky,
That mortals miss the loyal heats,
Which drove them erst to social feats;
Now, to a savage selfness grown,   35
Think nature barely serves for one;
With science poorly mask their hurt,
And vex the gods with question pert,
Immensely curious whether you
Still are rulers, or mildew?   40

Masters, I'm in pain with you;
Masters, I'll be plain with you;
In my palace of Castile,
I, a king, for kings can feel.
There my thoughts the matter roll,   45
And solve and oft resolve the whole.
And, for I'm styled Alphonse the Wise,
Ye shall not fail for sound advice.
Before ye want a drop of rain,
Hear the sentiment of Spain.   50

You have tried famine: no more try it;
Ply us now with a full diet;
Teach your pupils now with plenty;
For one sun supply us twenty.
I have thought it thoroughly over,—   55
State of hermit, state of lover;
We must have society,
We cannot spare variety.
Hear you, then, celestial fellows!
Fits not to be overzealous;   60
Steads not to work on the clean jump,

Nor wine nor brains perpetual pump.
Men and gods are too extense;
Could you slacken and condense?
Your rank overgrowths reduce   65
Till your kinds abound with juice?
Earth, crowded, cries, 'Too many men!'
My counsel is, kill nine in ten,
And bestow the shares of all
On the remnant decimal.   70
Add their nine lives to this cat;
Stuff their nine brains in his hat;
Make his frame and forces square
With the labors he must dare;
Thatch his flesh, and even his years   75
With the marble which he rears.
There, growing slowly old at ease,
No faster than his planted trees,
He may, by warrant of his age,
In schemes of broader scope engage.   80
So shall ye have a man of the sphere,
Fit to grace the solar year.

1846 || 1846

MITHRIDATES

Mithridates VI, king of Pontus, claimed descent from Alexander the Great and offered the principal military challenge to the Roman Empire in the first century BCE. He is supposed to have been an accomplished scholar, botanist, and linguist, and at the same time a thoroughly ruthless military chieftain. His name is most closely associated with his invention of a universal antidote to poison, with the aid of which he was said to have taken daily sublethal doses of those poisons he thought most likely to be used by plotters against his life. Edward Emerson judged that his father deployed Mithridates "as symbolic of the wise man who can find virtue in all things and escape the harm" (*W* 9:414). As A. E. Housman correctly said of Mithridates, "he died old." On the other hand, as Emerson noted in "The Tragic" (1844), "There are people who have an appetite for grief, pleasure is not strong enough and they crave pain, mithridatic stomachs which must be fed on poisoned bread, natures so doomed that no prosperity can soothe their ragged and dishevelled desolation" (*CW* 10:336).

MITHRIDATES

I cannot spare water or wine,
    Tobacco-leaf, or poppy, or rose;
From the earth-poles to the line,
    All between that works or grows,
Every thing is kin of mine.   5

Give me agates for my meat;
Give me cantharids to eat;
From air and ocean bring me foods,
From all zones and altitudes;—

From all natures, sharp and slimy,   10
    Salt and basalt, wild and tame:
Tree and lichen, ape, sea-lion,
    Bird, and reptile, be my game.

Ivy for my fillet band;
Blinding dog-wood in my hand;   15
Hemlock for my sherbet cull me,
And the prussic juice to lull me;

Swing me in the upas boughs,
Vampyre-fanned, when I carouse.

Too long shut in strait and few,   20
Thinly dieted on dew,
I will use the world, and sift it,
To a thousand humors shift it,
As you spin a cherry.
O doleful ghosts, and goblins merry!   25
O all you virtues, methods, mights,
Means, appliances, delights,
Reputed wrongs and braggart rights,
Smug routine, and things allowed,
Minorities, things under cloud!   30
Hither! take me, use me, fill me,
Vein and artery, though ye kill me!

                                                1846 || 1846

TO J. W.

It is not quite clear who "J. W." was. Edward Emerson supposed that he was John Weiss (1818–1879), "a young clergyman and an able writer, who had seemed to Mr. Emerson to dwell overmuch on Goethe's failings" (*W* 9:414). The identification seems odd, since Weiss, a college classmate of Thoreau's and an 1843 graduate of Harvard Divinity School, commented favorably, if sparingly, on Goethe (1749–1832) in the preface to his edition of Schiller's *Aesthetic Letters* (Boston, 1845). There he asserted that these men were the two giants of recent German literature. Attacks on Goethe's personal character were common at this time in moralistic New England, though the controversy by no means centered on the inconspicuous, new-minted clergyman at Watertown. The noted historian George Bancroft, for example, denounced Goethe as early as 1824, in the *North American Review,* and as late as 1839, in the *Christian Examiner,* a journal then edited by James Walker. Wofgang Menzel's hostility to Goethe suffused his book on *German Literature,* a volume in George Ripley's *Specimens of Foreign Standard Literature.* Reviewing this work in the *Dial* for January 1841, Theodore Parker called Menzel's diatribe "insane" (p. 332)—and, in the same issue, Margaret Fuller, translator of Johann Peter Eckermann's *Conversations with Goethe* (1839), agreed (pp. 340–347). The controversy over Goethe's morals was troublesome to the Transcendentalists, who regarded him as, simply, the most compelling literary figure of the preceding century and in many respects a model for their own practice: see Emerson's "Goethe, or the Writer" in *Representative Men* (*CW* 4:151–166). See also *JMN* 5:139 for some of Emerson's own closely held misgivings about Goethe's character, suggesting that the poem's censure of censure might in part have been aimed at himself.

TO J. W.

Set not thy foot on graves:
Hear what wine and roses say;
The mountain chase, the summer waves,
The crowded town, thy feet may well delay.

Set not thy foot on graves;   5
Nor seek to unwind the shroud
Which charitable Time
And Nature have allowed
To wrap the errors of a sage sublime.

Set not thy foot on graves: 10
Care not to strip the dead
Of his sad ornament,
His myrrh, and wine, and rings,
His sheet of lead,
And trophies buried: 15
Go, get them where he earned them when alive;
As resolutely dig or dive.

Life is too short to waste
In critic peep or cynic bark,
Quarrel or reprimand: 20
'Twill soon be dark;
Up! mind thine own aim, and
God speed the mark!

                                          1845? || 1846

HAMATREYA

During a trip to Vermont in July 1845, Emerson read the *Vishṅu Purāṅa* and copied the following passage into his journal:

> I have now given you a summary account of the sovereigns of the earth.—These, & other kings who with perishable frames have possessed this ever-enduring world, & who, blinded with deceptive notions of individual occupation, have indulged the feeling that suggests "This earth is mine,—it is my son's,—it belongs to my dynasty,—" have all passed away. So, many who reigned before them, many who succeeded them, & many who are yet to come, have ceased or will cease to be. Earth laughs, as if smiling with autumnal flowers to behold her kings unable to effect the subjugation of themselves. I will repeat to you, Maitreya, the stanzas that were chanted by Earth, & which the Muni Asita communicated to Janaka, whose banner was virtue.
>
> "How great is the folly of princes who are endowed with the faculty of reason, to cherish the confidence of ambition when they themselves are but foam upon the wave. Before they have subdued themselves, they seek to reduce their ministers, their servants, their subjects, under their authority; they then endeavour to overcome their foes. 'Thus,' say they, 'will we conquer the ocean-circled earth;' &, intent upon their project, behold not death, which is not far off. But what mighty matter is the subjugation of the sea girt earth, to one who can subdue himself. Emancipation from existence is the fruit of self-control. It is through infatuation that kings desire to possess me, whom their predecessors have been forced to leave, whom their fathers have not retained. Beguiled by the selfish love of sway, fathers contend with their sons, & brothers with brothers, for my possession. Foolishness has been the character of every king who has boasted, 'All this earth is mine—every thing is mine—it will be in my house forever;'—for he is dead. How is it possible that such vain desires should survive in the hearts of his descendants, who have seen their progenitor absorbed by the thirst of dominion, compelled to relinquish me whom he called his own, & tread the path of dissolution? When I hear a king sending word to another by his ambassador, 'This earth is mine; resign your pretensions to it,'—I am at first moved to violent laughter; but it soon subsides in pity for the infatuated fool.'"
>
> These were the verses, Maitreya, which Earth recited & by listen-

ing to which ambition fades away like snow before the sun. (*JMN* 9:321)

"Maitreya" is the name of the fifth Buddha, who is to come when the old teachings (dharma) have lapsed. According to an entry in notebook Oriental-ist, Maitreya means "hermit" (*TN* 2:135). The significance of Emerson's vari-ant, "Hamatreya," has not been discovered. His giving so sharply local an ap-plication of the exotic Buddhist text strikingly demonstrates his interest in the current relevance of ancient "ethnical scriptures." The language of the land-lords' satisfaction is well-observed Yankee vernacular and would sit well in a Frost poem.

HAMATREYA

Bulkeley, Hunt, Willard, Hosmer, Meriam, Flint,
Possessed the land which rendered to their toil
Hay, corn, roots, hemp, flax, apples, wool, and wood.
Each of these landlords walked amidst his farm,
Saying, ''Tis mine, my children's, and my name's: 5
How sweet the west wind sounds in my own trees!
How graceful climb those shadows on my hill!
I fancy these pure waters and the flags
Know me, as does my dog: we sympathize;
And, I affirm, my actions smack of the soil.'   10
Where are these men? Asleep beneath their grounds;
And strangers, fond as they, their furrows plough.
Earth laughs in flowers, to see her boastful boys
Earth-proud, proud of the earth which is not theirs;
Who steer the plough, but cannot steer their feet   15
Clear of the grave.
They added ridge to valley, brook to pond,
And sighed for all that bounded their domain.
'This suits me for a pasture; that's my park;
We must have clay, lime, gravel, granite-ledge,   20
And misty lowland, where to go for peat.
The land is well,—lies fairly to the south.
'Tis good, when you have crossed the sea and back,

To find the sitfast acres where you left them.'
Ah! the hot owner sees not Death, who adds   25
Him to his land, a lump of mould the more.
Hear what the Earth says:—

EARTH-SONG

'Mine and yours;
Mine, not yours.   30
Earth endures;
Stars abide—
Shine down in the old sea;
Old are the shores;
But where are old men?   35
I who have seen much,
Such have I never seen.

'The lawyer's deed
Ran sure,
In tail,   40
To them, and to their heirs
Who shall succeed,
Without fail,
Forevermore.

'Here is the land,   45
Shaggy with wood,
With its old valley,
Mound, and flood.
But the heritors?
Fled like the flood's foam,—   50
The lawyer, and the laws,
And the kingdom,
Clean swept herefrom.

'They called me theirs,
Who so controlled me;   55
Yet every one

Wished to stay, and is gone.
How am I theirs,
If they cannot hold me,
But I hold them?'   60

When I heard the Earth-song,
I was no longer brave;
My avarice cooled
Like lust in the chill of the grave.

1846 || 1846

GOOD-BYE

Composed in 1824, "Good-Bye" was the earliest-written of the poems that Emerson chose to collect, and perhaps for that reason was never one of his favorites. It refers to a period in Emerson's life after graduating from Harvard when he, his mother, and his brothers, needing to live frugally, moved from Boston into a pastoral exile in a retired corner of Roxbury. The slightly juvenile mood of renunciation seems to mask a sense of disappointment or exclusion, and likely of thwarted professional ambition. The work belongs to a poetic tradition of *contemptus mundi*, best exemplified in such poems as Sir Walter Ralegh's "The Lie," Shakespeare's sonnet 66, Alexander Pope's "Solitude," portions of Byron's *Childe Harold's Pilgrimage,* and various popular epitaphs.

For Emerson, of course, retirement from "the world" did not involve removal into a posthumous existence, but into a deeper acquaintance with nature, a development then explicitly encouraged by his aunt Mary Moody Emerson. As he told a friend at the time, "She was anxious that her nephew might hold high & reverential notions regarding [nature] as the temple where God & the Mind are to be studied & adored" (*L* 1:133).

GOOD-BYE

Good-bye, proud world! I'm going home:
Thou art not my friend, and I'm not thine.
Long through thy weary crowds I roam;
A river-ark on the ocean brine,
Long I've been tossed like the driven foam;   5
But now, proud world! I'm going home.

Good-bye to Flattery's fawning face;
To Grandeur with his wise grimace;
To upstart Wealth's averted eye;
To supple Office, low and high;   10
To crowded halls, to court and street;
To frozen hearts and hasting feet;
To those who go, and those who come;
Good-bye, proud world! I'm going home.

I am going to my own hearth-stone,   15
Bosomed in yon green hills alone,—

A secret nook in a pleasant land,
Whose groves the frolic fairies planned;
Where arches green, the livelong day,
Echo the blackbird's roundelay,   20
And vulgar feet have never trod
A spot that is sacred to thought and God.

O, when I am safe in my sylvan home,
I tread on the pride of Greece and Rome;
And when I am stretched beneath the pines,   25
Where the evening star so holy shines,
I laugh at the lore and the pride of man,
At the sophist schools, and the learned clan;
For what are they all, in their high conceit,
When man in the bush with God may meet?   30

1824 || 1839

THE RHODORA:
ON BEING ASKED, WHENCE IS THE FLOWER?

As collected in 1846, "The Rhodora" immediately followed "Good-Bye," composed a decade earlier. Both may be said to be about the attractions of rural seclusion, but the ten-year advance in the poet's maturity distinctly appears in the later poem, in its avoidance of allegorical figures, in the way that nature's presence is registered, and very much in the subtlety of the argument. Older readings of the poem (e.g., Matthiessen, pp. 48–50) unhelpfully stressed its affinities with eighteenth-century poetic traditions such as appear, for example, in William Cullen Bryant's moralistic "To a Waterfowl." With less dismissive intent, readings since then have pointed also to seventeenth-century antecedents, including George Herbert and the Ignatian meditation (e.g., Yoder, pp. 79–84). The older and simpler view made too little of the subject-object polarity that Emerson would shortly celebrate in *Nature* (1836) and which he anticipated here. "The greatest delight which the fields and woods minister," Emerson would write, "is the suggestion of an occult relation between man and the vegetable. I am not alone and unacknowledged" (*CW* 1:10). In April of 1834, shortly before writing the poem, he had for a second time left Boston to live in the quiet countryside, this time near Newton, Massachusetts. There he was in effect recuperating from his uncongenial and finally contentious ministry at the Second Church (1829–1832), from the anxiety and grief attending his brief first marriage to Ellen Tucker (1829–1831), and from the illness and exhaustion that occasioned his trip to Europe (1832–33). It was in Europe, at the Jardin des Plantes in Paris, where he first took note of the "occult relation" (*JMN* 4:198–200, 405–406). Knowledge of these circumstances helps to clarify the mutuality expressed in the poem between, on the one hand, the observer's sense of undeserved obscurity (see *JMN* 4:274–275), represented by his retreat to the countryside (in a sense "what brought [him] there"), and, on the other, the uncomplaining hiddenness of one suddenly eloquent, suddenly meaningful rhodora.

The poem's sophisticated architecture, its division into octaves, quatrains, and heroic couplets, combines formal symmetry with innovation, all the while remaining appropriately unobtrusive.

THE RHODORA:

ON BEING ASKED, WHENCE IS THE FLOWER?

In May, when sea-winds pierced our solitudes,
I found the fresh Rhodora in the woods,
Spreading its leafless blooms in a damp nook,
To please the desert and the sluggish brook.
The purple petals, fallen in the pool,   5
Made the black water with their beauty gay;
Here might the red-bird come his plumes to cool,
And court the flower that cheapens his array.
Rhodora! if the sages ask thee why
This charm is wasted on the earth and sky,   10
Tell them, dear, that if eyes were made for seeing,
Then Beauty is its own excuse for being:
Why thou wert there, O rival of the rose!
I never thought to ask, I never knew;
But, in my simple ignorance, suppose   15
The self-same Power that brought me there brought you.

1834 || 1839

THE HUMBLE-BEE

Two months into the presidency of Martin Van Buren, American banks started collapsing, the result of years of unrestrained speculation during the boom times of Andrew Jackson. As Emerson would shortly discover, the personal meaning of the Panic of 1837 was that the regular quarterly dividends from his bank stocks—a welcome supplement to his income from lecturing—failed to appear. On May 14 he declared that "the humblebee & the pine warbler seem to me the proper objects of attention in these disastrous times" (*JMN* 5:327), while the actual writing of the poem is acknowledged in an entry for May 9: "Yesterday in the woods I followed the fine humble bee with rhymes & fancies fine" (ibid.).

THE HUMBLE-BEE

Burly, dozing humble-bee,
Where thou art is clime for me.
Let them sail for Porto Rique,
Far-off heats through seas to seek;
I will follow thee alone,   5
Thou animated torrid-zone!
Zigzag steerer, desert cheerer,
Let me chase thy waving lines;
Keep me nearer, me thy hearer,
Singing over shrubs and vines.   10

Insect lover of the sun,
Joy of thy dominion!
Sailor of the atmosphere;
Swimmer through the waves of air;
Voyager of light and noon;   15
Epicurean of June;
Wait, I prithee, till I come
Within earshot of thy hum,—
All without is martyrdom.

When the south wind, in May days,   20
With a net of shining haze

Silvers the horizon wall,
And, with softness touching all,
Tints the human countenance
With a color of romance, 25
And, infusing subtle heats,
Turns the sod to violets,
Thou, in sunny solitudes,
Rover of the underwoods,
The green silence dost displace 30
With thy mellow, breezy bass.

Hot midsummer's petted crone,
Sweet to me thy drowsy tone
Tells of countless sunny hours,
Long days, and solid banks of flowers; 35
Of gulfs of sweetness without bound
In Indian wildernesses found;
Of Syrian peace, immortal leisure,
Firmest cheer, and bird-like pleasure.

Aught unsavory or unclean 40
Hath my insect never seen;
But violets and bilberry bells,
Maple-sap, and daffodels,
Grass with green flag half-mast high,
Succory to match the sky, 45
Columbine with horn of honey,
Scented fern, and agrimony,
Clover, catchfly, adder's-tongue,
And brier-roses, dwelt among;
All beside was unknown waste, 50
All was picture as he passed.

Wiser far than human seer,
Yellow-breeched philosopher!
Seeing only what is fair,
Sipping only what is sweet, 55
Thou dost mock at fate and care,

Leave the chaff, and take the wheat.
When the fierce north-western blast
Cools sea and land so far and fast,
Thou already slumberest deep;   60
Woe and want thou canst outsleep;
Want and woe, which torture us,
Thy sleep makes ridiculous.

1837 || 1839

BERRYING

Although this poem was written in the autumn of 1846, it was based on a journal entry from September 1841, featuring Emerson's autobiographical persona "Osman":

> O[sman] said that when he went a-berrying the devil got into the blueberries & tempted him to eat a bellyful, but if he came to a spring of water he would wash his hands & mouth & promise himself that he would eat no more. Instantly the devil would come to him again in the shape of larger & fairer berries than any he had yet found, & if he still passed them by, he would bring him blackberries, and if that would not serve, then grapes. He said, of one thing he was persuaded, that wisdom & berries grew on the same bushes, but that only one could ever be plucked at one time. (*JMN* 8:50)

Emerson read the poem in 1855 to a young protégé, Franklin Benjamin Sanborn (1831–1917), and, playing Sphinx, asked him what he thought it meant. "I hardly knew what to reply," recalled Sanborn, "where several meanings were possible; but said that he must have meant that Nature does not leave her least particle without a lesson for Man; that the moral of the delicious flavor of the low blackberry was 'Even so, what seems black to you in Man's destiny may have as fair an issue.'" Emerson smiled at this but withheld comment (Sanborn, p. 79).

BERRYING

'May be true what I had heard,—
Earth's a howling wilderness,
Truculent with fraud and force,'
Said I, strolling through the pastures,
And along the river-side.   5
Caught among the blackberry vines,
Feeding on the Ethiops sweet,
Pleasant fancies overtook me.
I said, 'What influence me preferred,
Elect, to dreams thus beautiful?'   10
The vines replied, 'And didst thou deem
No wisdom from our berries went?'

1846 || 1846

THE SNOW-STORM

When the heavy snowfall of December 29, 1834, struck Concord, Emerson was living in the upstairs back room of the Old Manse, the home of his step-grandfather, the Rev. Ezra Ripley. That evening he wrote in his journal:

> The great willowtree over my roof is the trumpet & accompaniment of the storm & gives due importance to every caprice of the gale and the trees in the avenue announce the same facts with equal din to the front tenants. Hoarse concert: they roar like the rigging of a ship in a tempest. (*JMN* 4:384)

The language about the trumpet and the annunciation, as Alan D. Hodder has pointed out (p. 47), reflects Emerson's adverse response to his grandfather's apocalyptic preaching. A paragraph written earlier the same evening, in which Emerson hoped he might eventually clarify "the distinction between a spiritual & a traditional religion," begins with an allusion to the storm: "To the music of the surly storm that thickens the darkness of the night abroad & rocks the walls & fans my cheek through the chinks & cracks, I would sing my strain though hoarse & small" (*JMN* 4:382). The journal entries of that day suggest Emerson's awareness that the end-of-the-world weather and the character of his religious speculations were connected, even as they would be again, in a famous passage from the Divinity School Address, in which he depicts another formalist Concord preacher, Barzillai Frost, as a merely "spectral" figure standing in his pulpit athwart the real snowstorm appearing in the window behind him (*CW* 1:85).

Probably within a day or two of the blizzard Emerson wrote "The Snow-Storm," first in prose (not his usual practice), yet with such intermittent capitalization as to show that he knew it was poetry already (*JMN* 6:246). Here the transformative power that descends out of "heaven" is no less the divine architect (deriving form from chaos) than the figure envisioned in traditional apocalypses. The prehistory of architecture, as of the other arts, lay for Emerson in the primary forms of nature, an insight central to the organic basis of his aesthetic theorizing in the 1830s, beginning with the first lecture he ever gave, which included a discussion of the beauty of falling and fallen snow (*EL* 1:15; cf. *JMN* 4:60–62). A brief but concentrated treatment of this natural artistry occurs in "History" (1841), where Emerson mentions having seen "a snow-drift along the sides of the stone wall which obviously gave the idea of the common architectural scroll to abut a tower" (*CW* 2:11).

The treatment of the poem by Carl F. Strauch in "The Year of Emerson's Poetic Maturity" mainly concerns Emerson's dependence on the writings of the Cambridge Platonist Ralph Cudworth, from which "spring directly" the poem's "central ideas": that "nature, in a frolic mood and in the briefest span of time, has created an architecture which the art of man can laboriously mimic only through long ages" (p. 374).

THE SNOW-STORM

Announced by all the trumpets of the sky,
Arrives the snow, and, driving o'er the fields,
Seems nowhere to alight: the whited air
Hides hills and woods, the river, and the heaven,
And veils the farm-house at the garden's end.   5
The sled and traveller stopped, the courier's feet
Delayed, all friends shut out, the housemates sit
Around the radiant fireplace, enclosed
In a tumultuous privacy of storm.

    Come see the north wind's masonry.   10
Out of an unseen quarry evermore
Furnished with tile, the fierce artificer
Curves his white bastions with projected roof
Round every windward stake, or tree, or door.
Speeding, the myriad-handed, his wild work   15
So fanciful, so savage, nought cares he
For number or proportion. Mockingly,
On coop or kennel he hangs Parian wreaths;
A swan-like form invests the hidden thorn;
Fills up the farmer's lane from wall to wall,   20
Maugre the farmer's sighs; and, at the gate,
A tapering turret overtops the work.
And when his hours are numbered, and the world
Is all his own, retiring, as he were not,
Leaves, when the sun appears, astonished Art   25
To mimic in slow structures, stone by stone,
Built in an age, the mad wind's night-work,
The frolic architecture of the snow.

1834 || 1841

WOODNOTES II

The two poems entitled "Woodnotes" are longish meditations on subjects drawn from nature but have otherwise little in common. "Woodnotes I" was a pastiche of four poems recalling a visit to the forests of Maine in 1835, written in the summer of that year and published in the *Dial* in October 1840. "Woodnotes II" is a longer and more unified poem, of greater philosophical interest, as it engages most of the themes that Emerson raised in his address of August 11, 1841, at Waterville College, published as "The Method of Nature" (*CW* 1:117–137). Before the poem's publication in the October 1841 issue of the *Dial*, Emerson referred to it, presumably in an earlier version, as the "Walden or Waldonian poems" and to a near-final version as "The Pine Tree" (*L* 2:405, 7:458). Lines 251–273 were a late addition, prompted by a picnic held at the "Cliff" above the western shore of Walden Pond, on June 7, 1841. This gathering was attended by Emerson and his family, Thoreau, a number of mothers with their children, and the single Caroline Sturgis—"my summer harp" (*L* 7:457). The picnic was captured in a contemporaneous journal entry: "At the Cliff & charged nature with emptiness. That was the expression of the wide amphitheatre to the blank eye. It seemed as if the curtain should every moment rise & this maternal cluck which filled the groves & all this ado & flutter of small creatures give place to what is truly great. But thus is the particular & near ever standing in eternal contrast to the grand horizon of sun & stars that shuts down or shuts never down above it" (*JMN* 8:494–495).

WOODNOTES II

As sunbeams stream through liberal space,
And nothing jostle or displace,
So waved the pine-tree through my thought,
And fanned the dreams it never brought.

'Whether is better the gift or the donor?   5
Come to me,'
Quoth the pine-tree,
'I am the giver of honor.
My garden is the cloven rock,
And my manure the snow;   10
And drifting sand-heaps feed my stock,
In summer's scorching glow.

Ancient or curious,
Who knoweth aught of us?
Old as Jove, 15
Old as Love,
Who of me
Tells the pedigree?
Only the mountains old,
Only the waters cold, 20
Only moon and star
My coevals are.
Ere the first fowl sung
My relenting boughs among,
Ere Adam wived, 25
Ere Adam lived,
Ere the duck dived,
Ere the bees hived,
Ere the lion roared,
Ere the eagle soared, 30
Light and heat, land and sea,
Spake unto the oldest tree.
Glad in the sweet and secret aid
Which matter unto matter paid,
The water flowed, the breezes fanned, 35
The tree confined the roving sand,
The sunbeam gave me to the sight,
The tree adorned the formless light,
And once again
O'er the grave of men 40
We shall talk to each other again
Of the old age behind,
Of the time out of mind,
Which shall come again.

'Whether is better the gift or the donor? 45
Come to me,'
Quoth the pine-tree,
'I am the giver of honor.
He is great who can live by me.

The rough and bearded forester   50
Is better than the lord;
God fills the scrip and canister,
Sin piles the loaded board.
The lord is the peasant that was,
The peasant the lord that shall be;   55
The lord is hay, the peasant grass,
One dry, and one the living tree.
Genius with my boughs shall flourish,
Want and cold our roots shall nourish.
Who liveth by the ragged pine   60
Foundeth a heroic line;
Who liveth in the palace hall
Waneth fast and spendeth all.
He goes to my savage haunts,
With his chariot and his care;   65
My twilight realm he disenchants,
And finds his prison there.

'What prizes the town and the tower?
Only what the pine-tree yields;
Sinew that subdued the fields;   70
The wild-eyed boy, who in the woods
Chants his hymn to hills and floods,
Whom the city's poisoning spleen
Made not pale, or fat, or lean;
Whom the rain and the wind purgeth,   75
Whom the dawn and the day-star urgeth,
In whose cheek the rose-leaf blusheth,
In whose feet the lion rusheth,
Iron arms, and iron mould,
That know not fear, fatigue, or cold.   80
I give my rafters to his boat,
My billets to his boiler's throat;
And I will swim the ancient sea,
To float my child to victory,
And grant to dwellers with the pine   85
Dominion o'er the palm and vine.

Westward I ope the forest gates,
The train along the railroad skates;
It leaves the land behind like ages past,
The foreland flows to it in river fast;   90
Missouri I have made a mart,
I teach Iowa Saxon art.
Who leaves the pine-tree, leaves his friend,
Unnerves his strength, invites his end.
Cut a bough from my parent stem,   95
And dip it in thy porcelain vase;
A little while each russet gem
Will swell and rise with wonted grace;
But when it seeks enlarged supplies,
The orphan of the forest dies.   100
Whoso walketh in solitude,
And inhabiteth the wood,
Choosing light, wave, rock, and bird,
Before the money-loving herd,
Into that forester shall pass,   105
From these companions, power and grace.
Clean shall he be, without, within,
From the old adhering sin.
Love shall he, but not adulate
The all-fair, the all-embracing Fate;   110
All ill dissolving in the light
Of his triumphant piercing sight.
Not vain, sour, nor frivolous;
Not mad, athirst, nor garrulous;
Grave, chaste, contented, though retired,   115
And of all other men desired.
On him the light of star and moon
Shall fall with purer radiance down;
All constellations of the sky
Shed their virtue through his eye.   120
Him Nature giveth for defence
His formidable innocence;
The mounting sap, the shells, the sea,
All spheres, all stones, his helpers be;

He shall never be old; 125
Nor his fate shall be foretold;
He shall meet the speeding year,
Without wailing, without fear;
He shall be happy in his love,
Like to like shall joyful prove; 130
He shall be happy whilst he woos,
Muse-born, a daughter of the Muse.
But if with gold she bind her hair,
And deck her breast with diamond,
Take off thine eyes, thy heart forbear, 135
Though thou lie alone on the ground.
The robe of silk in which she shines,
It was woven of many sins;
And the shreds
Which she sheds 140
In the wearing of the same,
Shall be grief on grief,
And shame on shame.

'Heed the old oracles,
Ponder my spells; 145
Song wakes in my pinnacles
When the wind swells.
Soundeth the prophetic wind,
The shadows shake on the rock behind,
And the countless leaves of the pine are strings 150
Tuned to the lay the wood-god sings.
    Hearken! Hearken!
If thou wouldst know the mystic song
Chanted when the sphere was young.
Aloft, abroad, the pæan swells; 155
O wise man! hear'st thou half it tells?
O wise man! hear'st thou the least part?
'Tis the chronicle of art.
To the open ear it sings
Sweet the genesis of things, 160
Of tendency through endless ages,
Of star-dust, and star-pilgrimages,

Of rounded worlds, of space and time,
Of the old flood's subsiding slime,
Of chemic matter, force, and form,   165
Of poles and powers, cold, wet, and warm:
The rushing metamorphosis,
Dissolving all that fixture is,
Melts things that be to things that seem,
And solid nature to a dream.   170
O, listen to the undersong—
The ever old, the ever young;
And, far within those cadent pauses,
The chorus of the ancient Causes!
Delights the dreadful Destiny   175
To fling his voice into the tree,
And shock thy weak ear with a note
Breathed from the everlasting throat.
In music he repeats the pang
Whence the fair flock of Nature sprang.   180
O mortal! thy ears are stones;
These echoes are laden with tones
Which only the pure can hear;
Thou canst not catch what they recite
Of Fate and Will, of Want and Right,   185
Of man to come, of human life,
Of Death, and Fortune, Growth, and Strife.'

    Once again the pine-tree sung:—
'Speak not thy speech my boughs among;
Put off thy years, wash in the breeze;   190
My hours are peaceful centuries.
Talk no more with feeble tongue;
No more the fool of space and time,
Come weave with mine a nobler rhyme.
Only thy Americans   195
Can read thy line, can meet thy glance,
But the runes that I rehearse
Understands the universe;
The least breath my boughs which tossed
Brings again the Pentecost;   200

To every soul resounding clear
In a voice of solemn cheer,—
"Am I not thine? Are not these thine?"
And they reply, "Forever mine!"
My branches speak Italian,   205
English, German, Basque, Castilian,
Mountain speech to Highlanders,
Ocean tongues to islanders,
To Fin, and Lap, and swart Malay,
To each his bosom-secret say.   210
    'Come learn with me the fatal song
Which knits the world in music strong,
Whereto every bosom dances,
Kindled with courageous fancies.
Come lift thine eyes to lofty rhymes,   215
Of things with things, of times with times,
Primal chimes of sun and shade,
Of sound and echo, man and maid,
The land reflected in the flood,
Body with shadow still pursued.   220
For Nature beats in perfect tune,
And rounds with rhyme her every rune,
Whether she work in land or sea,
Or hide underground her alchemy.
Thou canst not wave thy staff in air,   225
Or dip thy paddle in the lake,
But it carves the bow of beauty there,
And the ripples in rhymes the oar forsake.
The wood is wiser far than thou;
The wood and wave each other know.   230
Not unrelated, unaffied,
But to each thought and thing allied,
Is perfect Nature's every part,
Rooted in the mighty Heart.
But thou, poor child! unbound, unrhymed,   235
Whence camest thou, misplaced, mistimed?
Whence, O thou orphan and defrauded?
Is thy land peeled, thy realm marauded?

Who thee divorced, deceived, and left?
Thee of thy faith who hath bereft, 240
And torn the ensigns from thy brow,
And sunk the immortal eye so low?
Thy cheek too white, thy form too slender,
Thy gait too slow, thy habits tender
For royal man;—they thee confess 245
An exile from the wilderness,—
The hills where health with health agrees,
And the wise soul expels disease.
Hark! in thy ear I will tell the sign
By which thy hurt thou may'st divine. 250
When thou shalt climb the mountain cliff,
Or see the wide shore from thy skiff,
To thee the horizon shall express
Only emptiness and emptiness;
There lives no man of Nature's worth 255
In the circle of the earth;
And to thine eye the vast skies fall,
Dire and satirical,
On clucking hens, and prating fools,
On thieves, on drudges, and on dolls. 260
And thou shalt say to the Most High,
"Godhead! all this astronomy,
And fate, and practice, and invention,
Strong art, and beautiful pretension,
This radiant pomp of sun and star, 265
Throes that were, and worlds that are,
Behold! were in vain and in vain;—
It cannot be,—I will look again;
Surely now will the curtain rise,
And earth's fit tenant me surprise;— 270
But the curtain doth *not* rise,
And Nature has miscarried wholly
Into failure, into folly."

'Alas! thine is the bankruptcy,
Blessed Nature so to see. 275

Come, lay thee in my soothing shade,
And heal the hurts which sin has made.
I will teach the bright parable
Older than time,
Things undeclarable,   280
Visions sublime.
I see thee in the crowd alone;
I will be thy companion.
Quit thy friends as the dead in doom,
And build to them a final tomb;   285
Let the starred shade that nightly falls
Still celebrate their funerals,
And the bell of beetle and of bee
Knell their melodious memory.
Behind thee leave thy merchandise,   290
Thy churches, and thy charities;
And leave thy peacock wit behind;
Enough for thee the primal mind
That flows in streams, that breathes in wind.
Leave all thy pedant lore apart;   295
God hid the whole world in thy heart.
Love shuns the sage, the child it crowns,
And gives them all who all renounce.
The rain comes when the wind calls;
The river knows the way to the sea;   300
Without a pilot it runs and falls,
Blessing all lands with its charity;
The sea tosses and foams to find
Its way up to the cloud and wind;
The shadow sits close to the flying ball;   305
The date fails not on the palm-tree tall;
And thou,—go burn thy wormy pages,—
Shalt outsee seers, and outwit sages.
Oft didst thou thread the woods in vain
To find what bird had piped the strain;—   310
Seek not, and the little eremite
Flies gaily forth and sings in sight.

'Hearken once more!
I will tell thee the mundane lore.
Older am I than thy numbers wot;   315
Change I may, but I pass not.
Hitherto all things fast abide,
And anchored in the tempest ride.
Trenchant time behoves to hurry
All to yean and all to bury: 320
All the forms are fugitive,
But the substances survive.
Ever fresh the broad creation,
A divine improvisation,
From the heart of God proceeds,   325
A single will, a million deeds.
Once slept the world an egg of stone,
And pulse, and sound, and light was none;
And God said, "Throb!" and there was motion,
And the vast mass became vast ocean.   330
Onward and on, the eternal Pan,
Who layeth the world's incessant plan,
Halteth never in one shape,
But forever doth escape,
Like wave or flame, into new forms   335
Of gem, and air, of plants, and worms.
I, that today am a pine,
Yesterday was a bundle of grass.
He is free and libertine,
Pouring of his power the wine   340
To every age, to every race;
Unto every race and age
He emptieth the beverage;
Unto each, and unto all,
Maker and original.   345
The world is the ring of his spells,
And the play of his miracles.
As he giveth to all to drink,
Thus or thus they are and think.

He giveth little or giveth much, 350
To make them several or such.
With one drop sheds form and feature;
With the next a special nature;
The third adds heat's indulgent spark;
The fourth gives light which eats the dark; 355
Into the fifth himself he flings,
And conscious Law is King of kings.
Pleaseth him, the Eternal Child,
To play his sweet will, glad and wild;
As the bee through the garden ranges, 360
From world to world the godhead changes;
As the sheep go feeding in the waste,
From form to form he maketh haste;
This vault which glows immense with light
Is the inn where he lodges for a night. 365
What recks such Traveller if the bowers
Which bloom and fade like meadow flowers
A bunch of fragrant lilies be,
Or the stars of eternity?
Alike to him the better, the worse,— 370
The glowing angel, the outcast corse.
Thou metest him by centuries,
And lo! he passes like the breeze;
Thou seek'st in globe and galaxy,
He hides in pure transparency; 375
Thou askest in fountains and in fires,
He is the essence that inquires.
He is the axis of the star;
He is the sparkle of the spar;
He is the heart of every creature; 380
He is the meaning of each feature;
And his mind is the sky,
Than all it holds more deep, more high.'

1841 || 1841

MONADNOC

Mount Monadnoc (or Monadnock, as it is more usually written) is an isolated peak in Cheshire County in southern New Hampshire, near the towns of Troy, Jaffrey, Dublin, and Peterborough. Though sixty miles distant from Emerson's home in Concord, it is visible from a number of elevated points in or near the town. The poet briefly thought of building on a homesite across from the Old Manse "on Grandfather's hill facing Wachusett & Monadnoc & the setting sun" (*L* 1:445). He traveled to the mountain many times—first, perhaps, in 1838 on his way to deliver his oration on "Literary Ethics" at Dartmouth College (*L* 2:144). It was his excursion in June of 1846, however, that inspired the poem; he read the finished work to Bronson Alcott on June 28 (Alcott, p. 182; *L* 8:77).

Like "The Sphinx" and "Woodnotes II," "Monadnoc" is a meditation on nature's symbolism and its self-superseding effort to express its "secret" to the willing human mind (see ll. 272–275). In 1845–46 Emerson had failed with an earlier and more politically charged conception, in which Wachusett (a modest eminence near Princeton, Massachusetts) addressed Grand Monadnoc in protest against American militarism in the run-up to the Mexican War. Little of this inspiration survives in "Monadnoc," as the author's impulse to protest was simultaneously channeled into the "Ode, Inscribed to W. H. Channing." The poem "Wachusett" had been slated for inclusion in the 1847 *Poems*, but "Monadnoc" was in the end substituted for it (see *PN,* pp. 713–714, for the text of "Wachusett").

MONADNOC

Thousand minstrels woke within me,
    'Our music's in the hills;'—
Gayest pictures rose to win me,
    Leopard-colored rills.
'Up!—If thou knew'st who calls   5
To twilight parks of beech and pine,
High over the river intervals,
Above the ploughman's highest line,
Over the owner's farthest walls!
Up! where the airy citadel   10
O'erlooks the surging landscape's swell!
Let not unto the stones the Day

Her lily and rose, her sea and land display.
Read the celestial sign!
Lo! the south answers to the north;   15
Bookworm, break this sloth urbane;
A greater spirit bids thee forth
Than the gray dreams which thee detain.
Mark how the climbing Oreads
Beckon thee to their arcades!   20
Youth, for a moment free as they,
Teach thy feet to feel the ground,
Ere yet arrives the wintry day
When Time thy feet has bound.
Take the bounty of thy birth,   25
Taste the lordship of the earth.'

    I heard, and I obeyed,—
Assured that he who made the claim,
Well known, but loving not a name,
      Was not to be gainsaid.   30

Ere yet the summoning voice was still,
I turned to Cheshire's haughty hill.
From the fixed cone the cloud-rack flowed,
Like ample banner flung abroad
To all the dwellers in the plains   35
Round about, a hundred miles,
With salutation to the sea, and to the bordering isles.

In his own loom's garment dressed,
By his proper bounty blessed,
Fast abides this constant giver,   40
Pouring many a cheerful river;
To far eyes, an aerial isle
Unploughed, which finer spirits pile,
Which morn and crimson evening paint
For bard, for lover, and for saint;   45
The people's pride, the country's core,
Inspirer, prophet evermore;
Pillar which God aloft had set

So that men might it not forget;
It should be their life's ornament,   50
And mix itself with each event;
Gauge and calendar and dial,
Weatherglass and chemic phial,
Garden of berries, perch of birds,
Pasture of pool-haunting herds,   55
Graced by each change of sum untold,
Earth-baking heat, stone-cleaving cold.

The Titan heeds his sky-affairs,
Rich rents and wide alliance shares;
Mysteries of color daily laid   60
By morn and eve in light and shade;
And sweet varieties of chance,
And the mystic seasons' dance;
And thief-like step of liberal hours
Thawing snow-drift into flowers.   65
O, wondrous craft of plant and stone
By eldest science wrought and shown!

'Happy,' I said, 'whose home is here!
Fair fortunes to the mountaineer!
Boon Nature to his poorest shed   70
Has royal pleasure-grounds outspread.'
Intent, I searched the region round,
And in low hut my monarch found:—
Woe is me for my hope's downfall!
Is yonder squalid peasant all   75
That this proud nursery could breed
For God's vicegerency and stead?
Time out of mind, this forge of ores;
Quarry of spars in mountain pores;
Old cradle, hunting-ground, and bier   80
Of wolf and otter, bear and deer;
Well-built abode of many a race;
Tower of observance searching space;
Factory of river and of rain;
Link in the alps' globe-girding chain;   85

By million changes skilled to tell
What in the Eternal standeth well,
And what obedient Nature can;—
Is this colossal talisman
Kindly to plant, and blood, and kind,   90
But speechless to the master's mind?
I thought to find the patriots
In whom the stock of freedom roots:
To myself I oft recount
Tales of many a famous mount,—   95
Wales, Scotland, Uri, Hungary's dells;
Bards, Roys, Scanderbegs, and Tells.
Here Nature shall condense her powers,
Her music, and her meteors,
And lifting man to the blue deep   100
Where stars their perfect courses keep,
Like wise preceptor, lure his eye
To sound the science of the sky,
And carry learning to its height
Of untried power and sane delight: 105
The Indian cheer, the frosty skies,
Rear purer wits, inventive eyes,—
Eyes that frame cities where none be,
And hands that stablish what these see;
And by the moral of his place   110
Hint summits of heroic grace;
Man in these crags a fastness find
To fight pollution of the mind;
In the wide thaw and ooze of wrong,
Adhere like this foundation strong,   115
The insanity of towns to stem
With simpleness for stratagem.
But if the brave old mould is broke,
And end in churls the mountain folk,
In tavern cheer and tavern joke,   120
Sink, O mountain, in the swamp!
Hide in thy skies, O sovereign lamp!

Perish like leaves, the highland breed!
No sire survive, no son succeed!

Soft! let not the offended muse   125
Toil's hard hap with scorn accuse.
Many hamlets sought I then,
Many farms of mountain men.
Rallying round a parish steeple
Nestle warm the highland people,   130
Coarse and boisterous, yet mild,
Strong as giant, slow as child,
Smoking in a squalid room
Where yet the westland breezes come.
Masked in those rough guises lurk   135
Western magians,—here they work.
Sweat and season are their arts,
Their talismans are ploughs and carts;
And well the youngest can command
Honey from the frozen land;   140
With cloverheads the swamp adorn,
Change the running sand to corn;
For wolves and foxes, lowing herds,
And for cold mosses, cream and curds;
Weave wood to canisters and mats;   145
Drain sweet maple juice in vats.
No bird is safe that cuts the air
From their rifle or their snare;
No fish, in river or in lake,
But their long hands it thence will take;   150
And the country's flinty face,
Like wax, their fashioning skill betrays,
To fill the hollows, sink the hills,
Bridge gulfs, drain swamps, build dams and mills,
And fit the bleak and howling place   155
For gardens of a finer race.
The World-soul knows his own affair,
Forelooking, when he would prepare

For the next ages, men of mould
Well embodied, well ensouled,   160
He cools the present's fiery glow,
Sets the life-pulse strong but slow:
Bitter winds and fasts austere
His quarantines and grottos, where
He slowly cures decrepit flesh,   165
And brings it infantile and fresh.
Toil and tempest are the toys
And games to breathe his stalwart boys:
They bide their time, and well can prove,
If need were, their line from Jove;   170
Of the same stuff, and so allayed,
As that whereof the sun is made,
And of the fibre, quick and strong,
Whose throbs are love, whose thrills are song.

Now in sordid weeds they sleep,   175
In dulness now their secret keep;
Yet, will you learn our ancient speech,
These the masters who can teach.
Fourscore or a hundred words
All their vocal muse affords;   180
But they turn them in a fashion
Past clerks' or statesmen's art or passion.
I can spare the college bell,
And the learned lecture, well;
Spare the clergy and libraries,   185
Institutes and dictionaries,
For that hardy English root
Thrives here, unvalued, underfoot.
Rude poets of the tavern hearth,
Squandering your unquoted mirth,   190
Which keeps the ground, and never soars,
While Jake retorts, and Reuben roars;
Scoff of yeoman strong and stark,
Goes like bullet to its mark;

While the solid curse and jeer   195
Never balk the waiting ear.

On the summit as I stood,
O'er the floor of plain and flood,
Seemed to me the towering hill
Was not altogether still,   200
But a quiet sense conveyed;
If I err not, thus it said:—

'Many feet in summer seek,
Oft, my far-appearing peak;
In the dreaded winter time,   205
None save dappling shadows climb,
Under clouds, my lonely head,
Old as the sun, old almost as the shade.
And comest thou
To see strange forests and new snow,   210
And tread uplifted land?
And leavest thou thy lowland race,
Here amid clouds to stand?
And wouldst be my companion,
Where I gaze, and still shall gaze,   215
Thro' tempering nights and flashing days,
When forests fall, and man is gone,
Over tribes and over times,
At the burning Lyre,
Nearing me,   220
With its stars of northern fire,
In many a thousand years?

'Ah! welcome, if thou bring
My secret in thy brain;
To mountain-top may Muse's wing   225
With good allowance strain.
Gentle pilgrim, if thou know
The gamut old of Pan,
And how the hills began,

The frank blessings of the hill   230
Fall on thee, as fall they will.
'Tis the law of bush and stone,
Each can only take his own.

'Let him heed who can and will;
Enchantment fixed me here   235
To stand the hurts of time, until
In mightier chant I disappear.
     'If thou trowest
How the chemic eddies play,
Pole to pole, and what they say;   240
And that these gray crags
Not on crags are hung,
But beads are of a rosary
On prayer and music strung;
And, credulous, through the granite seeming,   245
Seest the smile of Reason beaming;—
Can thy style-discerning eye
The hidden-working Builder spy,
Who builds, yet makes no chips, no din,
With hammer soft as snowflake's flight;—   250
Knowest thou this?
O pilgrim, wandering not amiss!
Already my rocks lie light,
And soon my cone will spin.

'For the world was built in order,   255
And the atoms march in tune;
Rhyme the pipe, and Time the warder,
The sun obeys them, and the moon.
Orb and atom forth they prance,
When they hear from far the rune;   260
None so backward in the troop,
When the music and the dance
Reach his place and circumstance,
But knows the sun-creating sound,
And, though a pyramid, will bound.   265

'Monadnoc is a mountain strong,
Tall and good my kind among;
But well I know, no mountain can,
Zion or Meru, measure with man.
For it is on zodiacs writ,   270
Adamant is soft to wit:
And when the greater comes again
With my secret in his brain,
I shall pass, as glides my shadow
Daily over hill and meadow.   275

'Through all time, in light, in gloom,
Well I hear the approaching feet
On the flinty pathway beat
Of him that cometh, and shall come;
Of him who shall as lightly bear   280
My daily load of woods and streams,
As doth this round sky-cleaving boat
Which never strains its rocky beams;
Whose timbers, as they silent float,
Alps and Caucasus uprear,   285
And the long Alleganies here,
And all town-sprinkled lands that be,
Sailing through stars with all their history.

'Every morn I lift my head,
See New England underspread,   290
South from Saint Lawrence to the Sound,
From Katskill east to the sea-bound.
Anchored fast for many an age,
I await the bard and sage,
Who, in large thoughts, like fair pearl-seed,   295
Shall string Monadnoc like a bead.
Comes that cheerful troubadour,
This mound shall throb his face before,
As when, with inward fires and pain,
It rose a bubble from the plain.   300
When he cometh, I shall shed,

From this wellspring in my head,
Fountain-drop of spicier worth
Than all vintage of the earth.
There's fruit upon my barren soil   305
Costlier far than wine or oil.
There's a berry blue and gold,—
Autumn-ripe, its juices hold
Sparta's stoutness, Bethlehem's heart,
Asia's rancor, Athens' art,   310
Slowsure Britain's secular might,
And the German's inward sight.
I will give my son to eat
Best of Pan's immortal meat,
Bread to eat, and juice to drain;   315
So the coinage of his brain
Shall not be forms of stars, but stars,
Nor pictures pale, but Jove and Mars.
He comes, but not of that race bred
Who daily climb my specular head.   320
Oft as morning wreathes my scarf,
Fled the last plumule of the Dark,
Pants up hither the spruce clerk
From South Cove and City Wharf.
I take him up my rugged sides,   325
Half-repentant, scant of breath,—
Bead-eyes my granite chaos show,
And my midsummer snow;
Open the daunting map beneath,—
All his county, sea and land,   330
Dwarfed to measure of his hand;
His day's ride is a furlong space,
His city-tops a glimmering haze.
I plant his eyes on the sky-hoop bounding:
"See there the grim gray rounding   335
Of the bullet of the earth
Whereon ye sail,
Tumbling steep
In the uncontinented deep."

He looks on that, and he turns pale. 340
'Tis even so; this treacherous kite,
Farm-furrowed, town-incrusted sphere,
Thoughtless of its anxious freight,
Plunges eyeless on forever;
And he, poor parasite, 345
Cooped in a ship he cannot steer,—
Who is the captain he knows not,
Port or pilot trows not,—
Risk or ruin he must share.
I scowl on him with my cloud, 350
With my north wind chill his blood;
I lame him, clattering down the rocks;
And to live he is in fear.
Then, at last, I let him down
Once more into his dapper town, 355
To chatter, frightened, to his clan,
And forget me if he can.'

As in the old poetic fame
The gods are blind and lame,
And the simular despite 360
Betrays the more abounding might,
So call not waste that barren cone
Above the floral zone,
Where forests starve:
It is pure use;— 365
What sheaves like those which here we glean and bind
Of a celestial Ceres and the Muse?

Ages are thy days,
Thou grand affirmer of the present tense,
And type of permanence! 370
Firm ensign of the fatal Being,
Amid these coward shapes of joy and grief,
That will not bide the seeing!

Hither we bring
Our insect miseries to thy rocks; 375

And the whole flight, with folded wing,
Vanish, and end their murmuring,—
Vanish beside these dedicated blocks,
Which who can tell what mason laid?
Spoils of a front none need restore, 380
Replacing frieze and architrave;—
Yet flowers each stone rosette and metope brave;
Still is the haughty pile erect
Of the old building Intellect.

Complement of human kind, 385
Having us at vantage still,
Our sumptuous indigence,
O barren mound, thy plenties fill!
We fool and prate;
Thou art silent and sedate. 390
To myriad kinds and times one sense
The constant mountain doth dispense;
Shedding on all its snows and leaves,
One joy it joys, one grief it grieves.
Thou seest, O watchman tall, 395
Our towns and races grow and fall,
And imagest the stable good
For which we all our lifetime grope,
In shifting form the formless mind,
And though the substance us elude, 400
We in thee the shadow find.

Thou, in our astronomy
An opaker star,
Seen haply from afar,
Above the horizon's hoop, 405
A moment, by the railway troop,
As o'er some bolder height they speed,—
By circumspect ambition,
By errant gain,
By feasters and the frivolous,— 410
Recallest us,
And makest sane.

Mute orator! well skilled to plead,
And send conviction without phrase,
Thou dost succor and remede   415
The shortness of our days,
And promise, on thy Founder's truth,
Long morrow to this mortal youth.

1846 ‖ 1846

FABLE

Emerson's decision to place this short, comic poem immediately after the long, imposing "Monadnoc" in *Poems* (1847) is itself an instance of the dramatic conflict rehearsed in the parable. As he had said, "It is the right & property of all natural objects, of all genuine talents, of all native properties whatsoever, to be for their moment the top of the world, to exclude all other objects, & themselves monopolize the attention. A squirrel or a rabbit as I watch him bounding in the wood, not less than a lion fills the eye, is beautiful, sufficing, & stands then & there for nature; is the world" (*JMN* 7:199–200; May 26, 1839).

Edgar Allan Poe liked this poem, calling it "exceedingly *piquant* and *naive*" (Thomas and Jackson, p. 605). It was a favorite principally with children and was quickly reprinted from its first appearance in a gift-book (*The Diadem*, edited by Emerson's Philadelphia friend William H. Furness) in the March 1, 1846 issue of *Boston Gospel Teacher, and Sabbath School Contributor*. Perhaps because the Emerson children so much enjoyed it, "A Fable" was included in the 1876 *Selected Poems* against the advice of James Russell Lowell (*ETE* 2:196–197).

FABLE

The mountain and the squirrel
Had a quarrel;
And the former called the latter 'Little Prig.'
Bun replied,
'You are doubtless very big;   5
But all sorts of things and weather
Must be taken in together,
To make up a year
And a sphere.
And I think it no disgrace   10
To occupy my place.
If I'm not so large as you,
You are not so small as I,
And not half so spry.
I'll not deny you make   15
A very pretty squirrel track;
Talents differ; all is well and wisely put;
If I cannot carry forests on my back,
Neither can you crack a nut.'

1845 || 1845

ODE,
INSCRIBED TO W. H. CHANNING

One of the most challenging and rewarding of Emerson's poems, the "Ode, Inscribed to W. H. Channing" was written in the first week of June 1846 while the poet was on a brief excursion to New Hampshire's Mount Monadnoc. Over the previous two years, Emerson had taken a markedly more active role in the antislavery movement, having delivered major addresses on the annual abolitionist holiday of August 1 in 1844 and 1845, speaking, in the latter instance, from the same platform with William Henry Channing (1810–1884). A nephew of the late William Ellery Channing, the preeminent figure in American Unitarianism, the younger Channing was during the 1840s deeply interested in Fourierism and antislavery. He belonged to the Transcendentalist circle through his connections with its major journals, the *Western Messenger,* the *Dial,* and the *Present,* as well as such institutions as Brook Farm, where he was a favorite preacher, and the Boston Religious Union of Associationists, a Christian socialist organization. At the time Emerson's poem was published, Channing was identified with an emerging disunionist policy originally framed by radical abolitionists as a response to the Texas annexation controversy. When Texas formally entered the Union on December 29, 1845, many Americans feared not only the likelihood of war with Mexico but a decisive political triumph for the Southern slave power in the threatened imbalance of slave and free states. The administration of James K. Polk, in fact, secured a declaration of war against Mexico on May 11, 1846. Eight days later, with public feeling running high, a funeral (in the form of a massive political demonstration at Boston's Masonic Temple) was held for Charles Turner Torrey, a Salem minister who had died in Maryland State Prison, where he had been confined for helping slaves to escape. The "funeral eloquence" mentioned in line 34 was that of the occasion's main speaker, Rev. Joseph C. Lovejoy, brother of the abolitionist editor Elijah P. Lovejoy, notoriously the victim of a murderous proslavery mob in Alton, Illinois, in 1837. Emerson was in the audience to hear Lovejoy's eulogy for Torrey; he found it eloquent and moving (*JMN* 9:382, 418). Ten days later, on May 29, Channing gave his most important disunionist speech, at Boston's Faneuil Hall before the annual New England Anti-Slavery Convention.

No doubt some of the poem's power derives from the private history of the Channing-Emerson relationship. In an 1842 letter, Channing dissented from Emerson's emphasis on individualism as opposed to a cooperative approach to matters of reform: "*You deny the human Race,*" he said. "You stand, or rather seek to stand, a complete Adam. But you cannot do it" (quoted in Gougeon, *Virtue's Hero,* p. 71). Emerson, who had heard this charge before, responded first in journal entries, then by letters, and finally, and to greatest effect, in his poem. In an 1842 journal entry he had written,

I should write again to W. H. C. & say, He that unites himself to the
race separates himself from the Father but he who by love & con-
templation dwells with the father, from him the Race always pro-
ceeds filially & new, and the actual race feel in his presence their
degeneracy & his salutary redeeming force. Keep thyself pure from
the race. Come to them only as saviour, not as companion. (*JMN*
8:186)

Channing's view of the poet's duty in political matters echoed that of Samuel
Johnson in his criticism of Milton's "great promise and small performance"—
referring to behavior on Milton's part that Emerson understood very differ-
ently and clearly admired (*CW* 10:88).

ODE,

INSCRIBED TO W. H. CHANNING

Though loath to grieve
The evil time's sole patriot,
I cannot leave
My honied thought
For the priest's cant,   5
Or statesman's rant.

If I refuse
My study for their politique,
Which at the best is trick,
The angry Muse   10
Puts confusion in my brain.

But who is he that prates
Of the culture of mankind,
Of better arts and life?
Go, blindworm, go,   15
Behold the famous States
Harrying Mexico
With rifle and with knife!

Or who, with accent bolder,
Dare praise the freedom-loving mountaineer?   20

I found by thee, O rushing Contoocook!
And in thy valleys, Agiochook!
The jackals of the negro-holder.

The God who made New Hampshire
Taunted the lofty land   25
With little men;—
Small bat and wren
House in the oak:—
If earth-fire cleave
The upheaved land, and bury the folk,   30
The southern crocodile would grieve.

Virtue palters; Right is hence;
Freedom praised, but hid;
Funeral eloquence
Rattles the coffin-lid.   35

What boots thy zeal,
O glowing friend,
That would indignant rend
The northland from the south?
Wherefore? to what good end?   40
Boston Bay and Bunker Hill
Would serve things still;—
Things are of the snake.

The horseman serves the horse,
The neatherd serves the neat,   45
The merchant serves the purse,
The eater serves his meat;
'Tis the day of the chattel,
Web to weave, and corn to grind;
Things are in the saddle,   50
And ride mankind.

There are two laws discrete,
Not reconciled,—
Law for man, and law for thing;
The last builds town and fleet,   55

But it runs wild,
And doth the man unking.

'Tis fit the forest fall,
The steep be graded,
The mountain tunnelled,   60
The sand shaded,
The orchard planted,
The glebe tilled,
The prairie granted,
The steamer built.   65

Let man serve law for man;
Live for friendship, live for love,
For truth's and harmony's behoof;
The state may follow how it can,
As Olympus follows Jove.   70

   Yet do not I implore
The wrinkled shopman to my sounding woods,
Nor bid the unwilling senator
Ask votes of thrushes in the solitudes.
Every one to his chosen work;—   75
Foolish hands may mix and mar;
Wise and sure the issues are.
Round they roll till dark is light,
Sex to sex, and even to odd;—
The over-god   80
Who marries Right to Might,
Who peoples, unpeoples,—
He who exterminates
Races by stronger races,
Black by white faces,—   85
Knows to bring honey
Out of the lion;
Grafts gentlest scion
On pirate and Turk.

The Cossack eats Poland,   90
Like stolen fruit;

Her last noble is ruined,
Her last poet mute:
Straight, into double band
The victors divide;   95
Half for freedom strike and stand;—
The astonished Muse finds thousands at her side.

1846 || 1846

ASTRÆA

Astræa ("Star maiden"), the virgin daughter of Zeus and Themis, was goddess of Truth and Chastity, but preeminently of Justice (see l. 47). At the conclusion of the Greek Golden Age, she was the last of the immortals to consort with humans, who had begun to grow evil; finally, Zeus installed her in the heavens as the constellation Virgo.

Sometime in the late 1850s or 1860s Emerson considered changing the poem's title to "Γνωθι Σεαυτον," or "Know Thyself" (*CW* 9:153). It may be that "Astræa" is immediately followed by "Étienne de la Boéce" in *Poems* (1847) because Emerson thought of them as companion poems, or complementary treatments of the relation of self to other in friendship.

ASTRÆA

Thou the herald art who wrote
Thy rank, and quartered thine own coat.
There is no king nor sovereign state
That can fix a hero's rate;
Each to all is venerable,   5
Cap-a-pie invulnerable,
Until he write, where all eyes rest,
Slave or master on his breast.

I saw men go up and down,
In the country and the town,   10
With this tablet on their neck,—
'Judgment and a judge we seek.'
Not to monarchs they repair,
Nor to learned jurist's chair;
But they hurry to their peers,   15
To their kinsfolk and their dears;
Louder than with speech they pray,—
'What am I? companion, say.'
And the friend not hesitates
To assign just place and mates;   20
Answers not in word or letter,
Yet is understood the better;

Each to each a looking-glass,
Reflects his figure that doth pass.
Every wayfarer he meets   25
What himself declared repeats,
What himself confessed records,
Sentences him in his words;
The form is his own corporal form,
And his thought the penal worm.   30

Yet shine forever virgin minds,
Loved by stars and purest winds,
Which, o'er passion throned sedate,
Have not hazarded their state;
Disconcert the searching spy,   35
Rendering to a curious eye
The durance of a granite ledge
To those who gaze from the sea's edge.
It is there for benefit;
It is there for purging light;   40
There for purifying storms;
And its depths reflect all forms;
It cannot parley with the mean,—
Pure by impure is not seen.
For there's no sequestered grot,   45
Lone mountain tarn, or isle forgot,
But Justice, journeying in the sphere,
Daily stoops to harbor there.

? || 1846

ÉTIENNE DE LA BOÉCE

Emerson's celebrated essay on "Friendship" (1841), the best known of his many engagements with that subject, contributes largely to the conceptual background of "Étienne de la Boéce." Emerson's fascination with friendship, both as fact and as ideal, led him in the 1840s to submit his social relationships to extended analysis, while the inevitably philosophical cast of his thinking caused the friends involved—especially the women—to find him more aloof than they might have preferred. The poem "Étienne de la Boéce" was begun in 1843, nearly coinciding with Emerson's discovery (*JMN* 9:28) of a new translation of Montaigne's *Journey into Italy,* with its account of his friend Étienne (1530–1563). The latter's history seems largely irrelevant to the poem, yet it is noteworthy that he published the once famous *Discours de la servitude volontaire,* a pioneer exploration of passive resistance, or civil disobedience. An 1835 edition of this work carried a preface by Félicité de Lamennais, a Christian Socialist and reformer in whom a number of the Transcendentalists were interested.

ÉTIENNE DE LA BOÉCE

I serve you not, if you I follow,
Shadowlike, o'er hill and hollow;
And bend my fancy to your leading,
All too nimble for my treading.
When the pilgrimage is done,   5
And we've the landscape overrun,
I am bitter, vacant, thwarted,
And your heart is unsupported.
Vainly valiant, you have missed
The manhood that should yours resist,—   10
Its complement; but if I could,
In severe or cordial mood,
Lead you rightly to my altar,
Where the wisest Muses falter,
And worship that world-warming spark   15
Which dazzles me in midnight dark,
Equalizing small and large,
While the soul it doth surcharge,

That the poor is wealthy grown,
And the hermit never alone,—   20
The traveller and the road seem one
With the errand to be done,—
That were a man's and lover's part,
That were Freedom's whitest chart.

1843–1846 || 1846

SUUM CUIQUE

On April 26, 1834, while living in Newton, Massachusetts, Emerson wrote in his journal, "Rain rain. The good rain like a bad preacher does not know when to leave off" (*JMN* 4:281). Datelined "Newton, 1834" in the manuscript (*PN*, p. 18), the poem was probably written on or about that day. The Latin title means "to each his own." The poem's somber mood, no doubt reflecting Emerson's continued mourning for the loss of his first wife, Ellen, closely matches that of "Compensation," the next poem in the 1847 sequence.

SUUM CUIQUE

The rain has spoiled the farmer's day;
Shall sorrow put my books away?
    Thereby are two days lost:
Nature shall mind her own affairs;
I will attend my proper cares,   5
    In rain, or sun, or frost.

1834 || 1841

COMPENSATION

Emerson wrote this poem in November 1834, in New York City, where he had gone to officiate temporarily at the city's Second (Unitarian) Church. On arriving in New York, he learned of the death of his brother Edward Bliss Emerson in Puerto Rico, where he had gone in search of relief from his tubercular symptoms. "So falls one pile more of hope for this life" (*JMN* 4:325). Emerson was at the time still recovering from the shock of the unexpected death of a close friend, George Adams Sampson, whose eulogy he had delivered in August (*CS* 4:221–228). It was in this funereal mood, then, that Emerson, from his hotel room in Manhattan, witnessed the unusually raucous election of 1834, in which the party of Andrew Jackson and its candidate William L. Marcy prevailed against William H. Seward and the Whig "aristocracy" (*JMN* 4:330–334).

COMPENSATION

Why should I keep holiday
   When other men have none?
Why but because, when these are gay,
   I sit and mourn alone.

And why, when mirth unseals all tongues,   5
   Should mine alone be dumb?
Ah! late I spoke to silent throngs,
   And now their hour is come.

1834 || 1846

FORBEARANCE

Edward Emerson's note to this poem (*W* 9:430) suggested that it might refer to James Elliot Cabot (later, Emerson's literary executor) or to Henry David Thoreau. Neither identification is likely, however, since Emerson did not come to know Cabot until 1844 or 1845 (*L* 3:285–286, 7:621–623), and the sketch does not very closely fit Thoreau. Rather, it would seem to be a brief study in ideal friendship. "Forbearance" was published along with two other short poems, "The Park" and "Grace," in the *Dial* for January 1842, having been offered to editor Margaret Fuller as "my little contingent of particolored light infantry" (*L* 2:462, 464).

FORBEARANCE

Hast thou named all the birds without a gun?
Loved the wood-rose, and left it on its stalk?
At rich men's tables eaten bread and pulse?
Unarmed, faced danger with a heart of trust?
And loved so well a high behavior,   5
In man or maid, that thou from speech refrained,
Nobility more nobly to repay?
O, be my friend, and teach me to be thine!

1841? || 1842

THE PARK

Edward Emerson suggested (*W* 9:430) that the "yoke of conscience masterful" and the concluding reference to being led to the "Good" signified his father's strong residue of Puritan inheritance, constraints on feeling and expression less evident, perhaps, in the young friends he was making in the late 1830s and early '40s, including the elegant Southern belle Anna Barker (1813–1900) and her fiancé, the well-connected Samuel Gray Ward (1817–1907). Emerson discovered a beauty in the polish of their manners and their easy and self-confident movement through society, which he typically described in an imagery of wealth. Other poems on this theme include the motto "Manners" and the quatrain "A.H."

THE PARK

The prosperous and beautiful
  To me seem not to wear
The yoke of conscience masterful,
  Which galls me everywhere.

I cannot shake off the god;   5
  On my neck he makes his seat;
I look at my face in the glass,—
  My eyes his eyeballs meet.

Enchanters! enchantresses!
  Your gold makes you seem wise;   10
The morning mist within your grounds
  More proudly rolls, more softly lies.

Yet spake yon purple mountain,
  Yet said yon ancient wood,
That Night or Day, that Love or Crime,   15
  Leads all souls to the Good.

1841 || 1842

FORERUNNERS

Emerson composed this poem on May 3, 1845, as he walked home (thirty-five miles) from his visit to Worcester County's Mount Wachusett (*PN*, p. 795). It was a springtime version of the kind of excursion Thoreau described so well in "A Walk to Wachusett" nearly three years earlier. Emerson had promised some original poetry to his childhood friend William H. Furness, a Unitarian minister in Philadelphia, for a gift-book that Furness edited entitled *The Diadem*, and the deadline was at now at hand. On May 9, Emerson mailed off "Forerunners," together with "A Fable" and a piece called "Loss and Gain."

In a note at *W* 9:431, Edward Emerson pointed out the poem's dependence on a passage from the 1844 essay "Nature":

> I have seen the softness and beauty of the summer-clouds floating feathery overhead, enjoying, as it seemed, their height and privilege of motion, whilst yet they appeared not so much the drapery of this place and hour, as forelooking to some pavilions and gardens of festivity beyond. It is an odd jealousy: but the poet finds himself not near enough to his object. The pine-tree, the river, the bank of flowers before him, does not seem to be nature. Nature is still elsewhere. This or this is but outskirt and far-off reflection and echo of the triumph that has passed by, and is now at its glancing splendor and heyday, perchance in the neighboring fields, or, if you stand in the field, then in the adjacent woods. The present object shall give you this sense of stillness that follows a pageant which has just gone by." (*CW* 3:111; cf. the journal source at *JMN* 7:392)

FORERUNNERS

Long I followed happy guides,
I could never reach their sides;
Their step is forth, and, ere the day,
Breaks up their leaguer, and away.
Keen my sense, my heart was young,   5
Right good-will my sinews strung,
But no speed of mine avails
To hunt upon their shining trails.
On and away, their hasting feet
Make the morning proud and sweet;   10
Flowers they strew,—I catch the scent;

Or tone of silver instrument
Leaves on the wind melodious trace;
Yet I could never see their face.
On eastern hills I see their smokes,   15
Mixed with mist by distant lochs.
I met many travellers
Who the road had surely kept;
They saw not my fine revellers,—
These had crossed them while they slept.   20
Some had heard their fair report,
In the country or the court.
Fleetest couriers alive
Never yet could once arrive,
As they went or they returned,   25
At the house where these sojourned.
Sometimes their strong speed they slacken,
Though they are not overtaken;
In sleep their jubilant troop is near,—
I tuneful voices overhear;   30
It may be in wood or waste,—
At unawares 'tis come and past.
Their near camp my spirit knows
By signs gracious as rainbows.
I thenceforward, and long after,   35
Listen for their harp-like laughter,
And carry in my heart, for days,
Peace that hallows rudest ways.

1845 || 1845

GIVE ALL TO LOVE

One of the earliest journal passages bearing on Emerson's Platonic views of love and friendship dates from 1837:

> How little think the youth & maiden who are glancing at each other across a mixed company with eyes so full of mutual intelligence—how little think they of the precious fruit long hereafter to proceed from this now quite external stimulus. . . . By all the virtues that appear, by so much kindness, justice, fortitude &c, by so much are they made one. But all the vices are negations on either part & they are by so much two. At last they discover that all that at first drew them together was wholly caducous, had merely a prospective end like the scaffolding by which a house is built, & the unsuspected & wholly unconscious growth of principles from year to year is the real marriage foreseen & prepared from the first but wholly above their consciousness. (*JMN* 5:297–298)

More than three years later, on November 21, 1840, Emerson returned to the subject, evidently prompted by a suspicion that "Swedenborg exaggerates the Circumstance of marriage":

> All loves, all friendships are momentary. *Do you love me?* means at last *Do you see the same truth I see?* If you do, we are happy together: but when presently one of us passes into the perception of new truth, we are divorced and the force of all nature cannot hold us to each other. . . . No, Heaven is the marriage of all souls. We meet & worship an instant under the temple of one thought & part as though we parted not, to join another thought with other fellowships of joy. (*JMN* 7:532)

The sentiment that fastens on persons, Emerson felt, commonly opposes the law of change and growth, and so the worthy injunction to "give all to love" had to be distinguished from the unworthy injunction to "give all to the beloved." Some critics have argued that by extending the reach of his Transcendental philosophy to the subject of love, Emerson was bound to fail as a poet. On these debatable grounds Hyatt Waggoner maintained that "'Give All to Love' is as bad a poem as 'Love' is bad as an essay" (*Emerson as Poet*, pp. 199–200).

GIVE ALL TO LOVE

Give all to love;
Obey thy heart;
Friends, kindred, days,
Estate, good-fame,
Plans, credit, and the Muse,—   5
Nothing refuse.

'Tis a brave master;
Let it have scope:
Follow it utterly,
Hope beyond hope: 10
High and more high
It dives into noon,
With wing unspent,
Untold intent;
But it is a god,   15
Knows its own path,
And the outlets of the sky.

It was not for the mean;
It requireth courage stout,
Souls above doubt,   20
Valor unbending;
Such 'twill reward,—
They shall return
More than they were,
And ever ascending.   25

Leave all for love;
Yet, hear me, yet,
One word more thy heart behoved,
One pulse more of firm endeavor,—
Keep thee to-day,   30
To-morrow, forever,
Free as an Arab
Of thy beloved.

Cling with life to the maid;
But when the surprise,   35
First vague shadow of surmise
Flits across her bosom young
Of a joy apart from thee,
Free be she, fancy-free;
Nor thou detain her vesture's hem,   40
Nor the palest rose she flung
From her summer diadem.

Though thou loved her as thyself,
As a self of purer clay,
Though her parting dims the day,   45
Stealing grace from all alive;
Heartily know,
When half-gods go,
The gods arrive.

1846? || 1846

EROS

It is not known exactly when this poem was written, but it probably belongs to the period immediately following Emerson's work on the essays "Love" and "Friendship," a period when his correspondence with Margaret Fuller and Caroline Sturgis was much occupied with these themes. Despite its brevity it invites comparison to "Give All to Love" and to the "Initial, Dæmonic, and Celestial Love," here at the erotic center of *Poems* (1847).

EROS

The sense of the world is short,—
Long and various the report,—
   To love and be beloved;
Men and gods have not outlearned it;
And, how oft soe'er they've turned it,   5
   'Twill not be improved.

                    1841–1843? || 1844

INITIAL, DÆMONIC, AND CELESTIAL LOVE

This difficult suite of poems on love, allusive and esoteric by turns, has not attracted much attention beyond the observation that it expresses, from lowest to highest, the range of Plato's speculation in the *Phaedrus* and the *Symposium*. Given the slight differences in the numbering and subtitling of the poem's sections in the English and American editions of 1846, it would seem that Emerson regarded the second and third parts as a unit in balance against the first. Indeed the evidence suggests that the first section was written late in 1840 or early in 1841 and that it remained an independent work until the second and third sections were added some four years later. This asymmetry in the poem's structure has been reflected in the criticism. John S. Harrison, for example, ably discussed the Platonic background of the second and third parts, whereas Carl F. Strauch confined his remarks to the literary and mythic sources for "The Initial Love."

The best evidence for the early date of "The Initial Love" is its apparent implication in the epistolary conversation regarding love and friendship carried on during the fall of 1840 among Emerson, Caroline Sturgis, and Margaret Fuller. The origins of this protracted debate may well lie with Fuller's reading in 1839 of the relevant works of Plato and with what, early in 1840, she called her "search after Eros" (Meg McGavran Murray, 164 and 441, n. 8; *FuL* 2:105, 107). The influence of Plato on "The Initial Love" was also modulated through "Cupid's Conflict," a poem by the Cambridge Platonist Henry More (1614–1687) that Emerson had sent to Fuller with a request that it be reprinted in the *Dial*. The letter of November 4, 1840, conveying the request (*L* 2:354–355), was the first that Emerson had sent to Fuller since telling her that he would no longer entertain her increasingly impetuous discussion of their relationship. It is tempting, then, to see the poetic topos of Cupid in biographical terms and as related to the emotionally supercharged period between the marriage of Anna Barker and Samuel Gray Ward in October 1840 and the marriage of Ellery Channing and Ellen Fuller, Margaret's sister, the following September.

INITIAL, DÆMONIC, AND CELESTIAL LOVE

I.

THE INITIAL LOVE

Venus, when her son was lost,
Cried him up and down the coast,
In hamlets, palaces, and parks,

And told the truant by his marks,—
Golden curls, and quiver, and bow. 5
This befell how long ago!
Time and tide are strangely changed,
Men and manners much deranged:
None will now find Cupid latent
By this foolish antique patent. 10
He came late along the waste,
Shod like a traveller for haste;
With malice dared me to proclaim him,
That the maids and boys might name him.

Boy no more, he wears all coats, 15
Frocks, and blouses, capes, capotes;
He bears no bow, or quiver, or wand,
Nor chaplet on his head or hand.
Leave his weeds and heed his eyes,—
All the rest he can disguise. 20
In the pit of his eye's a spark
Would bring back day if it were dark;
And, if I tell you all my thought,
Though I comprehend it not,
In those unfathomable orbs 25
Every function he absorbs.
He doth eat, and drink, and fish, and shoot,
And write, and reason, and compute,
And ride, and run, and have, and hold,
And whine, and flatter, and regret, 30
And kiss, and couple, and beget,
By those roving eyeballs bold.

Undaunted are their courages,
Right Cossacks in their forages;
Fleeter they than any creature,— 35
They are his steeds, and not his feature;
Inquisitive, and fierce, and fasting,
Restless, predatory, hasting;
And they pounce on other eyes
As lions on their prey; 40

And round their circles is writ,
Plainer than the day,
Underneath, within, above,—
Love—love—love—love.
He lives in his eyes;   45
There doth digest, and work, and spin,
And buy, and sell, and lose, and win;
He rolls them with delighted motion,
Joy-tides swell their mimic ocean.
Yet holds he them with tortest rein,   50
That they may seize and entertain
The glance that to their glance opposes,
Like fiery honey sucked from roses.

He palmistry can understand,
Imbibing virtue by his hand   55
As if it were a living root;
The pulse of hands will make him mute;
With all his force he gathers balms
Into those wise, thrilling palms.

Cupid is a casuist,   60
A mystic, and a cabalist,—
Can your lurking thought surprise,
And interpret your device.
He is versed in occult science,
In magic, and in clairvoyance;   65
Oft he keeps his fine ear strained,
And Reason on her tiptoe pained
For aëry intelligence,
And for strange coincidence.
But it touches his quick heart   70
When Fate by omens takes his part,
And chance-dropped hints from Nature's sphere
Deeply soothe his anxious ear.

Heralds high before him run;
He has ushers many a one;   75
He spreads his welcome where he goes,

And touches all things with his rose.
All things wait for and divine him,—
How shall I dare to malign him,
Or accuse the god of sport?   80
I must end my true report,
Painting him from head to foot,
In as far as I took note,
Trusting well the matchless power
Of this young-eyed emperor   85
Will clear his fame from every cloud,
With the bards and with the crowd.

He is wilful, mutable,
Shy, untamed, inscrutable,
Swifter-fashioned than the fairies,   90
Substance mixed of pure contraries;
His vice some elder virtue's token,
And his good is evil-spoken.
Failing sometimes of his own,
He is headstrong and alone;   95
He affects the wood and wild,
Like a flower-hunting child;
Buries himself in summer waves,
In trees, with beasts, in mines, and caves;
Loves nature like a horned cow,   100
Bird, or deer, or caribou.

Shun him, nymphs, on the fleet horses!
He has a total world of wit;
O how wise are his discourses!
But he is the arch-hypocrite,   105
And, through all science and all art,
Seeks alone his counterpart.
He is a Pundit of the East,
He is an augur and a priest,
And his soul will melt in prayer,   110
But word and wisdom is a snare;
Corrupted by the present toy
He follows joy, and only joy.

There is no mask but he will wear;
He invented oaths to swear;   115
He paints, he carves, he chants, he prays,
And holds all stars in his embrace,
Godlike,—but 'tis for his fine pelf,
The social quintessence of self.
Well said I he is hypocrite,   120
And folly the end of his subtle wit!
He takes a sovran privilege
Not allowed to any liege;
For he does go behind all law,
And right into himself does draw;   125
For he is sovereignly allied,—
Heaven's oldest blood flows in his side,—
And interchangeably at one
With every king on every throne,
That no god dare say him nay,   130
Or see the fault, or seen betray:
He has the Muses by the heart,
And the Parcæ all are of his part.

His many signs cannot be told;
He has not one mode, but manifold,—   135
Many fashions and addresses,
Piques, reproaches, hurts, caresses,
Arguments, lore, poetry,
Action, service, badinage;
He will preach like a friar,   140
And jump like Harlequin;
He will read like a crier,
And fight like a Paladin.
Boundless is his memory;
Plans immense his term prolong;   145
He is not of counted age,
Meaning always to be young.
And his wish is intimacy,
Intimater intimacy,
And a stricter privacy;   150

The impossible shall yet be done,
And, being two, shall still be one.
As the wave breaks to foam on shelves,
Then runs into a wave again,
So lovers melt their sundered selves,   155
Yet melted would be twain.

II.

THE DÆMONIC AND THE CELESTIAL LOVE

DÆMONIC LOVE

Man was made of social earth,
Child and brother from his birth,
Tethered by a liquid cord
Of blood through veins of kindred poured.   160
Next his heart the fireside band
Of mother, father, sister, stand:
Names from awful childhood heard
Throbs of a wild religion stirred;—
Virtue, to love, to hate them, vice;   165
Till dangerous Beauty came, at last,
Till Beauty came to snap all ties;
The maid, abolishing the past,
With lotus wine obliterates
Dear memory's stone-incarved traits,   170
And, by herself, supplants alone
Friends year by year more inly known.
When her calm eyes opened bright,
All were foreign in their light.
It was ever the self-same tale,   175
The first experience will not fail;
Only two in the garden walked,
And with snake and seraph talked.

   But God said,
'I will have a purer gift;   180
There is smoke in the flame;
New flowerets bring, new prayers uplift,

And love without a name.
Fond children, ye desire
To please each other well;   185
Another round, a higher,
Ye shall climb on the heavenly stair,
And selfish preference forbear;
And in right deserving,
And without a swerving   190
Each from your proper state,
Weave roses for your mate.

'Deep, deep are loving eyes,
Flowed with naphtha fiery sweet;
And the point is paradise,   195
Where their glances meet:
Their reach shall yet be more profound,
And a vision without bound:
The axis of those eyes sun-clear
Be the axis of the sphere: 200
So shall the lights ye pour amain
Go, without check or intervals,
Through from the empyrean walls
Unto the same again.'

Close, close to men,   205
Like undulating layer of air,
Right above their heads,
The potent plain of Dæmons spreads.
Stands to each human soul its own,
For watch, and ward, and furtherance,   210
In the snares of Nature's dance;
And the lustre and the grace
To fascinate each youthful heart,
Beaming from its counterpart,
Translucent through the mortal covers,   215
Is the Dæmon's form and face.
To and fro the Genius hies,—
A gleam which plays and hovers
Over the maiden's head,

And dips sometimes as low as to her eyes.   220
Unknown, albeit lying near,
To men, the path to the Dæmon sphere;
And they that swiftly come and go
Leave no track on the heavenly snow.
Sometimes the airy synod bends,   225
And the mighty choir descends,
And the brains of men thenceforth,
In crowded and in still resorts,
Teem with unwonted thoughts:
As, when a shower of meteors   230
Cross the orbit of the earth,
And, lit by fringent air,
Blaze near and far,
Mortals deem the planets bright
Have slipped their sacred bars,   235
And the lone seaman all the night
Sails, astonished, amid stars.

Beauty of a richer vein,
Graces of a subtler strain,
Unto men these moonmen lend,   240
And our shrinking sky extend.
So is man's narrow path
By strength and terror skirted;
Also, (from the song the wrath
Of the Genii be averted!   245
The Muse the truth uncolored speaking,)
The Dæmons are self-seeking:
Their fierce and limitary will
Draws men to their likeness still.

The erring painter made Love blind,—   250
Highest Love who shines on all;
Him, radiant, sharpest-sighted god,
None can bewilder;
Whose eyes pierce
The universe,   255
Path-finder, road-builder,

Mediator, royal giver;
Rightly seeing, rightly seen,
Of joyful and transparent mien.
'Tis a sparkle passing   260
From each to each, from thee to me,
To and fro perpetually;
Sharing all, daring all,
Levelling, displacing
Each obstruction, it unites   265
Equals remote, and seeming opposites.
And ever and forever Love
Delights to build a road:
Unheeded Danger near him strides,
Love laughs, and on a lion rides.   270

But Cupid wears another face,
Born into Dæmons less divine:
His roses bleach apace,
His nectar smacks of wine.
The Dæmon ever builds a wall,   275
Himself encloses and includes,
Solitude in solitudes:
In like sort his love doth fall.
He is an oligarch;
He prizes wonder, fame, and mark;   280
He loveth crowns;
He scorneth drones;
He doth elect
The beautiful and fortunate,
And the sons of intellect,   285
And the souls of ample fate,
Who the Future's gates unbar,—
Minions of the Morning Star.
In his prowess he exults,
And the multitude insults.   290
His impatient looks devour
Oft the humble and the poor;
And, seeing his eye glare,

They drop their few pale flowers,
Gathered with hope to please, 295
Along the mountain towers,—
Lose courage, and despair.
He will never be gainsaid,—
Pitiless, will not be stayed;
His hot tyranny 300
Burns up every other tie.
Therefore comes an hour from Jove
Which his ruthless will defies,
And the dogs of Fate unties.
Shiver the palaces of glass; 305
Shrivel the rainbow-colored walls,
Where in bright Art each god and sibyl dwelt,
Secure as in the zodiac's belt;
And the galleries and halls,
Wherein every siren sung, 310
Like a meteor pass.
For this fortune wanted root
In the core of God's abysm,—
Was a weed of self and schism;
And ever the Dæmonic Love 315
Is the ancestor of wars,
And the parent of remorse.

CELESTIAL LOVE

Higher far,
Upward into the pure realm,
Over sun and star, 320
Over the flickering Dæmon film,
Thou must mount for love;
Into vision where all form
In one only form dissolves;
In a region where the wheel 325
On which all beings ride
Visibly revolves;
Where the starred, eternal worm

Girds the world with bound and term;
Where unlike things are like;   330
Where good and ill,
And joy and moan,
Melt into one.
There Past, Present, Future shoot
Triple blossoms from one root;   335
Substances at base divided
In their summits are united;
There the holy essence rolls,
One through separated souls;
And the sunny Æon sleeps   340
Folding Nature in its deeps,
And every fair and every good,
Known in part, or known impure,
To men below,
In their archetypes endure.   345
The race of gods,
Or those we erring own,
Are shadows flitting up and down
In the still abodes.
The circles of that sea are laws   350
Which publish and which hide the cause.

Pray for a beam
Out of that sphere,
Thee to guide and to redeem.

O, what a load   355
Of care and toil,
By lying use bestowed,
From his shoulders falls who sees
The true astronomy,
The period of peace.   360
Counsel which the ages kept
Shall the well-born soul accept.
As the overhanging trees
Fill the lake with images,—
As garment draws the garment's hem,   365

Men their fortunes bring with them.
By right or wrong,
Lands and goods go to the strong.
Property will brutely draw
Still to the proprietor;   370
Silver to silver creep and wind,
And kind to kind.

Nor less the eternal poles
Of tendency distribute souls.
There need no vows to bind   375
Whom not each other seek, but find.
They give and take no pledge or oath,—
Nature is the bond of both:
No prayer persuades, no flattery fawns,—
Their noble meanings are their pawns.   380
Plain and cold is their address,
Power have they for tenderness;
And, so thoroughly is known
Each other's counsel by his own,
They can parley without meeting;   385
Need is none of forms of greeting;
They can well communicate
In their innermost estate;
When each the other shall avoid,
Shall each by each be most enjoyed.   390

Not with scarfs or perfumed gloves
Do these celebrate their loves;
Not by jewels, feasts, and savors,
Not by ribbons or by favors,
But by the sun-spark on the sea,   395
And the cloud-shadow on the lea,
The soothing lapse of morn to mirk,
And the cheerful round of work.
Their cords of love so public are,
They intertwine the farthest star: 400
The throbbing sea, the quaking earth,
Yield sympathy and signs of mirth;

Is none so high, so mean is none,
But feels and seals this union;
Even the fell Furies are appeased,   405
The good applaud, the lost are eased.

Love's hearts are faithful, but not fond,
Bound for the just, but not beyond;
Not glad, as the low-loving herd,
Of self in other still preferred,   410
But they have heartily designed
The benefit of broad mankind.
And they serve men austerely,
After their own genius, clearly,
Without a false humility;   415
For this is Love's nobility,—
Not to scatter bread and gold,
Goods and raiment bought and sold;
But to hold fast his simple sense,
And speak the speech of innocence,   420
And with hand, and body, and blood,
To make his bosom-counsel good.
For he that feeds men serveth few;
He serves all who dares be true.

1840–41, 1845–46 || 1846

THE APOLOGY

When first published in *The Gift,* an 1844 anthology edited by William H. Furness, the poem retained its original title, "The Poet's Apology." It was probably written shortly before publication and in any event not before 1841 (see *CW* 9:220–221). In the cover letter to Furness, Emerson confessed to some uncertainty about the fourth stanza, which he had in fact transferred from another, unfinished poem (see *L* 7:593; *PN,* p. 844).

THE APOLOGY

Think me not unkind and rude
    That I walk alone in grove and glen;
I go to the god of the wood
    To fetch his word to men.

Tax not my sloth that I   5
    Fold my arms beside the brook;
Each cloud that floated in the sky
    Writes a letter in my book.

Chide me not, laborious band,
    For the idle flowers I brought;   10
Every aster in my hand
    Goes home loaded with a thought.

There was never mystery
    But 'tis figured in the flowers;
Was never secret history   15
    But birds tell it in the bowers.

One harvest from thy field
    Homeward brought the oxen strong;
A second crop thine acres yield,
    Which I gather in a song.   20

1841–1844 || 1844

MERLIN I

The origins of this poem can be traced to a conversation with Elizabeth Hoar (1814–1878), a family friend, on June 21, 1839, which led Emerson to conclude that although "you shall not speak truth in Prose,—you may in Verse" (*JMN* 7:218). A journal passage of a week later is recognizably the source of "Merlin I":

> Rhyme; not tinkling rhyme but grand Pindaric strokes as firm as the tread of a horse. Rhyme that vindicates itself as an art, the stroke of the bell of a cathedral. Rhyme which knocks at prose & dulness with the stroke of a cannon ball. Rhyme which builds out into Chaos & Old night a splendid architecture to bridge the impassable, & call aloud on all the children of morning that the Creation is recommencing. I wish to write such rhymes as shall not suggest a restraint but contrariwise the wildest freedom. (*JMN* 7:219)

Possibly these thoughts had relation to Emerson's concurrent experience as editor of Jones Very's *Essays and Poems* (Boston, 1839), which involved culling the sixty-six best sonnets from a submitted sample of two hundred. And yet Emerson's speculation about the strength and freedom of true poetic expression would not be lifted from his journal and "turned in a verse"—or connected to the bardic figure of Merlin—until 1845–46 (*W* 9:440–441; *JMN* 9:167–168; *L* 3:341).

MERLIN

I.

Thy trivial harp will never please
Or fill my craving ear;
Its chords should ring as blows the breeze,
Free, peremptory, clear.
No jingling serenader's art,   5
Nor tinkle of piano strings,
Can make the wild blood start
In its mystic springs.
The kingly bard
Must smite the chords rudely and hard,   10
As with hammer or with mace;

That they may render back
Artful thunder, which conveys
Secrets of the solar track,
Sparks of the supersolar blaze.   15
Merlin's blows are strokes of fate,
Chiming with the forest tone,
When boughs buffet boughs in the wood;
Chiming with the gasp and moan
Of the ice-imprisoned flood;   20
With the pulse of manly hearts;
With the voice of orators;
With the din of city arts;
With the cannonade of wars;
With the marches of the brave;   25
And prayers of might from martyrs' cave.

Great is the art,
Great be the manners, of the bard.
He shall not his brain encumber
With the coil of rhythm and number;   30
But, leaving rule and pale forethought,
He shall aye climb
For his rhyme.
'Pass in, pass in,' the angels say,
'In to the upper doors,   35
Nor count compartments of the floors,
But mount to paradise
By the stairway of surprise.'

Blameless master of the games,
King of sport that never shames,   40
He shall daily joy dispense
Hid in song's sweet influence.
Things more cheerly live and go,
What time the subtle mind
Sings aloud the tune whereto   45
Their pulses beat,
And march their feet,
And their members are combined.

By Sybarites beguiled,
He shall no task decline; 50
Merlin's mighty line
Extremes of nature reconciled,—
Bereaved a tyrant of his will,
And made the lion mild.
Songs can the tempest still, 55
Scattered on the stormy air,
Mould the year to fair increase,
And bring in poetic peace.

He shall not seek to weave,
In weak, unhappy times, 60
Efficacious rhymes;
Wait his returning strength.
Bird, that from the nadir's floor
To the zenith's top can soar,
The soaring orbit of the muse exceeds that journey's length. 65
Nor profane affect to hit
Or compass that, by meddling wit,
Which only the propitious mind
Publishes when 'tis inclined.
There are open hours 70
When the God's will sallies free,
And the dull idiot might see
The flowing fortunes of a thousand years;—
Sudden, at unawares,
Self-moved, fly-to the doors, 75
Nor sword of angels could reveal
What they conceal.

1845–46 || 1846

MERLIN II

Edward Emerson was surprised by his father's omission of this work from *Selected Poems* (1876), since it "well expressed his favorite idea of correspondence, universal rhyme and harmony in Nature, and compensation in life" (*W* 9:442). In illustration of this "favorite idea," Edward quoted from the article on Pythagoras in the *New American Cyclopædia* (1857–1866), edited by fellow Transcendentalists and erstwhile Brook Farmers, George Ripley and Charles A. Dana:

> The world subsists [according to Pythagoras] by the rhythmical order of its elements. Everywhere in Nature appear the two elements of the finite and the infinite which give rise to the elementary opposites of the universe, the odd and even, one and many, right and left, male and female, fixed and moved, straight and curved, light and darkness, square and oblong, good and bad.

According to a letter to Elizabeth Hoar, the poem was finished, along with its companion, in July 1846 (*L* 3:341).

MERLIN

II.

The rhyme of the poet
Modulates the king's affairs;
Balance-loving Nature
Made all things in pairs.
To every foot its antipode;   5
Each color with its counter glowed;
To every tone beat answering tones,
Higher or graver;
Flavor gladly blends with flavor;
Leaf answers leaf upon the bough;   10
And match the paired cotyledons.
Hands to hands, and feet to feet,
In one body grooms and brides;
Eldest rite, two married sides
In every mortal meet.   15
Light's far furnace shines,
Smelting balls and bars,

Forging double stars,
Glittering twins and trines.
The animals are sick with love,   20
Lovesick with rhyme;
Each with all propitious time
Into chorus wove.

Like the dancers' ordered band,
Thoughts come also hand in hand;   25
In equal couples mated,
Or else alternated;
Adding by their mutual gage,
One to other, health and age.
Solitary fancies go   30
Short-lived wandering to and fro,
Most like to bachelors,
Or an ungiven maid,
Not ancestors,
With no posterity to make the lie afraid,   35
Or keep truth undecayed.

Perfect-paired as eagle's wings,
Justice is the rhyme of things;
Trade and counting use
The self-same tuneful muse;   40
And Nemesis,
Who with even matches odd,
Who athwart space redresses
The partial wrong,
Fills the just period,   45
And finishes the song.

Subtle rhymes, with ruin rife,
Murmur in the house of life,
Sung by the Sisters as they spin;
In perfect time and measure they   50
Build and unbuild our echoing clay,
As the two twilights of the day
Fold us music-drunken in.

1845–46 || 1846

BACCHUS

Bacchus (or Dionysus), traditionally the god of wine and revelry, had been a figure of interest for Margaret Fuller, who in 1839–40 held out to her students in the Conversations the model of the Bacchantes, whose ecstatic chanting and dancing affirmed the god's passion (Meg McGavran Murray, p. 164). Charles Capper points out (1:302) that "in one Conversation, [Elizabeth] Peabody reported Fuller's contrast of Apollo as 'Genius' with Bacchus as 'Geniality': '[Bacchus's] whole life was triumph. Born of fire; a divine frenzy; the answer of the earth to the sun,—of the warmth of joy to the light of genius. He is beautiful, also; not severe in youthful beauty, like Apollo; but exuberant, and liable to excess'" (cf. *FuL* 2:118). The elements of exuberance and ecstasy also figure in a sentence from the *Phaedrus* that Emerson belatedly penciled in as a motto to "Bacchus" in a correction copy: "The man who is his own master knocks in vain at the doors of poetry" (*CW* 9:231–232).

In a letter to Elizabeth Hoar of July 27, 1846, Emerson mentioned "Bacchus" as among the poems he had written lately, adding that it was "not however translated from Hafiz" (*L* 3:341). Certainly the poem is close enough to Hafiz in tone, topic, and temperament to make the disavowal needful in speaking to one who knew of Emerson's recent fascination with the Persian poet. Hafiz wrote often of wine and wine drinking, notwithstanding the well-known Islamic proscriptions, using the references either metaphorically or as a rebuke to the moralistic rigidity of the orthodox. Emerson pointed out that "Hafiz does not write of wine & love in any mystical sense, further than that he uses wine as the symbol of intellectual freedom" (*TN* 2:120). Emerson's Protestant background asserts itself in "Bacchus" (as also in "Two Rivers") in a web of Eucharistic associations. Indeed, the poem draws on a wide range of religious traditions (echoed by the global and astronomical diversity of its spatial references) and makes them comport with what in the end has to be reckoned a secular, even a psychological, outlook. "Bacchus" is especially complex and evocative, particularly in the way its several blended mythologies resonate with the themes of the Merlin poems.

BACCHUS

Bring me wine, but wine which never grew
In the belly of the grape,
Or grew on vine whose tap-roots, reaching through
Under the Andes to the Cape,
Suffered no savor of the earth to scape.   5

Let its grapes the morn salute
From a nocturnal root,
Which feels the acrid juice
Of Styx and Erebus;
And turns the woe of Night,   10
By its own craft, to a more rich delight.

We buy ashes for bread;
We buy diluted wine;
Give me of the true,—
Whose ample leaves and tendrils curled   15
Among the silver hills of heaven,
Draw everlasting dew;
Wine of wine,
Blood of the world,
Form of forms, and mould of statures,   20
That I intoxicated,
And by the draught assimilated,
May float at pleasure through all natures;
The bird-language rightly spell,
And that which roses say so well.   25

Wine that is shed
Like the torrents of the sun
Up the horizon walls,
Or like the Atlantic streams, which run
When the South Sea calls.   30

Water and bread,
Food which needs no transmuting,
Rainbow-flowering, wisdom-fruiting
Wine which is already man,
Food which teach and reason can.   35

Wine which Music is,—
Music and wine are one,—
That I, drinking this,
Shall hear far Chaos talk with me;
Kings unborn shall walk with me;   40
And the poor grass shall plot and plan

What it will do when it is man.
Quickened so, will I unlock
Every crypt of every rock.

I thank the joyful juice   45
For all I know;—
Winds of remembering
Of the ancient being blow,
And seeming-solid walls of use
Open and flow.   50

Pour, Bacchus! the remembering wine;
Retrieve the loss of me and mine!
Vine for vine be antidote,
And the grape requite the lote!
Haste to cure the old despair,—   55
Reason in Nature's lotus drenched,
The memory of ages quenched;
Give them again to shine;
Let wine repair what this undid;
And where the infection slid,   60
A dazzling memory revive;
Refresh the faded tints,
Recut the aged prints,
And write my old adventures with the pen
Which on the first day drew,   65
Upon the tablets blue,
The dancing Pleiads and eternal men.

1846 || 1846

THE HOUSE

Emerson sent a copy of this poem to Ellen Sturgis Hooper, sister of Caroline Sturgis, on May 22, 1845, shortly after it was written. Earlier that month Emerson had assisted, with several friends, at the raising of Thoreau's cabin at Walden Pond, destined to become one of the most famous and least expensive houses in Massachusetts (*CW* 9:240; Harding, *Days*, pp. 180–181).

THE HOUSE

There is no architect
    Can build as the Muse can;
She is skilful to select
    Materials for her plan;

Slow and warily to choose   5
    Rafters of immortal pine,
Or cedar incorruptible,
    Worthy her design.

She threads dark Alpine forests,
    Or valleys by the sea,   10
In many lands, with painful steps,
    Ere she can find a tree.

She ransacks mines and ledges,
    And quarries every rock,
To hew the famous adamant   15
    For each eternal block.

She lays her beams in music,
    In music every one,
To the cadence of the whirling world
    Which dances round the sun;   20

That so they shall not be displaced
    By lapses or by wars,
But, for the love of happy souls,
    Outlive the newest stars.

1845 || 1846

GHASELLE:
FROM THE PERSIAN OF HAFIZ

On April 9, 1846, at Elizabeth Peabody's bookstore at 13 West Street, Boston, Emerson purchased Joseph von Hammer's two-volume translation (into German) of the fourteenth-century poet Hafiz, the *Diwan von Mohammed Schemsed-din Hafis* (Stuttgart and Tübingen, 1812–13) (see *L* 8:249, n. 66). This book quickly convinced Emerson that Hafiz was one of the great lyric poets of world literature; and indeed its acquisition marked an epoch in his own development as a writer. His translations from it were often fragmentary, desultory, and usually confined to his notebooks, but he was permanently inspired by the joy and unrestraint of this new poet's voice, to which he immediately paid indirect tribute in "Bacchus." Emerson certainly found the mystical or transcendental element in the Sufi poets congenial, though he paid little attention to their distinctive teachings; indeed, surprisingly, he uses the term "Sufi" only once in all his writings (*TN* 2:131). Emerson's portrait of Hafiz in the essay "Persian Poetry" (1858) stresses the poet's antinomian freedom: "Wrong shall not be wrong to Hafiz, for the name's sake. A law or statute is to him what a fence is to a nimble school-boy,—a temptation for a jump" (*CW* 8:132). The following poetic translation, one of two that Emerson published in *Poems* (1847), is taken from the *Diwan*, 1:106–107.

GHASELLE:
FROM THE PERSIAN OF HAFIZ

Of Paradise, O hermit wise,
    Let us renounce the thought;
Of old therein our names of sin
    Allah recorded not.

Who dear to God on earthly sod   5
    No rice or barley plants,
The same is glad that life is had,
    Though corn he wants.

O just fakir, with brow austere,
    Forbid me not the vine;   10
On the first day, poor Hafiz' clay
    Was kneaded up with wine.

Thy mind the mosque and cool kiosk,
    Spare fast and orisons;
Mine me allows the drinking-house,   15
    And sweet chase of the nuns.

He is no dervise, Heaven slights his service,
    Who shall refuse
There in the banquet to pawn his blanket
    For Schiraz' juice.   20

Who his friend's skirt or hem of his shirt
    Shall spare to pledge,
To him Eden's bliss and angel's kiss
    Shall want their edge.

Up! Hafiz, grace from high God's face   25
    Beams on thee pure;
Shy thou not hell, and trust thou well,
    Heaven is secure.

1846 || 1846

XENOPHANES

The prose germ of this poem is a journal entry of March 11, 1836: "All is in Each. Xenophanes complained in his old age that all things hastened back to Unity[,] Identity. He was weary of seeing the same thing in a tedious variety of forms" (*JMN* 5:136). Strauch ("The Year of Emerson's Poetic Maturity," pp. 365–369) mistakenly assigned the poem to 1834 but located the source of the anecdote in Joseph-Marie de Gérando, *Histoire comparée des systèmes de philosophie*, 2 vols. (Paris, 1822–23), 1:460, from a section on Xenophanes and the Greek Eleatic school. The idea of the "All in Each in Nature" (as Madame de Staël, in *Germany* [1813], had derived it from Goethe) was known to Emerson as early as 1821, when his aunt Mary Moody Emerson quoted the relevant passage in a letter: "The german philosophers professed 'two general opinions' for guides in studying the sciences;—'one that the universe is made after the model of the human soul; the other that the analogy of every part of the universe, with it's [sic] *whole*, is so close that the same idea is constantly reflected from the whole in every part & from every part in the whole'" (p. 143; cf. Cole, p. 167). Emerson was prompted to write the poem when, on March 20, 1836, the chain of sources had circled round again to Goethe: "Only last evening I found the following sentence in Goethe, a comment and consent to my speculations on the All in Each in Nature this last week. 'Every existing thing is an analogon of all existing things. Thence appears to us Being ever, at once sundered & connected. If we follow the analogy too far all things confound themselves in identity. If we avoid it, then all things scatter into infinity. In both cases, observation is at a stand, in the one as too lively, in the other as dead'" (*JMN* 5:138). The former option seems to have taken hold of Xenophanes, whose resulting impression of monotony is registered in Emerson's poem in a version of dramatic monologue. For Emerson, who saw the unity and diversity at once, the idea of All in Each had immediate application in his theory of poetic expression: "This metonymy, or seeing the same sense in things so diverse, gives a pure pleasure. Every one of a million times we find a charm in the metamorphosis. It makes us dance and sing. All men are so far poets" ("Poetry and Imagination," *CW* 8:12–13; cf. *LL* 1:303).

XENOPHANES

By fate, not option, frugal Nature gave
One scent to hyson and to wall-flower,
One sound to pine-groves and to waterfalls,
One aspect to the desert and the lake.

It was her stern necessity: all things   5
Are of one pattern made; bird, beast, and flower,
Song, picture, form, space, thought, and character
Deceive us, seeming to be many things,
And are but one. Beheld far off, they part
As God and devil; bring them to the mind,   10
They dull its edge with their monotony.
To know one element, explore another,
And in the second reappears the first.
The specious panorama of a year
But multiplies the image of a day,—   15
A belt of mirrors round a taper's flame;
And universal Nature, through her vast
And crowded whole, an infinite paroquet,
Repeats one note.

                                                        1836 || 1846

BLIGHT

Written in July 1843, the poem was published in the January 1844 issue of the *Dial* with the title "The Times. A Fragment." Emerson supplied its final title when he prepared copy for *Poems* in 1846, possibly influenced by a journal entry from April of that year: "Some times I seem to move in a constellation. I think my birth has fallen in the thick of the Milky Way: and again I fancy the American Blight & English narrowness & German defectiveness & French surface have bereaved the time of all worth" (*JMN* 9:359). William Stowe has described Emerson's treatment in this poem of the three forms of botanical knowledge: "local knowledge of common names, occult knowledge of specific virtues, and abstract knowledge of and union with the order of the universe" (p. 574).

BLIGHT

Give me truths;
For I am weary of the surfaces,
And die of inanition. If I knew
Only the herbs and simples of the wood,
Rue, cinquefoil, gill, vervain, and agrimony,   5
Blue-vetch, and trillium, hawkweed, sassafras,
Milkweeds, and murky brakes, quaint pipes, and sundew,
And rare and virtuous roots, which in these woods
Draw untold juices from the common earth,
Untold, unknown, and I could surely spell   10
Their fragrance, and their chemistry apply
By sweet affinities to human flesh,
Driving the foe and stablishing the friend,—
O, that were much, and I could be a part
Of the round day, related to the sun   15
And planted world, and full executor
Of their imperfect functions.
But these young scholars, who invade our hills,
Bold as the engineer who fells the wood,
And travelling often in the cut he makes,   20
Love not the flower they pluck, and know it not,

And all their botany is Latin names.
The old men studied magic in the flowers,
And human fortunes in astronomy,
And an omnipotence in chemistry,   25
Preferring things to names, for these were men,
Were unitarians of the united world,
And, wheresoever their clear eye-beams fell,
They caught the footsteps of the SAME. Our eyes
Are armed, but we are strangers to the stars,   30
And strangers to the mystic beast and bird,
And strangers to the plant and to the mine.
The injured elements say, 'Not in us;'
And night and day, ocean and continent,
Fire, plant, and mineral say, 'Not in us,'   35
And haughtily return us stare for stare.
For we invade them impiously for gain;
We devastate them unreligiously,
And coldly ask their pottage, not their love.
Therefore they shove us from them, yield to us   40
Only what to our griping toil is due;
But the sweet affluence of love and song,
The rich results of the divine consents
Of man and earth, of world beloved and lover,
The nectar and ambrosia, are withheld;   45
And in the midst of spoils and slaves, we thieves
And pirates of the universe, shut out
Daily to a more thin and outward rind,
Turn pale and starve. Therefore, to our sick eyes,
The stunted trees look sick, the summer short,   50
Clouds shade the sun, which will not tan our hay,
And nothing thrives to reach its natural term;
And life, shorn of its venerable length,
Even at its greatest space is a defeat,
And dies in anger that it was a dupe;   55
And, in its highest noon and wantonness,
Is early frugal, like a beggar's child;
Even in the hot pursuit of the best aims

And prizes of ambition, checks its hand,
Like Alpine cataracts frozen as they leaped,   60
Chilled with a miserly comparison
Of the toy's purchase with the length of life.

1843 || 1844

MUSKETAQUID

"Musketaquid" is the Indian name for the notoriously languid Concord River, on whose banks, before the Revolution, Emerson's grandfather had built "The Old Manse," northward of Concord center. It was from there, probably on February 21, 1835, that Emerson wrote to his fiancée, Lydia Jackson, at Plymouth, hoping to make her think well of the town, his family's ancestral home, and urging that it become their marital home as well. He pointed out that he had "promised" to write a poem in praise of the river—"whenever the tardy, callow muse shall new moult her feathers. River large & inkstand little, deep & deep would blend their voices" (*L* 1:440; cf. *L* 7:237–238). Emerson did not fulfill his promise, however, until 1843 or 1844, by which time the river had ceased to be the poem's main focus.

MUSKETAQUID

Because I was content with these poor fields,
Low, open meads, slender and sluggish streams,
And found a home in haunts which others scorned,
The partial wood-gods overpaid my love,
And granted me the freedom of their state,   5
And in their secret senate have prevailed
With the dear, dangerous lords that rule our life,
Made moon and planets parties to their bond,
And through my rock-like, solitary wont
Shot million rays of thought and tenderness.   10
For me, in showers, in sweeping showers, the spring
Visits the valley;—break away the clouds,—
I bathe in the morn's soft and silvered air,
And loiter willing by yon loitering stream.
Sparrows far off, and nearer, April's bird,   15
Blue-coated,—flying before from tree to tree,
Courageous, sing a delicate overture
To lead the tardy concert of the year.
Onward and nearer rides the sun of May;
And wide around, the marriage of the plants   20
Is sweetly solemnized. Then flows amain
The surge of summer's beauty; dell and crag,

Hollow and lake, hill-side, and pine arcade,
Are touched with genius. Yonder ragged cliff
Has thousand faces in a thousand hours.   25

Beneath low hills, in the broad interval
Through which at will our Indian rivulet
Winds mindful still of sannup and of squaw,
Whose pipe and arrow oft the plough unburies,
Here in pine houses built of new-fallen trees,   30
Supplanters of the tribe, the farmers dwell.
Traveller, to thee, perchance, a tedious road,
Or, it may be, a picture; to these men,
The landscape is an armory of powers,
Which, one by one, they know to draw and use.   35
They harness beast, bird, insect, to their work;
They prove the virtues of each bed of rock,
And, like the chemist mid his loaded jars,
Draw from each stratum its adapted use
To drug their crops or weapon their arts withal.   40
They turn the frost upon their chemic heap,
They set the wind to winnow pulse and grain,
They thank the spring-flood for its fertile slime,
And, on cheap summit-levels of the snow,
Slide with the sledge to inaccessible woods   45
O'er meadows bottomless. So, year by year,
They fight the elements with elements,
(That one would say, meadow and forest walked,
Transmuted in these men to rule their like,)
And by the order in the field disclose   50
The order regnant in the yeoman's brain.

What these strong masters wrote at large in miles,
I followed in small copy in my acre;
For there's no rood has not a star above it;
The cordial quality of pear or plum   55
Ascends as gladly in a single tree
As in broad orchards resonant with bees;
And every atom poises for itself,
And for the whole. The gentle deities

Showed me the lore of colors and of sounds,   60
The innumerable tenements of beauty,
The miracle of generative force,
Far-reaching concords of astronomy
Felt in the plants, and in the punctual birds;
Better, the linked purpose of the whole,   65
And, chiefest prize, found I true liberty
In the glad home plain-dealing nature gave.
The polite found me impolite; the great
Would mortify me, but in vain; for still
I am a willow of the wilderness,   70
Loving the wind that bent me. All my hurts
My garden spade can heal. A woodland walk,
A quest of river-grapes, a mocking thrush,
A wild-rose, or rock-loving columbine,
Salve my worst wounds.   75
For thus the wood-gods murmured in my ear:
'Dost love our manners? Canst thou silent lie?
Canst thou, thy pride forgot, like nature pass
Into the winter night's extinguished mood?
Canst thou shine now, then darkle,   80
And being latent feel thyself no less?
As, when the all-worshipped moon attracts the eye,
The river, hill, stems, foliage are obscure,
Yet envies none, none are unenviable.'

1843–44? || 1846

DIRGE

Beginning with "Musketaquid" and continuing with "Dirge," "Threnody," and the "Concord Hymn," these last four poems of the 1847 sequence develop local and personal themes, all in a subdued and melancholy commemorative tone.

In conveying the manuscript of "Dirge" to his old friend William H. Furness for publication in *The Gift,* Emerson wrote on March 12, 1845, that it was "composed . . . by me one afternoon, years ago, as I walked in the woods & on the narrow plain through which our Concord River flows . . . and remembered my brothers Edward & Charles, to whom as to me this place was in boyhood & youth all 'the country' which we knew. . . . My sister Elizabeth Hoar [betrothed to Emerson's brother Charles before his death in 1836], who first persuaded me to print some rhymes, is fond of these verses, so I draw them out of their sad recess for you. Their cadence was so agreeable that I should have printed them in the Dial but for their personality" (*L* 7:592).

Written in 1838, "Dirge" memorializes Emerson's younger brothers Charles Chauncy and Edward Bliss, who died in 1834, and recalls their many summer visits, as children, to the Concord home of their step-grandfather, Ezra Ripley (1751–1841). In *Emerson in Concord,* the poet's son pointed out that the family took refuge there for a period during the War of 1812, when prices in Boston spiked and poverty threatened. The boys in their play favored the great meadows east of the Old Manse and liked as well "Cæsar's Woods" and "Peter's Field," retired places named for slaves who lived there before the Revolution.

DIRGE

Knows he who tills this lonely field,
    To reap its scanty corn,
What mystic fruit his acres yield
    At midnight and at morn?

In the long sunny afternoon,   5
    The plain was full of ghosts;
I wandered up, I wandered down,
    Beset by pensive hosts.

The winding Concord gleamed below,
    Pouring as wide a flood   10
As when my brothers, long ago,
    Came with me to the wood.

But they are gone,—the holy ones
    Who trod with me this lovely vale;
The strong, star-bright companions   15
    Are silent, low, and pale.

My good, my noble, in their prime,
    Who made this world the feast it was,
Who learned with me the lore of time,
    Who loved this dwelling-place!   20

They took this valley for their toy,
    They played with it in every mood;
A cell for prayer, a hall for joy,—
    They treated nature as they would.

They colored the horizon round;   25
    Stars flamed and faded as they bade;
All echoes hearkened for their sound,—
    They made the woodlands glad or mad.

I touch this flower of silken leaf,
    Which once our childhood knew;   30
Its soft leaves wound me with a grief
    Whose balsam never grew.

Hearken to yon pine-warbler
    Singing aloft in the tree!
Hearest thou, O traveller,   35
    What he singeth to me?

Not unless God made sharp thine ear
    With sorrow such as mine,
Out of that delicate lay could'st thou
    Its heavy tale divine.   40

'Go, lonely man,' it saith;
    'They loved thee from their birth;
Their hands were pure, and pure their faith,—
    There are no such hearts on earth.

'Ye drew one mother's milk,   45
    One chamber held ye all;

A very tender history
   Did in your childhood fall.

'Ye cannot unlock your heart,
   The key is gone with them;   50
The silent organ loudest chants
   The master's requiem.'

1838 || 1844

THRENODY

Emerson's first-born child, Waldo, died at 8:15 PM on Thursday, January 27, 1842, at the age of five. On the previous Sunday Emerson had taken him through inclement weather to services at the First Parish Church, just then reopened after extensive renovations. On Monday the child came down with what seemed to be a cold, and Lidian supposed he had contracted it on his excursion the day before. The symptoms rapidly grew worse and the family physician, Dr. Josiah Bartlett, was called in. He diagnosed the illness as Scarlet Fever, or Scarlatina. The available palliatives were ineffective since the cause of the disease, a bacterial infection, was at the time unknown. Shortly after the onset of delirium, Waldo died.

Earlier, in 1838, two years after the death of his brother Charles, four years after the death of his brother Edward, and seven years after the death of his much-beloved first wife, Ellen, Emerson told the poet Jones Very "that I had never suffered, & that I could scarce bring myself to feel a concern for the safety & life of my nearest friends that would satisfy them: that I saw clearly that if my wife, my child, my mother, should be taken from me, I should still remain whole with the same capacity of cheap enjoyment from all things. I should not grieve enough, although I love them. But could I make them feel what I feel—the boundless resources of the soul,—remaining entire when particular threads of relation are snapped,—I should then dismiss forever the little remains of uneasiness I have in regard to them" (*JMN* 7:132). This is the position that the death of Waldo tested and that "Threnody" works out.

Emerson family tradition held that the poem's first half (the lament) was written in the spring immediately following the event and that the second half (the consolation) had to wait for the grief to subside, as though a weak "philosophy" had been overmatched or that the articulation of the loss had become traumatically separated from Emerson's ways of confronting it. A closer examination of the manuscripts and related evidence shows that the poem was substantially written between October 1842 and the following spring, though Emerson was reluctant to show it to friends until January 1844 (*CW* 9:289–290).

Often praised as one of Emerson's finest poems, and arguably one of the great nineteenth-century elegies, "Threnody" has, in the opinion of Oliver Wendell Holmes, "the dignity of 'Lycidas' without its refrigerating classicism" (p. 333).

THRENODY

The South-wind brings
Life, sunshine, and desire,
And on every mount and meadow
Breathes aromatic fire;
But over the dead he has no power,   5
The lost, the lost, he cannot restore;
And, looking over the hills, I mourn
The darling who shall not return.

I see my empty house,
I see my trees repair their boughs;   10
And he, the wondrous child,
Whose silver warble wild
Outvalued every pulsing sound
Within the air's cerulean round,—
The hyacinthine boy, for whom   15
Morn well might break and April bloom,—
The gracious boy, who did adorn
The world whereinto he was born,
And by his countenance repay
The favor of the loving Day,—   20
Has disappeared from the Day's eye;
Far and wide she cannot find him;
My hopes pursue, they cannot bind him.
Returned this day, the South-wind searches,
And finds young pines and budding birches;   25
But finds not the budding man;
Nature, who lost, cannot remake him;
Fate let him fall, Fate can't retake him;
Nature, Fate, men, him seek in vain.

And whither now, my truant wise and sweet,   30
O, whither tend thy feet?
I had the right, few days ago,
Thy steps to watch, thy place to know;
How have I forfeited the right?
Hast thou forgot me in a new delight?   35

I hearken for thy household cheer,
O eloquent child!
Whose voice, an equal messenger,
Conveyed thy meaning mild.
What though the pains and joys 40
Whereof it spoke were toys
Fitting his age and ken,
Yet fairest dames and bearded men,
Who heard the sweet request,
So gentle, wise, and grave, 45
Bended with joy to his behest,
And let the world's affairs go by,
Awhile to share his cordial game,
Or mend his wicker wagon-frame,
Still plotting how their hungry ear 50
That winsome voice again might hear;
For his lips could well pronounce
Words that were persuasions.

Gentlest guardians marked serene
His early hope, his liberal mien; 55
Took counsel from his guiding eyes
To make this wisdom earthly wise.
Ah, vainly do these eyes recall
The school-march, each day's festival,
When every morn my bosom glowed 60
To watch the convoy on the road;
The babe in willow wagon closed,
With rolling eyes and face composed;
With children forward and behind,
Like Cupids studiously inclined; 65
And he the chieftain paced beside,
The centre of the troop allied,
With sunny face of sweet repose,
To guard the babe from fancied foes.
The little captain innocent 70
Took the eye with him as he went;
Each village senior paused to scan

And speak the lovely caravan.
From the window I look out
To mark thy beautiful parade,   75
Stately marching in cap and coat
To some tune by fairies played;—
A music heard by thee alone
To works as noble led thee on.

Now Love and Pride, alas! in vain,   80
Up and down their glances strain.
The painted sled stands where it stood;
The kennel by the corded wood;
The gathered sticks to stanch the wall
Of the snow-tower, when snow should fall;   85
The ominous hole he dug in the sand,
And childhood's castles built or planned;
His daily haunts I well discern,—
The poultry-yard, the shed, the barn,—
And every inch of garden ground   90
Paced by the blessed feet around,
From the roadside to the brook
Whereinto he loved to look.
Step the meek birds where erst they ranged;
The wintry garden lies unchanged;   95
The brook into the stream runs on;
But the deep-eyed boy is gone.

On that shaded day,
Dark with more clouds than tempests are,
When thou didst yield thy innocent breath   100
In birdlike heavings unto death,
Night came, and Nature had not thee;
I said, 'We are mates in misery.'
The morrow dawned with needless glow;
Each snowbird chirped, each fowl must crow;   105
Each tramper started; but the feet
Of the most beautiful and sweet
Of human youth had left the hill
And garden,—they were bound and still.

There's not a sparrow or a wren,   110
There's not a blade of autumn grain,
Which the four seasons do not tend,
And tides of life and increase lend;
And every chick of every bird,
And weed and rock-moss is preferred.   115
O ostrich-like forgetfulness!
O loss of larger in the less!
Was there no star that could be sent,
No watcher in the firmament,
No angel from the countless host   120
That loiters round the crystal coast,
Could stoop to heal that only child,
Nature's sweet marvel undefiled,
And keep the blossom of the earth,
Which all her harvests were not worth?   125
Not mine,—I never called thee mine,
But Nature's heir,—if I repine,
And seeing rashly torn and moved
Not what I made, but what I loved,
Grow early old with grief that thou   130
Must to the wastes of Nature go,—
'Tis because a general hope
Was quenched, and all must doubt and grope.
For flattering planets seemed to say
This child should ills of ages stay,   135
By wondrous tongue, and guided pen,
Bring the flown Muses back to men.
Perchance not he but Nature ailed,
The world and not the infant failed.
It was not ripe yet to sustain   140
A genius of so fine a strain,
Who gazed upon the sun and moon
As if he came unto his own,
And, pregnant with his grander thought,
Brought the old order into doubt.   145
His beauty once their beauty tried;
They could not feed him, and he died,

And wandered backward as in scorn,
To wait an æon to be born.
Ill day which made this beauty waste, 150
Plight broken, this high face defaced!
Some went and came about the dead;
And some in books of solace read;
Some to their friends the tidings say;
Some went to write, some went to pray; 155
One tarried here, there hurried one;
But their heart abode with none.
Covetous death bereaved us all,
To aggrandize one funeral.
The eager fate which carried thee 160
Took the largest part of me:
For this losing is true dying;
This is lordly man's down-lying,
This his slow but sure reclining,
Star by star his world resigning. 165

O child of paradise,
Boy who made dear his father's home,
In whose deep eyes
Men read the welfare of the times to come,
I am too much bereft. 170
The world dishonored thou hast left.
O truth's and nature's costly lie!
O trusted broken prophecy!
O richest fortune sourly crossed!
Born for the future, to the future lost! 175

The deep Heart answered, 'Weepest thou?
Worthier cause for passion wild
If I had not taken the child.
And deemest thou as those who pore,
With aged eyes, short way before,— 180
Think'st Beauty vanished from the coast
Of matter, and thy darling lost?
Taught he not thee—the man of eld,

Whose eyes within his eyes beheld
Heaven's numerous hierarchy span   185
The mystic gulf from God to man?
To be alone wilt thou begin
When worlds of lovers hem thee in?
To-morrow, when the masks shall fall
That dizen Nature's carnival,   190
The pure shall see by their own will,
Which overflowing Love shall fill,
'Tis not within the force of fate
The fate-conjoined to separate.
But thou, my votary, weepest thou?   195
I gave thee sight—where is it now?
I taught thy heart beyond the reach
Of ritual, bible, or of speech;
Wrote in thy mind's transparent table,
As far as the incommunicable;   200
Taught thee each private sign to raise,
Lit by the supersolar blaze.
Past utterance, and past belief,
And past the blasphemy of grief,
The mysteries of Nature's heart;   205
And though no Muse can these impart,
Throb thine with Nature's throbbing breast,
And all is clear from east to west.

'I came to thee as to a friend;
Dearest, to thee I did not send   210
Tutors, but a joyful eye,
Innocence that matched the sky,
Lovely locks, a form of wonder,
Laughter rich as woodland thunder,
That thou might'st entertain apart   215
The richest flowering of all art:
And, as the great all-loving Day
Through smallest chambers takes its way,
That thou might'st break thy daily bread
With prophet, savior, and head;   220

That thou might'st cherish for thine own
The riches of sweet Mary's Son,
Boy-Rabbi, Israel's paragon.
And thoughtest thou such guest
Would in thy hall take up his rest? 225
Would rushing life forget her laws,
Fate's glowing revolution pause?
High omens ask diviner guess;
Not to be conned to tediousness.
And know my higher gifts unbind 230
The zone that girds the incarnate mind.
When the scanty shores are full
With Thought's perilous, whirling pool;
When frail Nature can no more,
Then the Spirit strikes the hour: 235
My servant Death, with solving rite,
Pours finite into infinite.

'Wilt thou freeze love's tidal flow,
Whose streams through nature circling go?
Nail the wild star to its track 240
On the half-climbed zodiac?
Light is light which radiates,
Blood is blood which circulates,
Life is life which generates,
And many-seeming life is one,— 245
Wilt thou transfix and make it none?
Its onward force too starkly pent
In figure, bone, and lineament?
Wilt thou, uncalled, interrogate,
Talker! the unreplying Fate? 250
Nor see the genius of the whole
Ascendant in the private soul,
Beckon it when to go and come,
Self-announced its hour of doom?
Fair the soul's recess and shrine, 255
Magic-built to last a season;
Masterpiece of love benign;

Fairer that expansive reason
Whose omen 'tis, and sign.
Wilt thou not ope thy heart to know   260
What rainbows teach, and sunsets show?
Verdict which accumulates
From lengthening scroll of human fates,
Voice of earth to earth returned,
Prayers of saints that inly burned,—   265
Saying, *What is excellent,*
As God lives, is permanent;
Hearts are dust, hearts' loves remain;
Heart's love will meet thee again.
Revere the Maker; fetch thine eye   270
Up to his style, and manners of the sky.
Not of adamant and gold
Built he heaven stark and cold;
No, but a nest of bending reeds,
Flowering grass, and scented weeds;   275
Or like a traveller's fleeing tent,
Or bow above the tempest bent;
Built of tears and sacred flames,
And virtue reaching to its aims;
Built of furtherance and pursuing,   280
Not of spent deeds, but of doing.
Silent rushes the swift Lord
Through ruined systems still restored,
Broadsowing, bleak and void to bless,
Plants with worlds the wilderness;   285
Waters with tears of ancient sorrow
Apples of Eden ripe to-morrow.
House and tenant go to ground,
Lost in God, in Godhead found.'

1842–43 || 1846

CONCORD HYMN

SUNG AT THE COMPLETION OF THE BATTLE MONUMENT, JULY 4, 1837

The first battle of the American Revolution occurred on April 19, 1775, at Concord's North Bridge, between British troops sent out from Boston by General Thomas Gage and a body of hastily assembled minutemen from Concord, Acton, and Lincoln. This bridge lay virtually in Emerson's grandfather's backyard—that is, immediately behind the historic Old Manse, built in 1769 by William Emerson, the town's minister. He was present on the fateful day "to animate and encourage his people," according to local historian Lemuel Shattuck (p. 105). He was likewise with the American forces two months later at Boston's Bunker Hill. Afterward he served as an army chaplain, fell ill at Fort Ticonderoga, and died in Rutland, Vermont, in October 1776, on his way home (*William Emerson*, pp. 71–75). He was succeeded in the Concord pulpit by Ezra Ripley, who married Emerson's widow and occupied the Old Manse until his own death, in 1841. The people of Concord took a strong interest in the town's Revolutionary history because their minister did: Ripley published his *History of the Fight at Concord* in 1827 to counter claims from nearby Lexington that the Revolution had begun there. He pointed out that during the predawn encounter at Lexington only the British had fired, killing several. Thus it was at Concord, hours later, that Britain was first forcibly and effectually resisted. After publishing his book, Ripley led the effort to place a memorial at the site of the battle bridge, donating a small plot of land on which an appropriate monument would be erected. The committee of arrangements wrangled at length over the wording to be inscribed on the obelisk, rejecting submissions from Ripley, Shattuck, and Emerson himself (all too long for the space available), and settled at last on a concise formula by local physician Edward Jarvis (see Jarvis, p. 223). In consequence of these delays, the dedication was postponed from April 19, 1836, to July 4, 1837. Asked to provide a hymn for the occasion, Emerson wrote it in June (*L* 2:85, n. 121). Copies were printed in broadside and the hymn sung to the tune of Old Hundred by a choir that included Thoreau, but not Emerson, who, with his family, was gone from town that day (Harding, *Days*, p. 48).

This "perfect little poem," as Oliver Wendell Holmes called it (p. 332), was for many years a staple in the schoolroom, though not because its crystal clarity exempts it from being misread. Bliss Perry cited an instance:

> As for the Concord Hymn, my recollection is that a student came up after a class-room discussion of the poem, and said: "My teacher in the Normal School told us that there were four mistakes in the first stanza:

1. The bridge had no arch. It was laid on flat stringers.
2. We don't know that there was any flag.
3. There was no battle-array to justify the word 'embattled'; just a straggling crowd of farmers.
4. The farthest point at which the shots were heard was South Acton. (quoted in Strauch, Diss., p. 554)

One effect of this joke is to recoup a sense of Emerson's audaciousness in the figurative language of line 4, largely lost to us through too frequent quotation. In one of the four surviving copies of the broadside printing, one of the hundred or so original singers underscored the line and wrote next to it in the margin a single word—"poetical" (Ives, pl. 2).

CONCORD HYMN

SUNG AT THE COMPLETION OF THE BATTLE MONUMENT, JULY 4, 1837

By the rude bridge that arched the flood,
　　Their flag to April's breeze unfurled,
Here once the embattled farmers stood,
　　And fired the shot heard round the world.

The foe long since in silence slept;　　　　　　　　　5
　　Alike the conqueror silent sleeps;
And Time the ruined bridge has swept
　　Down the dark stream which seaward creeps.

On this green bank, by this soft stream,
　　We set today a votive stone,　　　　　　　　　10
That memory may their deed redeem,
　　When, like our sires, our sons are gone.

Spirit, that made those heroes dare
　　To die, and leave their children free,
Bid Time and Nature gently spare　　　　　　　　15
　　The shaft we raise to them and thee.

1837　||　1837

FROM

*May-Day and
Other Pieces*

(1867)

MAY-DAY

The title poem in Emerson's second collection, *May-Day and Other Pieces* (1867)—at 663 lines his longest work in verse—was a challenging, personally rewarding composition, praised at the time by some readers but never a critical success. The young William Dean Howells damned it with faint praise in an influential review in the *Atlantic Monthly*, implying that for all its many fine passages its quirky structure failed to track adequately the well-known sequence of the onset of a New England spring. This criticism was taken to heart by the poet, who wanted to exclude it from the 1876 *Selected Poems*, and by the poet's children, Ellen and Edward, who, in separate editorial interventions, rearranged and in parts rewrote it, hoping to improve its chronology and so save it for reprinting. The version given here is based on the original, authorized text of 1867; the reader may decide whether the inconsecutiveness of its development is as much an obstacle to enjoyment as was supposed at one time. The poem's hint of stream-of-consciousness arguably fits a celebratory aim. Its interest in history relates emotionally to its post–Civil-War situation and works to recover the kind of day that "Shall to the planet overpay / The ravage of a year of war" (ll. 274–275). Like Whittier's "Snow-Bound," Emerson's poem finds solace and reparation in the recollection of a child's joyous relation to the gifts of nature.

Criticism of the poem's structure, however, cannot be quite dismissed, since the work combines some shorter passages independently written over a lengthy period, going as far back as 1838. The topic of Spring was a perennial favorite with Emerson, providing inspiration for verse jottings not obviously intended for inclusion in "May-Day." These he indexed in his notebooks under the heading "Spring." Many such fragments did indeed find a place in the poem's finally extemporized structure, including a long section (ll. 480–602) that in 1876 was extracted and published under the title "The Harp." Emerson's intention to produce a single long poem on the subject of Spring appears not to have taken definite form much before the Civil War years.

MAY-DAY

Daughter of Heaven and Earth, coy Spring,
With sudden passion languishing,
Maketh all things softly smile,
Painteth pictures mile on mile,
Holds a cup with cowslip-wreaths,   5
Whence a smokeless incense breathes.

Girls are peeling the sweet willow,
Poplar white, and Gilead tree,
And troops of boys
Shouting with whoop and hilloa   10
And hip, hip, three times three.
The air is full of whistlings bland;
What was that I heard
Out of the hazy land?
Harp of the wind, or song of bird,   15
Or clapping of shepherd's hands,
Or vagrant booming of the air,
Voice of a meteor lost in day?
Such tidings of the starry sphere
Can this elastic air convey.   20
Or haply 'twas the cannonade
Of the pent and darkened lake,
Cooled by the pendent mountain's shade,
Whose deeps, till beams of noonday break,
Afflicted moan, and latest hold   25
Even into May the iceberg cold.
Was it a squirrel's pettish bark,
Or clarionet of jay? or hark,
Where yon wedged line the Nestor leads,
Steering north with raucous cry   30
Through tracts and provinces of sky,
Every night alighting down
In new landscapes of romance,
Where darkling feed the clamorous clans
By lonely lakes to men unknown.   35
Come the tumult whence it will,
Voice of sport, or rush of wings,
It is a sound, it is a token
That the marble sleep is broken,
And a change has passed on things.   40

Beneath the calm, within the light,
A hid unruly appetite
Of swifter life, a surer hope,

Strains every sense to larger scope,
Impatient to anticipate   45
The halting steps of aged Fate.
Slow grows the palm, too slow the pearl:
When Nature falters, fain would zeal
Grasp the felloes of her wheel,
And grasping give the orbs another whirl.   50
Turn swiftlier round, O tardy ball!
And sun this frozen side,
Bring hither back the robin's call,
Bring back the tulip's pride.

Why chidest thou the tardy Spring?   55
The hardy bunting does not chide;
The blackbirds make the maples ring
With social cheer and jubilee;
The redwing flutes his *o-ka-lee,*
The robins know the melting snow;   60
The sparrow meek, prophetic-eyed,
Her nest beside the snowdrift weaves,
Secure the osier yet will hide
Her callow brood in mantling leaves;
And thou, by science all undone,   65
Why only must thy reason fail
To see the southing of the sun?

As we thaw frozen flesh with snow,
So Spring will not, foolish fond,
Mix polar night with tropic glow,   70
Nor cloy us with unshaded sun,
Nor wanton skip with bacchic dance,
But she has the temperance
Of the gods, whereof she is one,—
Masks her treasury of heat   75
Under east-winds crossed with sleet.
Plants and birds and humble creatures
Well accept her rule austere;
Titan-born, to hardy natures
Cold is genial and dear.   80

As Southern wrath to Northern right
Is but straw to anthracite;
As in the day of sacrifice,
When heroes piled the pyre,
The dismal Massachusetts ice   85
Burned more than others' fire,
So Spring guards with surface cold
The garnered heat of ages old:
Hers to sow the seed of bread,
That man and all the kinds be fed;   90
And, when the sunlight fills the hours,
Dissolves the crust, displays the flowers.

The world rolls round,—mistrust it not,—
Befalls again what once befell;
All things return, both sphere and mote,   95
And I shall hear my bluebird's note,
And dream the dream of Auburn dell.

When late I walked, in earlier days,
All was stiff and stark;
Knee-deep snows choked all the ways,   100
In the sky no spark;
Firm-braced I sought my ancient woods,
Struggling through the drifted roads;
The whited desert knew me not,
Snow-ridges masked each darling spot;   105
The summer dells, by genius haunted,
One arctic moon had disenchanted.
All the sweet secrets therein hid
By Fancy, ghastly spells undid.
Eldest mason, Frost, had piled   110
With wicked ingenuity
Swift cathedrals in the wild.
The piny hosts were sheeted ghosts
In the star-lit minster aisled.
I found no joy: the icy wind   115
Might rule the forest to his mind.
Who would freeze in frozen brakes?

Back to books and sheltered home,
And wood-fire flickering on the walls,
To hear, when, 'mid our talk and games,   120
Without the baffled north-wind calls.
But soft! a sultry morning breaks;
The cowslips make the brown brook gay;
A happier hour, a longer day.
Now the sun leads in the May,   125
Now desire of action wakes,
And the wish to roam.

The caged linnet in the Spring
Hearkens for the choral glee,
When his fellows on the wing   130
Migrate from the Southern Sea.
When trellised grapes their flowers unmask,
And the new-born tendrils twine,
The old wine darkling in the cask
Feels the bloom on the living vine,   135
And bursts the hoops at hint of Spring:
And so perchance, in Adam's race,
Of Eden's bower some dream-like trace
Survived the Flight, and swam the Flood,
And wakes the wish in youngest blood   140
To tread the forfeit Paradise,
And feed once more the exile's eyes;
And ever when the happy child
In May beholds the blooming wild,
And hears in heaven the bluebird sing,   145
'Onward,' he cries, 'your baskets bring,—
In the next field is air more mild,
And o'er yon hazy crest is Eden's balmier Spring.'

Not for a regiment's parade,
Nor evil laws or rulers made,   150
Blue Walden rolls its cannonade,
But for a lofty sign
Which the Zodiac threw,
That the bondage-days are told,

And waters free as winds shall flow. 155
Lo! how all the tribes combine
To rout the flying foe.
See, every patriot oak-leaf throws
His elfin length upon the snows,
Not idle, since the leaf all day 160
Draws to the spot the solar ray,
Ere sunset quarrying inches down,
And half way to the mosses brown;
While the grass beneath the rime
Has hints of the propitious time, 165
And upward pries and perforates
Through the cold slab a thousand gates,
Till green lances peering through
Bend happy in the welkin blue.

April cold with dropping rain 170
Willows and lilacs brings again,
The whistle of returning birds,
And trumpet-lowing of the herds.
The scarlet maple-keys betray
What potent blood hath modest May. 175
What fiery force the earth renews,
The wealth of forms, the flush of hues;
Joy shed in rosy waves abroad
Flows from the heart of Love, the lord.

Hither rolls the storm of heat; 180
I feel its finer billows beat
Like a sea which me infolds;
Heat with viewless fingers moulds,
Swells, and mellows, and matures,
Paints, and flavors, and allures, 185
Bird and briar inly warms,
Still enriches and transforms,
Gives the reed and lily length,
Adds to oak and oxen strength,
Boils the world in tepid lakes, 190

Burns the world, yet burnt remakes;
Enveloping heat, enchanted robe,
Wraps the daisy and the globe,
Transforming what it doth infold,
Life out of death, new out of old,   195
Painting fawns' and leopards' fells,
Seethes the gulf-encrimsoning shells,
Fires gardens with a joyful blaze
Of tulips, in the morning's rays.
The dead log touched bursts into leaf,   200
The wheat-blade whispers of the sheaf.
What god is this imperial Heat,
Earth's prime secret, sculpture's seat?
Doth it bear hidden in its heart
Water-line patterns of all art,   205
All figures, organs, hues, and graces?
Is it Dædalus? is it Love?
Or walks in mask almighty Jove,
And drops from Power's redundant horn
All seeds of beauty to be born?   210

Where shall we keep the holiday,
And duly greet the entering May?
Too strait and low our cottage doors,
And all unmeet our carpet floors;
Nor spacious court, nor monarch's hall,   215
Suffice to hold the festival.
Up and away! where haughty woods
Front the liberated floods:
We will climb the broad-backed hills,
Hear the uproar of their joy;   220
We will mark the leaps and gleams
Of the new-delivered streams,
And the murmuring rivers of sap
Mount in the pipes of the trees,
Giddy with day, to the topmost spire,   225
Which for a spike of tender green

Bartered its powdery cap;
And the colors of joy in the bird,
And the love in its carol heard,
Frog and lizard in holiday coats,   230
And turtle brave in his golden spots;
We will hear the tiny roar
Of the insects evermore,
While cheerful cries of crag and plain
Reply to the thunder of river and main.   235

As poured the flood of the ancient sea
Spilling over mountain chains,
Bending forests as bends the sedge,
Faster flowing o'er the plains,—
A world-wide wave with a foaming edge   240
That rims the running silver sheet,—
So pours the deluge of the heat
Broad northward o'er the land,
Painting artless paradises,
Drugging herbs with Syrian spices,   245
Fanning secret fires which glow
In columbine and clover-blow,
Climbing the northern zones,
Where a thousand pallid towns
Lie like cockles by the main,   250
Or tented armies on a plain.
The million-handed sculptor moulds
Quaintest bud and blossom folds,
The million-handed painter pours
Opal hues and purple dye;   255
Azaleas flush the island floors,
And the tints of heaven reply.

Wreaths for the May! for happy Spring
Today shall all her dowry bring,
The love of kind, the joy, the grace,   260
Hymen of element and race,
Knowing well to celebrate

With song and hue and star and state,
With tender light and youthful cheer,
The spousals of the new-born year.   265
Lo Love's inundation poured
Over space and race abroad!

Spring is strong and virtuous,
Broad-sowing, cheerful, plenteous,
Quickening underneath the mould   270
Grains beyond the price of gold.
So deep and large her bounties are,
That one broad, long midsummer day
Shall to the planet overpay
The ravage of a year of war.   275

Drug the cup, thou butler sweet,
And send the nectar round;
The feet that slid so long on sleet
Are glad to feel the ground.
Fill and saturate each kind   280
With good according to its mind,
Fill each kind and saturate
With good agreeing with its fate,
Willow and violet, maiden and man.

The bittersweet, the haunting air   285
Creepeth, bloweth everywhere;
It preys on all, all prey on it,
Blooms in beauty, thinks in wit,
Stings the strong with enterprise,
Makes travellers long for Indian skies,   290
And, where it comes, this courier fleet
Fans in all hearts expectance sweet,
As if tomorrow should redeem
The vanished rose of evening's dream.
By houses lies a fresher green,   295
On men and maids a ruddier mien,
As if Time brought a new relay

Of shining virgins every May,
And Summer came to ripen maids
To a beauty that not fades.   300

The ground-pines wash their rusty green,
The maple-tops their crimson tint,
On the soft path each track is seen,
The girl's foot leaves its neater print.
The pebble loosened from the frost   305
Asks of the urchin to be tossed.
In flint and marble beats a heart,
The kind Earth takes her children's part,
The green lane is the school-boy's friend,
Low leaves his quarrel apprehend,   310
The fresh ground loves his top and ball,
The air rings jocund to his call,
The brimming brook invites a leap,
He dives the hollow, climbs the steep.
The youth reads omens where he goes,   315
And speaks all languages the rose.
The wood-fly mocks with tiny noise
The far halloo of human voice;
The perfumed berry on the spray
Smacks of faint memories far away.   320
A subtle chain of countless rings
The next unto the farthest brings,
And, striving to be man, the worm
Mounts through all the spires of form.

I saw the bud-crowned Spring go forth,   325
Stepping daily onward north
To greet staid ancient cavaliers
Filing single in stately train.
And who, and who are the travellers?
They were Night and Day, and Day and Night,   330
Pilgrims wight with step forthright.
I saw the Days deformed and low,
Short and bent by cold and snow;
The merry Spring threw wreaths on them,

Flower-wreaths gay with bud and bell; 335
Many a flower and many a gem,
They were refreshed by the smell,
They shook the snow from hats and shoon,
They put their April raiment on;
And those eternal forms, 340
Unhurt by a thousand storms,
Shot up to the height of the sky again
And danced as merrily as young men.
I saw them mask their awful glance
Sidewise meek in gossamer lids, 345
And to speak my thought if none forbids,
It was as if the eternal gods,
Tired of their starry periods,
Hid their majesty in cloth
Woven of tulips and painted moth. 350
On carpets green the maskers march
Below May's well-appointed arch,
Each star, each god, each grace amain,
Every joy and virtue speed,
Marching duly in her train, 355
And fainting Nature at her need
Is made whole again.

'Twas the vintage-day of field and wood
When magic wine for bards is brewed;
Every tree and stem and chink 360
Gushed with syrup to the brink:
The air stole into the streets of towns,
And betrayed the fund of joy
To the high-school and medalled boy:
On from hall to chamber ran, 365
From youth to maid, from boy to man,
To babes, and to old eyes as well.
'Once more,' the old man cried, 'ye clouds,
Airy turrets purple-piled,
Which once my infancy beguiled, 370
Beguile me with the wonted spell.

I know ye skilful to convoy
The total freight of hope and joy
Into rude and homely nooks,
Shed mocking lustres on shelf of books,   375
On farmer's byre, on meadow-pipes,
Or on a pool of dancing chips.
I care not if the pomps you show
Be what they soothfast appear,
Or if yon realms in sunset glow   380
Be bubbles of the atmosphere.
And if it be to you allowed
To fool me with a shining cloud,
So only new griefs are consoled
By new delights, as old by old,   385
Frankly I will be your guest,
Count your change and cheer the best.
The world hath overmuch of pain,—
If Nature give me joy again,
Of such deceit I'll not complain.'   390

Ah! well I mind the calendar,
Faithful through a thousand years,
Of the painted race of flowers,
Exact to days, exact to hours,
Counted on the spacious dial   395
Yon broidered zodiac girds.
I know the pretty almanac
Of the punctual coming-back,
On their due days, of the birds.
I marked them yestermorn,   400
A flock of finches darting
Beneath the crystal arch,
Piping, as they flew, a march,—
Belike the one they used in parting
Last year from yon oak or larch.   405
Dusky sparrows in a crowd,
Diving, darting northward free,
Suddenly betook them all,

Every one to his hole in the wall,
Or to his niche in the apple-tree.   410
I greet with joy the choral trains
Fresh from palms and Cuba's canes.
Best gems of Nature's cabinet,
With dews of tropic morning wet,
Beloved of children, bards, and Spring,   415
O birds, your perfect virtues bring,
Your song, your forms, your rhythmic flight,
Your manners for the heart's delight,
Nestle in hedge, or barn, or roof,
Here weave your chamber weatherproof,   420
Forgive our harms, and condescend
To man as to a lubber friend,
And, generous, teach his awkward race
Courage, and probity, and grace!

Poets praise that hidden wine   425
Hid in milk we drew
At the barrier of Time,
When our life was new.
We had eaten fairy fruit,
We were quick from head to foot,   430
All the forms we looked on shone
As with diamond dews thereon.
What cared we for costly joys,
The Museum's far-fetched toys?
Gleam of sunshine on the wall   435
Poured a deeper cheer than all
The revels of the Carnival.
We a pine-grove did prefer
To a marble theatre,
Could with gods on mallows dine,   440
Nor cared for spices or for wine.
Wreaths of mist and rainbows spanned,
Arch on arch, the grimmest land;
Whistle of a woodland bird
Made the pulses dance,   445

Note of horn in valleys heard
Filled the region with romance.

None can tell how sweet,
How virtuous, the morning air;
Every accent vibrates well;   450
Not alone the wood-bird's call,
Or shouting boys that chase their ball,
Pass the height of minstrel skill,
But the plowman's thoughtless cry,
Lowing oxen, sheep that bleat,   455
And the joiner's hammer-beat,
Softened are above their will.
All grating discords melt,
No dissonant note is dealt,
And though thy voice be shrill   460
Like rasping file on steel,
Such is the temper of the air,
Echo waits with art and care,
And will the faults of song repair.

So by remote Superior Lake,   465
And by resounding Mackinac,
When northern storms the forest shake,
And billows on the long beach break,
The artful Air doth separate
Note by note all sounds that grate,   470
Smothering in her ample breast
All but godlike words,
Reporting to the happy ear
Only purified accords.
Strangely wrought from barking waves,   475
Soft music daunts the Indian braves,—
Convent-chanting which the child
Hears pealing from the panther's cave
And the impenetrable wild.

One musician is sure,   480
His wisdom will not fail,
He has not tasted wine impure,

Nor bent to passion frail.
Age cannot cloud his memory,
Nor grief untune his voice,   485
Ranging down the ruled scale
From tone of joy to inward wail,
Tempering the pitch of all
In his windy cave.
He all the fables knows,   490
And in their causes tells,—
Knows Nature's rarest moods,
Ever on her secret broods.
The Muse of men is coy,
Oft courted will not come;   495
In palaces and market squares
Entreated, she is dumb;
But my minstrel knows and tells
The counsel of the gods,
Knows of Holy Book the spells,   500
Knows the law of Night and Day,
And the heart of girl and boy,
The tragic and the gay,
And what is writ on Table Round
Of Arthur and his peers,   505
What sea and land discoursing say
In sidereal years.
He renders all his lore
In numbers wild as dreams,
Modulating all extremes,—   510
What the spangled meadow saith
To the children who have faith;
Only to children children sing,
Only to youth will spring be spring.

Who is the Bard thus magnified?   515
When did he sing? and where abide?

Chief of song where poets feast
Is the wind-harp which thou seest
In the casement at my side.

Æolian harp, 520
How strangely wise thy strain!
Gay for youth, gay for youth,
(Sweet is art, but sweeter truth,)
In the hall at summer eve
Fate and Beauty skilled to weave. 525
From the eager opening strings
Rung loud and bold the song.
Who but loved the wind-harp's note?
How should not the poet doat
On its mystic tongue, 530
With its primeval memory,
Reporting what old minstrels said
Of Merlin locked the harp within,—
Merlin paying the pain of sin,
Pent in a dungeon made of air,— 535
And some attain his voice to hear,
Words of pain and cries of fear,
But pillowed all on melody,
As fits the griefs of bards to be.
And what if that all-echoing shell, 540
Which thus the buried Past can tell,
Should rive the Future, and reveal
What his dread folds would fain conceal?
It shares the secret of the Earth,
And of the kinds that owe her birth. 545
Speaks not of self that mystic tone,
But of the Overgods alone:
It trembles to the cosmic breath,—
As it heareth, so it saith;
Obeying meek the primal Cause, 550
It is the tongue of mundane laws.
And this, at least, I dare affirm,
Since genius too has bound and term,
There is no bard in all the choir,
Not Homer's self, the poet sire, 555
Wise Milton's odes of pensive pleasure,
Or Shakspeare, whom no mind can measure,

Nor Collins' verse of tender pain,
Nor Byron's clarion of disdain,
Scott, the delight of generous boys,   560
Or Wordsworth, Pan's recording voice,—
Not one of all can put in verse,
Or to this presence could rehearse,
The sights and voices ravishing
The boy knew on the hills in Spring   565
When pacing through the oaks he heard
Sharp queries of the sentry-bird,
The heavy grouse's sudden whirr,
The rattle of the kingfisher;
Saw bonfires of the harlot flies   570
In the lowland, when day dies;
Or marked, benighted and forlorn,
The first far signal-fire of morn.
These syllables that Nature spoke,
And the thoughts that in him woke,   575
Can adequately utter none
Save to his ear the wind-harp lone.
And best can teach its Delphian chord
How Nature to the soul is moored,
If once again that silent string,   580
As erst it wont, would thrill and ring.

Not long ago, at eventide,
It seemed, so listening, at my side
A window rose, and, to say sooth,
I looked forth on the fields of youth: 585
I saw fair boys bestriding steeds,
I knew their forms in fancy weeds,
Long, long concealed by sundering fates,
Mates of my youth,—yet not my mates,
Stronger and bolder far than I,   590
With grace, with genius, well attired,
And then as now from far admired,
Followed with love
They knew not of,

With passion cold and shy.   595
O joy, for what recoveries rare!
Renewed, I breathe Elysian air,
See youth's glad mates in earliest bloom,—
Break not my dream, obtrusive tomb!
Or teach thou, Spring! the grand recoil   600
Of life resurgent from the soil
Wherein was dropped the mortal spoil.

Soft on the south-wind sleeps the haze:
So on thy broad mystic van
Lie the opal-colored days,   605
And waft the miracle to man.
Soothsayer of the eldest gods,
Repairer of what harms betide,
Revealer of the inmost powers
Prometheus proffered, Jove denied;   610
Disclosing treasures more than true,
Or in what far tomorrow due;
Speaking by the tongues of flowers,
By the ten-tongued laurel speaking,
Singing by the oriole songs,   615
Heart of bird the man's heart seeking;
Whispering hints of treasure hid
Under Morn's unlifted lid,
Islands looming just beyond
The dim horizon's utmost bound;—   620
Who can, like thee, our rags upbraid
Or taunt us with our hope decayed?
Or who like thee persuade,
Making the splendor of the air,
The morn and sparkling dew, a snare?   625
Or who resent
Thy genius, wiles, and blandishment?

There is no orator prevails
To beckon or persuade
Like thee the youth or maid: 630
Thy birds, thy songs, thy brooks, thy gales,

Thy blooms, thy kinds,
Thy echoes in the wilderness,
Soothe pain, and age, and love's distress,
Fire fainting will, and build heroic minds.   635

For thou, O Spring! canst renovate
All that high God did first create,
Be still his arm and architect,
Rebuild the ruin, mend defect;
Chemist to vamp old worlds with new,   640
Coat sea and sky with heavenlier blue,
New-tint the plumage of the birds,
And slough decay from grazing herds,
Sweep ruins from the scarped mountain,
Cleanse the torrent at the fountain,   645
Purge alpine air by towns defiled,
Bring to fair mother fairer child,
Not less renew the heart and brain,
Scatter the sloth, wash out the stain,
Make the aged eye sun-clear,   650
To parting soul bring grandeur near.
Under gentle types, my Spring
Masks the might of Nature's king,
An energy that searches thorough
From Chaos to the dawning morrow;   655
Into all our human plight,
The soul's pilgrimage and flight;
In city or in solitude,
Step by step, lifts bad to good,
Without halting, without rest,   660
Lifting Better up to Best;
Planting seeds of knowledge pure,
Through earth to ripen, through heaven endure.

1862–1866 || 1867

THE ADIRONDACS

The plan of an excursion into the primitive wilderness of New York's Adirondack region (as the name is now more often spelled) was formed between poet and *Atlantic Monthly* editor James Russell Lowell and a painter friend of his, William James Stillman, who had recently moved to Cambridge following his brief editorship in New York of *The Crayon,* America's first art journal. Stillman quickly attracted notice for the landscapes he exhibited at this time, including one that he called "The Procession of the Pines," a sublime scene painted at Follansbee Pond in the manner of the Hudson River artists, particularly of his teacher, Frederick Edwin Church, and Church's friend Sanford R. Gifford. It was Gifford who had urged on him the advantages of painting in the seclusion of wild Adirondack scenery, and Stillman had accepted the hint fervently, for many years making annual trips to the northern wilderness. He may also have been influenced in going there by a book published in 1849 with the Thoreauvian title *The Adirondack; Or, Life in the Woods,* by Joel T. Headley, like Stillman a graduate of Union College in Schenectady.

Stillman's circle of acquaintance in Cambridge and Boston expanded rapidly after a first visit in 1855, and Lowell, who befriended him and contributed poems to *The Crayon,* introduced him to members of the recently established Saturday Club. In 1857 Stillman organized the first of several camping trips to Follansbee Pond. On this trip Stillman escorted Lowell's brother-in-law, Dr. Estes Howe, together with Howe's best friend, John Holmes, brother of Oliver Wendell Holmes. This excursion was so successful that a more ambitious one was scheduled for the next summer. Howe and Holmes would return with five new campers from the Saturday Club: Emerson and Lowell; Louis Agassiz, professor of natural history at Harvard; Judge Ebenezer Rockwood Hoar, of Concord, soon to be elevated to the Supreme Judicial Court of Massachusetts; and the convivial Horatio Woodman, founder of the Saturday Club. Two additional invitees were, like Howe and Holmes, not members of the Club: Jeffries Wyman, Harvard professor of anatomy and president of the Boston Society of Natural History, and Dr. Amos Binney, a young friend and patron of Stillman. Henry Wadsworth Longfellow had been invited, but on hearing that Emerson had purchased a double-barreled gun (a combination rifle and shotgun), he expressed an urgent wish to be excused (Longfellow, 4:92). Nor was he the only one concerned on this point.

Setting out on Monday, August 2, 1858, Emerson, along with most of the party, arrived by nightfall in the town of Lake George, New York, at the southern end of the Champlain Valley. The next day they traveled "down the Lake" to Burlington, Vermont, crossed by steamer to Port Kent, then by stage the short distance to Keeseville, New York, where they joined Stillman. There they were greeted by a large crowd of Keeseville folk hoping to get a glimpse of

Agassiz, who had been in the news for declining an invitation from Louis Napoleon to head the natural history museum in Paris, the Jardin des Plantes. On Wednesday morning the party set out, as Emerson records, "in strong country carts" (l. 6) down the rough road along the Ausable River to the village of Saranac Lake, the site of "Martin's Beach." This was in fact a hotel operated by William F. Martin, who specialized in outfitting just such camping expeditions as this one. William H. H. Murray wrote ten years later that "Martin is one of the few men in the world who seem to know how 'to keep a hotel.' At his house you can easily and cheaply obtain your entire outfit for a trip of any length. Here it is that the celebrated Long Lake guides, with their unrivalled boats, principally resort. Here, too, many of the Saranac guides, some of them surpassed by none, make their headquarters" (p. 47).

Provisioned, and with eight guides hired and assigned, the party traversed Lower Saranac Lake, then passed by the Saranac River to Round Lake, now known as Middle Saranac Lake. After crossing that, they were assisted by their guides over a portage to Upper Saranac Lake, the lower end of which they rowed across to a second portage, the mile-long "Indian Carry," at the end of which they found, at Stony Creek Ponds, the log house of Stephen C. Martin, William Martin's brother and Stillman's own favorite guide and life-long friend. The party rested there during a day of rain before setting out, at ten o'clock on Friday morning, across the Ponds to the Raquette River and thence to the marshy inlet at the north end of Follansbee Pond, discovering there a good-sized lake hemmed in on three sides by high hills, covered by mixed pine and hardwood forests, themselves overseen by mountain peaks miles farther off. At Follansbee they occupied what Lowell dubbed "Camp Maple," in some part rustically constructed by Stillman less than a week before. The delighted visitors from Boston, Cambridge, and Concord stayed about ten days, until August 16 (*L* 8:573). Emerson's unpublished Account Books show that he was home by the evening of the 17th, bringing to a close what Paul Schneider has identified as a landmark in the history of American ecotourism (p. 9).

In *Emerson as Poet*, Hyatt Waggoner suggested that "The Adirondacs" was among the very best of Emerson's late poems, even though its "perfectly conventional blank verse" contributed nothing new, in a prosodical way, to his poetic achievement (p. 109). Nevertheless Emerson's imperfectly regular blank verse has its surprises: the diction swings amusingly between the two rewards of the demotic and the resplendent, and the poem becomes a travelogue, taking the reader from prosaic Keeseville to loud Bog River, not omitting along the way "the midge, mosquito, and the fly"—to come at last upon an "Oreads' fended Paradise" where "Some mystic hint accosts the vigilant" (ll. 177, 198, 207). Of course the Paradise was "fended" in fact by brawny, unlettered Saranac guides, whose society put the scholars and professors to a radical test of relevance (the test of the "red flannel"), contributing largely to a sophisticated mock-heroic tone that one does not meet with everywhere in Emerson. And the sudden intrusion into wildest nature of the century's technological sublime (the presence of a future not quite arrived, in the midst of a past not quite gone) is the surprise that in the end composes the poem structurally and accounts for much of its intellectual interest.

THE ADIRONDACS

A JOURNAL

Dedicated to my fellow-travellers in August, 1858.

> Wise and polite,—and if I drew
> Their several portraits, you would own
> Chaucer had no such worthy crew,
> Nor Boccace in Decameron.

We crossed Champlain to Keeseville with our friends,   5
Thence, in strong country carts, rode up the forks
Of the Ausable stream, intent to reach
The Adirondac lakes. At Martin's Beach
We chose our boats; each man a boat and guide,—
Ten men, ten guides, our company all told.   10

    Next morn, we swept with oars the Saranac,
With skies of benediction, to Round Lake,
Where all the sacred mountains drew around us,
Taháwus, Seward, MacIntyre, Baldhead,
And other Titans without muse or name.   15
Pleased with these grand companions, we glide on,
Instead of flowers, crowned with a wreath of hills,
And made our distance wider, boat from boat,
As each would hear the oracle alone.
By the bright morn the gay flotilla slid   20
Through files of flags that gleamed like bayonets,
Through gold-moth-haunted beds of pickerel flower,
Through scented banks of lilies white and gold,
Where the deer feeds at night, the teal by day,
On through the Upper Saranac, and up   25
Père Raquette stream, to a small tortuous pass

Winding through grassy shallows in and out,
Two creeping miles of rushes, pads, and sponge,
To Follansbee Water, and the Lake of Loons.

    Northward the length of Follansbee we rowed,   30
Under low mountains, whose unbroken ridge
Ponderous with beechen forest sloped the shore.
A pause and council: then, where near the head
On the east, a bay makes inward to the land
Between two rocky arms, we climb the bank,   35
And in the twilight of the forest noon
Wield the first axe these echoes ever heard.
We cut young trees to make our poles and thwarts,
Barked the white spruce to weatherfend the roof,
Then struck a light, and kindled the camp-fire.   40

    The wood was sovran with centennial trees,—
Oak, cedar, maple, poplar, beech, and fir,
Linden and spruce. In strict society
Three conifers, white, pitch, and Norway pine,
Five-leaved, three-leaved, and two-leaved, grew thereby.   45
Our patron pine was fifteen feet in girth,
The maple eight, beneath its shapely tower.

    'Welcome!' the wood god murmured through the leaves,—
'Welcome, though late, unknowing, yet known to me.'
Evening drew on; stars peeped through maple boughs,   50
Which o'erhung, like a cloud, our camping fire.
Decayed millennial trunks, like moonlight flecks,
Lit with phosphoric crumbs the forest floor.

    Ten scholars, wonted to lie warm and soft
In well-hung chambers daintily bestowed,   55
Lie here on hemlock boughs, like Sacs and Sioux,
And greet unanimous the joyful change.
So fast will Nature acclimate her sons,
Though late returning to her pristine ways.
Off soundings, seamen do not suffer cold,   60
And, in the forest, delicate clerks, unbrowned,
Sleep on the fragrant brush, as on down beds.

Up with the dawn, they fancied the light air
That circled freshly in their forest dress
Made them to boys again. Happier that they   65
Slipped off their pack of duties, leagues behind,
At the first mounting of the giant stairs.
No placard on these rocks warned to the polls,
No door-bell heralded a visitor,
No courier waits, no letter came or went,   70
Nothing was ploughed, or reaped, or bought, or sold;
The frost might glitter, it would blight no crop,
The falling rain will spoil no holiday.
We were made freemen of the forest laws,
All dressed, like Nature, fit for her own ends,   75
Essaying nothing she cannot perform.

        In Adirondac lakes,
At morn or noon, the guide rows bareheaded:
Shoes, flannel shirt, and kersey trousers make
His brief toilette: at night, or in the rain,
He dons a surcoat which he doffs at morn: 80
A paddle in the right hand, or an oar,
And in the left, a gun, his needful arms.
By turns we praised the stature of our guides,
Their rival strength and suppleness, their skill
To row, to swim, to shoot, to build a camp,   85
To climb a lofty stem, clean without boughs
Full fifty feet, and bring the eaglet down:
Temper to face wolf, bear, or catamount,
And wit to trap or take him in his lair.
Sound, ruddy men, frolic and innocent,   90
In winter, lumberers; in summer, guides;
Their sinewy arms pull at the oar untired
Three times ten thousand strokes, from morn to eve.

    Look to yourselves, ye polished gentlemen!
No city airs or arts pass current here.   95
Your rank is all reversed: let men of cloth
Bow to the stalwart churls in overalls:

They are the doctors of the wilderness,
And we the low-prized laymen.
In sooth, red flannel is a saucy test   100
Which few can put on with impunity.
What make you, master, fumbling at the oar?
Will you catch crabs? Truth tries pretension here.
The sallow knows the basket-maker's thumb;
The oar, the guide's. Dare you accept the tasks   105
He shall impose, to find a spring, trap foxes,
Tell the sun's time, determine the true north,
Or stumbling on through vast self-similar woods
To thread by night the nearest way to camp?

 Ask you, how went the hours?   110
All day we swept the lake, searched every cove,
North from Camp Maple, south to Osprey Bay,
Watching when the loud dogs should drive in deer,
Or whipping its rough surface for a trout;
Or bathers, diving from the rock at noon;   115
Challenging Echo by our guns and cries;
Or listening to the laughter of the loon;
Or, in the evening twilight's latest red,
Beholding the procession of the pines;
Or, later yet, beneath a lighted jack,   120
In the boat's bow, a silent night-hunter
Stealing with paddle to the feeding grounds
Of the red deer, to aim at a square mist.
Hark to that muffled roar! a tree in the woods
Is fallen: but hush! it has not scared the buck   125
Who stands astonished at the meteor light,
Then turns to bound away,—is it too late?

 Sometimes we tried our rifles at a mark,
Six rods, sixteen, twenty, or forty-five;
Sometimes our wits at sally and retort,   130
With laughter sudden as the crack of rifle;
Or parties scaled the near acclivities
Competing seekers of a rumored lake,

Whose unauthenticated waves we named
Lake Probability,—our Carbuncle,   135
Long sought, not found.

        Two Doctors in the camp
Dissected the slain deer, weighed the trout's brain,
Captured the lizard, salamander, shrew,
Crab, mice, snail, dragon-fly, minnow, and moth;
Insatiate skill in water or in air   140
Waved the scoop-net, and nothing came amiss;
The while, one leaden pot of alcohol
Gave an impartial tomb to all the kinds.
Not less the ambitious botanist sought plants,
Orchis and gentian, fern, and long whip-scirpus,   145
Rosy polygonum, lake-margin's pride,
Hypnum, and hydnum, mushroom, sponge, and moss,
Or harebell nodding in the gorge of falls.
Above, the eagle flew, the osprey screamed,
The raven croaked, owls hooted, the woodpecker   150
Loud hammered, and the heron rose in the swamp.
As water poured through hollows of the hills
To feed this wealth of lakes and rivulets,
So Nature shed all beauty lavishly
From her redundant horn.

        Lords of this realm,   155
Bounded by dawn and sunset, and the day
Rounded by hours where each outdid the last
In miracles of pomp, we must be proud,
As if associates of the sylvan gods.
We seemed the dwellers of the zodiac,   160
So pure the Alpine element we breathed,
So light, so lofty pictures came and went.
We trode on air, contemned the distant town,
Its timorous ways, big trifles, and we planned
That we should build, hard-by, a spacious lodge,   165
And how we should come hither with our sons,
Hereafter,—willing they, and more adroit.

Hard fare, hard bed, and comic misery,—
The midge, the blue-fly, and the mosquito
Painted our necks, hands, ankles, with red bands: 170
But, on the second day, we heed them not,
Nay, we saluted them Auxiliaries,
Whom earlier we had chid with spiteful names.
For who defends our leafy tabernacle
From bold intrusion of the travelling crowd,—   175
Who but the midge, musquito, and the fly,
Which past endurance sting the tender cit,
But which we learn to scatter with a smudge,
Or baffle by a veil, or slight by scorn?

Our foaming ale we drunk from hunters' pans,   180
Ale, and a sup of wine. Our steward gave
Venison and trout, potatoes, beans, wheat-bread;
All ate like abbots, and, if any missed
Their wonted convenance, cheerly hid the loss
With hunters' appetite, and peals of mirth.   185
And Stillman, our guides' guide, and Commodore,
Crusoe, Crusader, Pius Æneas, said aloud,
"Chronic dyspepsia never came from eating
Food indigestible":—then murmured some,
Others applauded him who spoke the truth.   190

Nor doubt but visitings of graver thought
Checked in these souls the turbulent heyday
'Mid all the hints and glories of the home.
For who can tell what sudden privacies
Were sought and found, amid the hue and cry   195
Of scholars furloughed from their tasks, and let
Into this Oreads' fended Paradise,
As chapels in the city's thoroughfares,
Whither gaunt Labor slips to wipe his brow,
And meditate a moment on Heaven's rest.   200
Judge with what sweet surprises Nature spoke
To each apart, lifting her lovely shows
To spiritual lessons pointed home.

And as through dreams in watches of the night,
So through all creatures in their form and ways   205
Some mystic hint accosts the vigilant,
Not clearly voiced, but waking a new sense
Inviting to new knowledge, one with old.
Hark to that petulant chirp! what ails the warbler?
Mark his capricious ways to draw the eye.   210
Now soar again. What wilt thou, restless bird,
Seeking in that chaste blue a bluer light,
Thirsting in that pure for a purer sky?

   And presently the sky is changed; O world!
What pictures and what harmonies are thine!   215
The clouds are rich and dark, the air serene,
So like the soul of me, what if 'twere me?
A melancholy better than all mirth.
Comes the sweet sadness at the retrospect,
Or at the foresight of obscurer years?   220
Like yon slow-sailing cloudy promontory,
Whereon the purple iris dwells in beauty
Superior to all its gaudy skirts.
And, that no day of life may lack romance,
The spiritual stars rise nightly, shedding down   225
A private beam into each several heart.
Daily the bending skies solicit man,
The seasons chariot him from this exile,
The rainbow hours bedeck his glowing chair,
The storm-winds urge the heavy weeks along,   230
Suns haste to set, that so remoter lights
Beckon the wanderer to his vaster home.

   With a vermilion pencil mark the day
When of our little fleet three cruising skiffs
Entering Big Tupper, bound for the foaming Falls   235
Of loud Bog River, suddenly confront
Two of our mates returning with swift oars.
One held a printed journal waving high
Caught from a late-arriving traveller,
Big with great news, and shouted the report   240

For which the world had waited, now firm fact,
Of the wire-cable laid beneath the sea,
And landed on our coast, and pulsating
With ductile fire. Loud, exulting cries
From boat to boat, and to the echoes round,   245
Greet the glad miracle. Thought's new-found path
Shall supplement henceforth all trodden ways,
Match God's equator with a zone of art,
And lift man's public action to a height
Worthy the enormous cloud of witnesses,   250
When linkèd hemispheres attest his deed.
We have few moments in the longest life
Of such delight and wonder as there grew,—
Nor yet unsuited to that solitude:
A burst of joy, as if we told the fact   255
To ears intelligent; as if gray rock
And cedar grove and cliff and lake should know
This feat of wit, this triumph of mankind;
As if we men were talking in a vein
Of sympathy so large, that ours was theirs,   260
And a prime end of the most subtle element
Were fairly reached at last. Wake, echoing caves!
Bend nearer, faint day-moon! Yon thundertops,
Let them hear well! 'tis theirs as much as ours.

    A spasm throbbing through the pedestals   265
Of Alp and Andes, isle and continent,
Urging astonished Chaos with a thrill
To be a brain, or serve the brain of man.
The lightning has run masterless too long;
He must to school, and learn his verb and noun,   270
And teach his nimbleness to earn his wage,
Spelling with guided tongue man's messages
Shot through the weltering pit of the salt sea.
And yet I marked, even in the manly joy
Of our great-hearted Doctor in his boat,   275
(Perchance I erred,) a shade of discontent;
Or was it for mankind a generous shame,

As of a luck not quite legitimate,
Since fortune snatched from wit the lion's part?
Was it a college pique of town and gown,   280
As one within whose memory it burned
That not academicians, but some lout,
Found ten years since the California gold?
And now, again, a hungry company
Of traders, led by corporate sons of trade,   285
Perversely borrowing from the shop the tools
Of science, not from the philosophers,
Had won the brightest laurel of all time.
'Twas always thus, and will be; hand and head
Are ever rivals: but, though this be swift,   290
The other slow,—this the Prometheus,
And that the Jove,—yet, howsoever hid,
It was from Jove the other stole his fire,
And, without Jove, the good had never been.
It is not Iroquois or cannibals,   295
But ever the free race with front sublime,
And these instructed by their wisest too,
Who do the feat, and lift humanity.
Let not him mourn who best entitled was,
Nay, mourn not one: let him exult,   300
Yea, plant the tree that bears best apples, plant,
And water it with wine, nor watch askance
Whether thy sons or strangers eat the fruit:
Enough that mankind eat, and are refreshed.

We flee away from cities, but we bring   305
The best of cities with us, these learned classifiers,
Men knowing what they seek, armed eyes of experts.
We praise the guide, we praise the forest life;
But will we sacrifice our dear-bought lore
Of books and arts and trained experiment,   310
Or count the Sioux a match for Agassiz?
O no, not we! Witness the shout that shook
Wild Tupper Lake; witness the mute all-hail
The joyful traveller gives, when on the verge

Of craggy Indian wilderness he hears   315
From a log-cabin stream Beethoven's notes
On the piano, played with master's hand.
'Well done!' he cries, 'the bear is kept at bay,
The lynx, the rattlesnake, the flood, the fire;
All the fierce enemies, ague, hunger, cold,   320
This thin spruce roof, this clayed log-wall,
This wild plantation will suffice to chase.
Now speed the gay celerities of art,
What in the desert was impossible
Within four walls is possible again,—   325
Culture and libraries, mysteries of skill,
Traditioned fame of masters, eager strife
Of keen competing youths, joined or alone,
To outdo each other, and extort applause.
Mind wakes a new-born giant from her sleep.   330
Twirl the old wheels! Time takes fresh start again,
On for a thousand years of genius more.'

    The holidays were fruitful, but must end;
One August evening had a cooler breath;
Into each mind intruding duties crept;   335
Under the cinders burned the fires of home;
Nay, letters found us in our paradise;
So in the gladness of the new event
We struck our camp, and left the happy hills.
The fortunate star that rose on us sank not;   340
The prodigal sunshine rested on the land,
The rivers gambolled onward to the sea,
And Nature, the inscrutable and mute,
Permitted on her infinite repose
Almost a smile to steal to cheer her sons,   345
As if one riddle of the Sphinx were guessed.

                                         1858 || 1867

BRAHMA

"Hamatreya" had been the first fruit of Emerson's reading in the *Vishńu Puráńa;* "Brahma" was the second. As early as 1845, when he borrowed the Hindu text from James Elliot Cabot, Emerson copied into his notebook the germinal passages from which the two poems eventually grew (*JMN* 9:319, 321). "Hamatreya" was composed in time for inclusion in the 1847 *Poems,* but "Brahma" would not achieve its final form for more than a decade. In March or April of 1847 Emerson repeated the prose source ("What living creature slays or is slain? What living creature preserves or is preserved? Each is his own destroyer or preserver, as he follows evil or good") and turned it into a quatrain in a series of drafts (*JMN* 9:354, 10:36–37; *PN,* pp. 307, 361). Then in the summer of 1856, inspired by reading Thoreau's copy of *The Upanishads* (*L* 5:70–71), Emerson took a fresh approach to the subject and produced the familiar sixteen-line version that he would publish in the November 1857 inaugural issue of the *Atlantic Monthly.*

As Robert Richardson has astutely suggested, the meaning of the *Vishńu Puráńa* for Emerson concentrated in the idea of identity: "Identity, identity! friend & foe are of one stuff, and the stuff is such & so much that the variations of surface are unimportant" (*JMN* 9:322; Richardson, p. 408). Emerson had developed this uncanny sense of collapsed bipolarity some years earlier in remarking the way in which dreams show that "every act, every thought, every cause is bipolar, and in the act is contained the counter-action. If I strike, I am struck; if I chase, I am pursued" ("Demonology," *EL* 3:155; cf. *JMN* 5:475). What Richardson calls Emerson's "politics of identity" may be seen at work in the "Concord Hymn" and the "Ode . . . to W. H. Channing," but "Brahma" is its exposition.

BRAHMA

If the red slayer think he slays,
    Or if the slain think he is slain,
They know not well the subtle ways
    I keep, and pass, and turn again.

Far or forgot to me is near;
    Shadow and sunlight are the same;
The vanished gods to me appear;
    And one to me are shame and fame.

5

They reckon ill who leave me out;
    When me they fly, I am the wings;   10
I am the doubter and the doubt,
    And I the hymn the Brahmin sings.

The strong gods pine for my abode,
    And pine in vain the sacred Seven;
But thou, meek lover of the good!   15
    Find me, and turn thy back on heaven.

1856 || 1857

FREEDOM

On August 7, 1853, Julia Griffiths, secretary of the Ladies' Anti-Slavery Society of Rochester, New York, wrote to Emerson to solicit a contribution to the second annual volume of her *Autographs for Freedom,* a fundraising effort in support of the work of her friend Frederick Douglass. These volumes were among the first designedly interracial literary projects in American history. On October 24, Emerson responded with his poem "Freedom" (*L* 8:379).

Emerson supposed that much talking on the slavery question was both fatally easy and morally superfluous and that overwrought rhetoric and long discourses ought to be left entirely to the doomed party, the defenders of slavery (*JMN* 9:126–128). At the Boston funeral of the abolitionist Charles T. Torrey in 1846, it had seemed "almost too late to say anything for freedom,—the battle is already won" (*JMN* 9:400). Certainly it had never been enough for Emerson as poet or orator simply to say again what others had said, or to offer a conformable public opinion in place of a deep and personal enactment of freedom. The poet's contribution—his contribution—would be to enlarge and transform the meanings that had been in play in casual and less considered ways in anti-slavery discourse. In one of his topical notebooks, Emerson quoted some striking lines by his friend Caroline Sturgis Tappan on the radical indirection of the poet's relation to slavery and freedom:

> Toil not to free the slave from chains,
> Strive not to give the laborer rest,
> Unless rich beauty fill the plains,
> The freeman wanders still unblest. (*TN* 1:120)

FREEDOM

Once I wished I might rehearse
Freedom's pæan in my verse,
That the slave who caught the strain
Should throb until he snapped his chain.
But the Spirit said, 'Not so;   5
Speak it not, or speak it low;
Name not lightly to be said,
Gift too precious to be prayed,
Passion not to be expressed
But by heaving of the breast: 10
Yet,—wouldst thou the mountain find

Where this deity is shrined,
Who gives to seas and sunset skies
Their unspent beauty of surprise,
And, when it lists him, waken can   15
Brute or savage into man;
Or, if in thy heart he shine,
Blends the starry fates with thine,
Draws angels nigh to dwell with thee,
And makes thy thoughts archangels be;   20
Freedom's secret wilt thou know?—
Counsel not with flesh and blood;
Loiter not for cloak or food;
Right thou feelest, rush to do.'

1853 || 1853

ODE SUNG IN THE TOWN HALL, CONCORD, JULY 4, 1857

In poems that Emerson wrote for public and commemorative occasions, invariably at the invitation of his local community, he typically found an organizing point of reference in the close accord of nature's beauty and heroic phases of human action—in other words, in the necessary consents of plot and setting. In this Fourth-of-July ode, the bright midsummer sunshine of the first and last stanzas blends with the human meanings of freedom and independence to glorify the place of home. This slightly jingoistic celebration of unity between benign geography and handsome traits of character prepares the reader for claims about "race," which, in turn, serve Emerson as propositional grounds for feeling good about the society he lives in. Emerson had just the year before published *English Traits* (1856), with a chapter on "Race" that might well make a modern reader marvel. There he explains the dominant power of the British Empire (exemplary in so many ways) as an effect of "Saxon" strength and capacity for adaptation, and yet he introduces qualification, mixture, and nuance into all his affirmations.

The Fourth-of-July festivities held in Concord in 1857 had the additional purpose of raising funds for the newly opened Sleepy Hollow cemetery on Bedford Street, a project in which Emerson had been much involved. On July 8 he had the remains of his mother and son reinterred in a plot where, in 1882, he would himself be buried (*JMN* 14:154).

ODE SUNG IN THE TOWN HALL, CONCORD, JULY 4, 1857

O tenderly the haughty day
    Fills his blue urn with fire;
One morn is in the mighty heaven,
    And one in our desire.

The cannon booms from town to town,   5
    Our pulses are not less,
The joy-bells chime their tidings down,
    Which children's voices bless.

For He that flung the broad blue fold
    O'er-mantling land and sea,   10
One third part of the sky unrolled
    For the banner of the free.

The men are ripe of Saxon kind
    To build an equal state,—
To take the statute from the mind,   15
    And make of duty fate.

United States! the ages plead,—
    Present and Past in under-song,—
Go put your creed into your deed,
    Nor speak with double tongue.   20

For sea and land don't understand,
    Nor skies without a frown
See rights for which the one hand fights
    By the other cloven down.

Be just at home; then write your scroll   25
    Of honor o'er the sea,
And bid the broad Atlantic roll,
    A ferry of the free.

And, henceforth, there shall be no chain,
    Save underneath the sea   30
The wires shall murmur through the main
    Sweet songs of LIBERTY.

The conscious stars accord above,
    The waters wild below,
And under, through the cable wove,   35
    Her fiery errands go.

For He that worketh high and wise,
    Nor pauses in his plan,
Will take the sun out of the skies
    Ere freedom out of man.   40

              1857 || 1857

BOSTON HYMN

READ IN MUSIC HALL, JANUARY 1, 1863

On the afternoon of New Year's Day, 1863, as Abraham Lincoln signed the Emancipation Proclamation, a great jubilee was held in Boston's Music Hall. Emerson there read his poem to a crowd of three thousand as a last-minute addition to the festivities, serving as prologue to orchestral works by Beethoven and Rossini. Henry James, Jr., recalled "the momentousness of the occasion, the vast excited multitude, the crowded platform and the tall, spare figure of Emerson, in the midst, reading out the stanzas. . . . I well remember the immense effect with which his beautiful voice pronounced the lines—

> 'Pay ransom to the owner
> And fill the bag to the brim.
> Who is the owner? The slave is owner,
> And ever was. Pay *him!*'" (pp. 27–28)

The old proposal to end slavery by compensating slave owners—a plan that as late as 1855 even Emerson supported (*LL* 2:13–14)—had become official United States policy on April 10, 1862, when a congressional joint resolution committed the government to pay for slaves wherever and whenever a state might adopt a policy of gradual emancipation (*Statutes at Large* . . . , vol. 12 [Boston, 1863], p. 617). This was of course a conservative anti-slavery measure, one that acknowledged the property rights of slave owners and even accepted their estimates of the cash value of African Americans. It was widely supposed that uncompensated emancipation would amount to an unconstitutional taking and as such would have no defensible basis in law. The Emancipation Proclamation, issued by Lincoln in his capacity as commander in chief, freed slaves in the eleven states then in rebellion. The border states kept their slaves and the Southern Confederacy ignored the proclamation. Only in such places as Boston was there any considerable rejoicing, and then only when the measure was seen—as Emerson presented it—as a magnificent vehicle of justice and equity and not (as many regarded it) as an act of dubious legality, announced for purely pragmatic reasons, impossible to enforce, and therefore of wholly uncertain effect. Emerson's "Boston Hymn" went far toward establishing the towering prestige of Lincoln's Proclamation as a classic American document.

The poem had been commissioned by John Sullivan Dwight, Emerson's friend from the days of the Transcendental Club, who was now editor of *Dwight's Journal of Music* and the organizer of the Music Hall celebration. As Carl F. Strauch has shown, Emerson began the poem on December 18 and did not finish until December 31, the day before the event, which explains its absence from the printed program ("The Background").

Hours after the event, on the evening of January 1, Emerson read his poem again during a party at the home of the wealthy Medford industrialist George Luther Stearns, a Republican activist and a member of the "Secret Six" of John Brown's backers. Others attending the party included Wendell Phillips; William Lloyd Garrison; Samuel Gridley Howe (another of the "Secret Six") and his wife, Julia Ward Howe; Bronson Alcott; Samuel Longfellow (brother of the poet); Judge Martin F. Conway, a colleague of Brown's from Kansas; and Edwin A. Brackett, a sculptor, whose marble bust of John Brown, recently on display at the Boston Athenaeum, was now being returned to the home of its owners, Mr. and Mrs. Stearns (*CW* 9:378–381; Cheney, pp. xxxii–xxxiii). This second, more private celebration made it clear how much of the credit for Emancipation was felt by this group to be owing to the activity of the martyr Brown. Indeed, the connection to Brown offers an explanation of Emerson's decision to cast the poem as a moral and political charge from God to the Pilgrims. Brown himself consciously modeled the Pilgrim mythology, believing that he was descended from Peter Brown, who arrived on the *Mayflower* in 1620. So he told the Stearnses' son in an autobiographical letter that Emerson admired, and which in turn became part of the Brown mythology when it was published in James Redpath's *Public Life of Capt. John Brown* (Boston, 1860), a book dedicated to Brown partisans Emerson, Wendell Phillips, and Thoreau.

BOSTON HYMN

READ IN MUSIC HALL, JANUARY 1, 1863

The word of the Lord by night
To the watching Pilgrims came,
As they sat by the seaside,
And filled their hearts with flame.

God said, I am tired of kings,   5
I suffer them no more;
Up to my ear the morning brings
The outrage of the poor.

Think ye I made this ball
A field of havoc and war,   10
Where tyrants great and tyrants small
Might harry the weak and poor?

My angel,—his name is Freedom,—
Choose him to be your king;

He shall cut pathways east and west,   15
And fend you with his wing.

Lo! I uncover the land
Which I hid of old time in the West,
As the sculptor uncovers the statue
When he has wrought his best;   20

I show Columbia, of the rocks
Which dip their foot in the seas
And soar to the air-borne flocks
Of clouds, and the boreal fleece.

I will divide my goods;   25
Call in the wretch and slave:
None shall rule but the humble,
And none but Toil shall have.

I will have never a noble,
No lineage counted great: 30
Fishers and choppers and plowmen
Shall constitute a state.

Go, cut down trees in the forest,
And trim the straightest boughs;
Cut down trees in the forest,   35
And build me a wooden house.

Call the people together,
The young men and the sires,
The digger in the harvest-field,
Hireling, and him that hires;   40

And here in a pine state-house
They shall choose men to rule
In every needful faculty,
In church, and state, and school.

Lo, now! if these poor men   45
Can govern the land and sea,
And make just laws below the sun,
As planets faithful be.

And ye shall succor men;
'Tis nobleness to serve;   50
Help them who cannot help again:
Beware from right to swerve.

I break your bonds and masterships,
And I unchain the slave:
Free be his heart and hand henceforth   55
As wind and wandering wave.

I cause from every creature
His proper good to flow:
As much as he is and doeth,
So much he shall bestow.   60

But, laying hands on another
To coin his labor and sweat,
He goes in pawn to his victim
For eternal years in debt.

Today unbind the captive,   65
So only are ye unbound;
Lift up a people from the dust,
Trump of their rescue, sound!

Pay ransom to the owner,
And fill the bag to the brim.   70
Who is the owner? The slave is owner,
And ever was. Pay him.

Oh North! give him beauty for rags,
And honor, O South! for his shame;
Nevada! coin thy golden crags   75
With Freedom's image and name.

Up! and the dusky race
That sat in darkness long,—
Be swift their feet as antelopes,
And as behemoth strong.   80

Come, East and West and North,
By races, as snow-flakes,

And carry my purpose forth,
Which neither halts nor shakes.

My will fulfilled shall be,   85
For, in daylight or in dark,
My thunderbolt has eyes to see
His way home to the mark.

1862 ‖ 1863

VOLUNTARIES

"Voluntaries" memorializes the gallantry and sacrifice of Colonel Robert Gould Shaw, the twenty-five-year-old commanding officer of the Massachusetts Fifty-Fourth Infantry Regiment, who died with 116 of his men in the assault on Fort Wagner, at Charleston harbor, on July 18, 1863. The Massachusetts Fifty-Fourth was, famously, the first Union regiment composed of free Northern blacks. Its existence was largely owing to the efforts of Massachusetts governor John Albion Andrew, who persuaded the Lincoln administration to admit African American soldiers into the army's ranks. Also instrumental in organizing and supporting the regiment were a number of wealthy Boston abolitionists, including some of Emerson's friends in the Saturday Club, such as John Murray Forbes, George Luther Stearns, Wendell Phillips, and, most significantly, Francis George Shaw, father of the regiment's volunteer leader, the quickly martyred Colonel Shaw.

In many respects the first months' history of the Fifty-Fourth, culminating in the heroic demonstration at Fort Wagner, was the rolling out of a Transcendentalist and reform mythology, grounded in the more than lingering example of John Brown, of the sacrificial white leader who in dying for the freedom of slaves would expiate the guilt accrued through decades of cowardly inaction. It was a culturally decisive mythology, immensely helpful to the war effort, and one to which, in the end, even the history of Lincoln was assimilated.

One of the emotional keys to the poem lies in the curious fact that when Governor Andrew wished to appoint young Shaw to the command of the new regiment—having chosen him for his staunch abolitionism and prior military experience—he put the question first to Shaw's father, who was requested, if he approved, to forward the enclosed commission to his son. This makes Frank Shaw (1809–1882) a crucial unnamed presence in the work and the occasion of the poem's important economy of fathers and sons. Indeed, it was in a literal sense to the elder Shaw in his capacity as father that Emerson addressed the work, having sent a copy to him on September 10 (*L* 9:113–114).

Emerson had known Francis George Shaw since the late 1820s, when he and Emerson's younger brothers attended Harvard together. They remained in touch after Shaw left college early to tend to his father's extensive business interests, those especially in the Caribbean (Bosco and Myerson, p. 145). The Shaw family controlled one of the largest mercantile fortunes of that period and had a way of marrying into other such fortunes, and yet Frank Shaw gradually turned away from the culture of capitalism (under the influence of Emerson's sermons, according to his biographer) and became an increasingly active social reformer and abolitionist (Foote, pp. 30–32). Early drawn to Transcendentalism, he and his wife (a sister of Caroline Sturgis) moved from Boston to Roxbury in 1841 to be near Brook Farm, which they supported financially, and to cultivate the friendships in particular of Margaret Fuller and Theodore Parker. A Fourierist, Shaw contributed frequently to the *Harbinger*, translated a French biography of Fourier and a novel, *Consuelo*, by George Sand. When Brook Farm closed, Shaw and his family moved to Staten Island, began attending the Brooklyn church of Henry Ward Beecher, and got to know Beecher's sister, Harriet Beecher Stowe, whose *Uncle Tom's Cabin* (1851–52) was an enduring point of fascination for his young son Robert. It was apparently at this time that Frank Shaw made the acquaintance of Emerson's friend Henry James, Sr., whose son Garth Wilkinson James, while serving as an adjutant under R. G. Shaw, was wounded at Fort Wagner.

Emerson felt multiply connected to the project of the Massachusetts Fifty-Fourth: when asked by one of Shaw's Roxbury relatives to speak at a recruiting and fundraising rally on its behalf, he did so—at Chickering Hall on March 20, 1863—though it is likely that he was acting also at the suggestion of George L. Stearns and with the encouragement of his own daughters, close friends of Robert's sister Pauline (*L* 5:318, 320; *JMN* 15:210–213; Gougeon, *Virtue's Hero*, pp. 294–301). The fact that Emerson's frail nineteen-year-old son Edward was chafing to leave Harvard and enlist in the army was surely an emotional complication.

It is difficult to appreciate fully the cultural significance of the death of young Robert Gould Shaw. The commemorative volume assembled by his parents in 1864—*Memorial RGS*—offers a context for Emerson's poem more helpful and indicative than its first public appearance in the *Atlantic Monthly* for October 1863. In that privately printed volume, Emerson's poem figures among tributes from family members James Russell Lowell and George W. Curtis, friends Lydia Maria Child and Harriet Martineau, Henry Ward Beecher and Harriet Beecher Stowe, Louis Agassiz, Thomas Wentworth Higginson, J. L. Motley, William Lloyd Garrison, Charles Sumner, and the elder Henry James. There were tributes as well from black abolitionists Henry Highland Garnet, Charlotte Forten, Harriet Jacobs, and Joshua B. Smith. Smith, an escaped slave from North Carolina, had been taken in and employed by the Shaw family; later and for many years he was a successful caterer in Boston and a leading figure in the Boston Vigilance Committee. Still later he headed the fundraising for the high-relief bronze memorial to Shaw and his black troops by Augustus Saint-Gaudens installed on the edge of Boston Common facing the State House.

VOLUNTARIES

I.

Low and mournful be the strain,
Haughty thought be far from me;
Tones of penitence and pain,
Moanings of the tropic sea;
Low and tender in the cell   5
Where a captive sits in chains,
Crooning ditties treasured well
From his Afric's torrid plains.
Sole estate his sire bequeathed—
Hapless sire to hapless son—   10
Was the wailing song he breathed,
And his chain when life was done.

What his fault, or what his crime?
Or what ill planet crossed his prime?
Heart too soft and will too weak   15
To front the fate that crouches near,—
Dove beneath the vulture's beak;—
Will song dissuade the thirsty spear?
Dragged from his mother's arms and breast,
Displaced, disfurnished here,   20
His wistful toil to do his best
Chilled by a ribald jeer.
Great men in the Senate sate,
Sage and hero, side by side,
Building for their sons the State,   25
Which they shall rule with pride.
They forbore to break the chain
Which bound the dusky tribe,
Checked by the owners' fierce disdain,
Lured by "Union" as the bribe.   30
Destiny sat by, and said,
'Pang for pang your seed shall pay,
Hide in false peace your coward head,
I bring round the harvest-day.'

II.

Freedom all winged expands,   35
Nor perches in a narrow place;
Her broad van seeks unplanted lands;
She loves a poor and virtuous race.
Clinging to a colder zone
Whose dark sky sheds the snow-flake down,   40
The snow-flake is her banner's star,
Her stripes the boreal streamers are.
Long she loved the Northman well;
Now the iron age is done,
She will not refuse to dwell   45
With the offspring of the Sun;
Foundling of the desert far,
Where palms plume, siroccos blaze,
He roves unhurt the burning ways
In climates of the summer star.   50
He has avenues to God
Hid from men of Northern brain,
Far beholding, without cloud,
What these with slowest steps attain.
If once the generous chief arrive   55
To lead him willing to be led,
For freedom he will strike and strive,
And drain his heart till he be dead.

III.

In an age of fops and toys,
Wanting wisdom, void of right,   60
Who shall nerve heroic boys
To hazard all in Freedom's fight,—
Break sharply off their jolly games,
Forsake their comrades gay,
And quit proud homes and youthful dames,   65
For famine, toil, and fray?
Yet on the nimble air benign
Speed nimbler messages,

That waft the breath of grace divine
To hearts in sloth and ease.   70
So nigh is grandeur to our dust,
So near is God to man,
When Duty whispers low, *Thou must,*
The youth replies, *I can.*

IV.

O, well for the fortunate soul   75
Which Music's wings infold,
Stealing away the memory
Of sorrows new and old!
Yet happier he whose inward sight,
Stayed on his subtile thought,   80
Shuts his sense on toys of time,
To vacant bosoms brought.
But best befriended of the God
He who, in evil times,
Warned by an inward voice,   85
Heeds not the darkness and the dread,
Biding by his rule and choice,
Feeling only the fiery thread
Leading over heroic ground,
Walled with mortal terror round,   90
To the aim which him allures,
And the sweet heaven his deed secures.
Peril around all else appalling,
Cannon in front and leaden rain,
Him Duty through the clarion calling   95
To the van called not in vain.

Stainless soldier on the walls,
Knowing this,—and knows no more,—
Whoever fights, whoever falls,
Justice conquers evermore,   100
Justice after as before,—
And he who battles on her side,
God, though he were ten times slain,

Crowns him victor glorified,
Victor over death and pain; 105
Forever: but his erring foe,
Self-assured that he prevails,
Looks from his victim lying low,
And sees aloft the red right arm
Redress the eternal scales. 110
He, the poor foe, whom angels foil,
Blind with pride, and fooled by hate,
Writhes within the dragon coil,
Reserved to a speechless fate.

V.

Blooms the laurel which belongs 115
To the valiant chief who fights;
I see the wreath, I hear the songs
Lauding the Eternal Rights,
Victors over daily wrongs:
Awful victors, they misguide 120
Whom they will destroy,
And their coming triumph hide
In our downfall, or our joy:
They reach no term, they never sleep,
In equal strength through space abide; 125
Though, feigning dwarfs, they crouch and creep,
The strong they slay, the swift outstride:
Fate's grass grows rank in valley clods,
And rankly on the castled steep,—
Speak it firmly,—these are gods, 130
All are ghosts beside.

1863 || 1863

LOVE AND THOUGHT

None of the notebook drafts offers evidence about the date of composition, though it may be significant that "Cupido," another poem on the same topic, likely dates to 1843, which coincides as well with the writing of "The Initial, Daemonic, and Celestial Love." The central conceit of "Love and Thought" may derive from Emerson's observation in a letter of January 24, 1843, to Samuel Gray Ward: "I think the two first friends must have been travel[l]ers" (*L* 7:521). This letter was written in a lonely mood from a city (Philadelphia) that he found especially devoid of interest and that contained no persons with whom he could intelligently converse. "If the world was all Philadelphia," he explained to Ward, "although the poultry- & dairy-market would be admirable, I fear suicide would exceedingly prevail."

LOVE AND THOUGHT

Two well-assorted travellers use
The highway, Eros and the Muse.
From the twins is nothing hidden,
To the pair is naught forbidden;
Hand in hand the comrades go   5
Every nook of nature through:
Each for other they were born,
Each can other best adorn;
They know one only mortal grief
Past all balsam or relief,   10
When, by false companions crossed,
The pilgrims have each other lost.

1843? || 1867

RUBIES

Emerson's experience in the early 1840s with certain younger friends—notably Margaret Fuller and Caroline Sturgis—confirmed his belief that his constitutionally cool personality made him less helpful, less available, and less a center of genuine affection than he would have preferred. Among his many expressions of this feeling is a journal entry of November 11, 1842:

> That which he [the generic "selfish man"] wishes most of all is to be lifted to some higher platform so that he may see beyond his present fear the trans-alpine good, so that his fear, his coldness, his custom may be broken up like fragments of ice melted & carried away in the great stream of goodwill. . . . We desire to be made great: we desire to be touched with that fire that shall command all this ice to stream; that I shall be a benefit thoroughly, thoroughly. (*JMN* 8:253; used in "New England Reformers," *CW* 3:163)

RUBIES

They brought me rubies from the mine,
    And held them to the sun;
I said, they are drops of frozen wine
    From Eden's vats that run.

I looked again,—I thought them hearts   5
    Of friends to friends unknown;
Tides that should warm each neighboring life
    Are locked in sparkling stone.

But fire to thaw that ruddy snow,
    To break enchanted ice,   10
And give love's scarlet tides to flow,—
    When shall that sun arise?

1855? || 1867

MERLIN'S SONG

The best discussion of the sources for "Merlin's Song" is the article by Kenneth Walter Cameron, "The Potent Song in Emerson's Merlin Poems." The "potent song" figures not only in the Merlin poems proper, but in "Woodnotes II," "Freedom," "Two Rivers," and elsewhere as well. The motif is a principal point of contact between Emerson and the bardic tradition, with which he first became acquainted in 1816 through William Godwin's *Life of Geoffrey Chaucer* (Cameron, p. 26). A few years later he copied a crucial passage from this book into his journal:

> I know a song by which I soften & inchant the arms of my enemies
> & render their weapons of none effect. I know a song which I need
> only to sing when men have loaded me with bonds for the moment
> I sing it my chains fall in pieces & I walk forth at liberty. I know a
> song useful to all mankind; for as soon as hatred inflames the sons
> of men, the moment I sing it they are appeased. I know a song of
> such virtue, that were I caught in a storm, I can hush the winds, &
> render the air perfectly calm. (*JMN* 1:371)

A short while later Emerson found the passage again, quoted this time in an issue of the Boston *Monthly Anthology* for November 1807 and versified by an unnamed contributor as "The Song of a Runic Bard" (Cameron, p. 24). Years later, on July 26, 1847, Emerson borrowed from the Harvard College library a copy of Paul Henri Mallet's *Northern Antiquities.* Either at this time or when he subsequently acquired a copy of his own (Harding, *Emerson's Library,* p. 181), he discovered the source from which Godwin had quoted: "The Runic Chapter, or the Magic of Odin" (Cameron, p. 27). In 1853, among notes he was taking while researching *English Traits,* Emerson copied the passage once more (*JMN* 13:171). Then in 1856 he produced three brief prose imitations based on the germinal passage and followed these by two lines of verse, the last of "Merlin's Song": "Yet they who hear it shed their age / And take their youth again" (*JMN* 14:73–74).

Cameron concluded (p. 28) that the potent song motif allowed Emerson to indulge his sense of the transformative, immortality-conferring effect of inspired poetry, and his belief that such poetry "works" by bringing into play the divine indwelling Reason, disarming the ordinary functions of the Understanding, and so producing the mystical restoration to wholeness announced by the Orphic Poet at the end of *Nature* (1836). This immoderate estimate of the capacities of language (and of the highest conception of the uses of poetry) is certainly not confined to the bardic tradition, though Emerson found it, time and again, convincingly expressed there (see Adkins). In most esoteric and all Gnostic systems of belief, a certain (nonstandard or "poetic") way of knowing is in itself redemptive. One finds this principle memorably set forth, for example, in the Gnostic *Gospel of Thomas,* when Jesus says, "Whoever finds the interpretation of these sayings will not experience death" (Robinson, p. 126). When we speak of the "vitality" of some poetic expression—because we have an *experience* of it—we have some version of this meaning in mind.

MERLIN'S SONG

Of Merlin wise I learned a song,—
Sing it low, or sing it loud,
It is mightier than the strong,
And punishes the proud.
I sing it to the surging crowd,—   5
Good men it will calm and cheer,
Bad men it will chain and cage.
In the heart of the music peals a strain
Which only angels hear;
Whether it waken joy or rage,   10
Hushed myriads hark in vain,
Yet they who hear it shed their age,
And take their youth again.

1856? || 1867

THE ROMANY GIRL

Emerson's interest in Gypsies had been sparked by the works of the English linguist and travel-writer George Borrow (1803–1881). In 1842 Emerson reviewed *The Zincali; or, An Account of the Gypsies in Spain* (1841) in the *Dial* and published a shorter notice of Borrow's *Bible in Spain* (1843) a year later. His library eventually included *Lavengro, the Scholar, the Gypsy, the Priest* (1851) as well as its sequel, *The Romany Rye* (1857). In March 1843, presumably when reading *The Bible in Spain*, Emerson made a journal entry that would serve, years later, as the germ for the second stanza of "The Romany Girl": "Gypsies & militia captains, paddies & Chinese, all manner of cunning & pragmatical men and a few fine women, a strange world made up of such oddities; the only beings that belong to the horizon being the fine women" (*JMN* 8:345). In his remarks on *The Zincali*, Emerson gave his opinion that Borrow overstated the wretchedness and isolation of the Gypsies, that he did not disclose the "resources and compensation" that must exist. "It is an aristocracy of rags, and suffering, and vice, yet as exclusive as the patricians of wealth and power. . . . The condition of the Gypsy may be bad enough, tried by the scale of English comfort, and yet appear tolerable and pleasant to the Gypsy, who finds attractions in his out-door way of living, his freedom, and sociability, which the Agent of the Bible Society [i.e., Borrow] does not reckon" (*CW* 10:196).

Emerson continued to refer to Borrow, generally enlisting him in support of a recommendation of noble savagery against the effete manners of the hypercivilized. "I much prefer the heathenism of Indians & Gypsies," he wrote in 1853, recalling "Borrow's story of the squinting gypsies to whom he read St John's gospel" (*JMN* 13:158). Two years later he listed *Lavengro* first among illustrations of "Real power" (*JMN* 13:394). A few pages later in the journal Emerson began to identify that power, first in what appears to be prose: "The sun goes down, & with it the coarseness of my attire: the moon rises, and with it the power of my beauty"—followed then by drafts of the poem's first stanza (*JMN* 13:396–397).

The poem was one of four that Emerson published in the inaugural issue of the *Atlantic Monthly*, in November 1857. It was a favorite with his daughter Ellen, who was gratified on one occasion to hear a friend remark that "Your Father's 'Romany Girl' is better Gypsy, infinitely!" than George Eliot's 1868 poem, "The Spanish Gypsy" (*ETE* 1:503).

THE ROMANY GIRL

The sun goes down, and with him takes
The coarseness of my poor attire;
The fair moon mounts, and aye the flame
Of Gypsy beauty blazes higher.

Pale Northern girls! you scorn our race;   5
You captives of your air-tight halls,
Wear out in-doors your sickly days,
But leave us the horizon walls.

And if I take you, dames, to task,
And say it frankly without guile,   10
Then you are Gypsies in a mask,
And I the lady all the while.

If, on the heath, below the moon,
I court and play with paler blood,
Me false to mine dare whisper none,—   15
One sallow horseman knows me good.

Go, keep your cheek's rose from the rain,
For teeth and hair with shopmen deal;
My swarthy tint is in the grain,
The rocks and forest know it real.   20

The wild air bloweth in our lungs,
The keen stars twinkle in our eyes,
The birds gave us our wily tongues,
The panther in our dances flies.

You doubt we read the stars on high,   25
Nathless we read your fortunes true;
The stars may hide in the upper sky,
But without glass we fathom you.

1855 ‖ 1857

DAYS

Emerson did not often comment on his own poems, but early in 1852 he made the following remarkable entry in his journal:

> I find one state of mind does not remember or conceive of another state. Thus I have written within a twelvemonth verses ("Days") which I do not remember the composition or correction of, & could not write the like today, & have only for proof of their being mine, various external evidences as, the MS. in which I find them, & the circumstance that I have sent copies of them to friends, &c &c. Well, if they had been better, if it had been a noble poem, perhaps it would have only more entirely taken up the ladder into heaven. (*JMN* 13:10)

The passage, then, assigns composition to 1851—as firmly, perhaps, as it refers the writing of the poem to a process of the unconscious mind. Emerson's estimating the quality of a poem by the degree to which its author has forgotten having struggled with its creation provides an important hint about its history. As Robert D. Richardson, Jr., has noted, "The perception behind 'Days,' the nagging regretful sense that the days are gods, each one laden with gifts we are never quite able to take, was expressed scores of times in Emerson's notes, letters, and journals" (p. 178). By the time he was ready to commit the poem to paper, Emerson had been revolving the idea so constantly and for so long a period that he had come to inhabit it.

The early, fragmentary anticipations of "Days" seem each to express some salient but subordinate aspect of the finished poem—as, for example, among the earliest, some lines of 1825 that depict Emerson's commitment to a career in the church as removing him from an ordinary history of hopes and disappointment:

> Days that come dancing on fraught with delights
> Dash our blown hopes as they limp heavily by. (*JMN* 2:405)

Two years later, sick and discouraged, he implicitly compared his case to that of Job: "My days run onward like the weaver's beam [cf. Job 7:6]. They have no honour among men, they have no grandeur in the view of the invisible world. It is as if a net of meanness were drawn around aspiring men thro' which their eyes are kept on mighty objects but the subtile fence is forever interposed" (*JMN* 3:78–79; cf. Richardson, pp. 78–79). The imagery here anticipates the "pleached" garden of the poem, signifying one fenced off from the world by the interwoven branches of a hedge, for the design and growing up of which, of course, the gardener is himself responsible. Among other, early, and at times morbid, developments of this theme, might be cited "My days roll by me," one of Emerson's few regular sonnets (*JMN* 3:36), and the quatrain "The days pass over me," written in 1831 in the wake of his first wife's death (see p. 256 below).

In "Doctrine of the Hands" (1837), Emerson redirected the evolving mythology toward the comic possibilities:

> Silent and passive and as it were sulkily nature offers every morning her wealth to man. She is immensely rich: he is welcome to her entire goods; but she speaks no word, will not beckon or cough, only leaves all her doors ajar—hall, storeroom, and cellar. He may do as he will: if he takes her hint and uses her goods, she speaks no word; if he blunders and starves, she says nothing. (*EL* 2:235)

In a letter to Margaret Fuller in October 1840, with his mind on reform and the Brook Farm experiment, he supposed that "The morning & evening cannot touch us with their delicate fingers, [&] the finer hints of all beneficent spirits are lost on the flannel & buckram customs in which we wrap ourselves warm." Here "custom" is the old "subtile fence" that keeps a bountiful providence at bay. "Heaven walks among us ordinarily muffled in such triple or tenfold disguises that the wisest are deceived & no one suspects the days to be gods" (*L* 2:342).

In 1844 Emerson tried out on his aunt Mary the idea that the days are "gods" and found her willing to concede that, yes, they are "(little) gods," originating, like us, with their Father, adding, however, with characteristically free orthography, "how many of them in touching our earth instead of strenght receive dingy feeble aspects some robed like harliquins, some habited like gaity or pomp" (Mary Moody Emerson, p. 455).

In a letter to Lidian of September 3, 1846, written as he was assembling *Poems*, Emerson gave the old idea a Gnostic twist, saying that "though days go smoothly enough they do not bring me in their fine timely wallets the alms I incessantly beg of them." What he particularly wanted from them turns out to be a version of the "potent song" of the Merlin poems: "Where are the melodies, where the unattainable words, where the efficacious rhymes, that make night & day alike, good luck & bad, and abolish all that is called fortune or glory, before the serenity & security of him that heareth these? Where? Where? If Eddy knows them, send him back by car or boat or cloud. No, he is only the theme of these. One day that strange revolution & Declaration of Independence which occurs in human breasts may befal in his, & he may know himself & these, and begin to murmur incantations of his own" (*L* 3:344). As in the Gnostic religion, so in Emerson's, self-knowledge is the key to world-knowledge: both alike are redemptive, and both sustain the language of poetry.

The approaches in prose grow closer. On May 24, 1847, Emerson wrote in his journal: "The days come & go like muffled & veiled figures sent from a distant friendly party, but they say nothing, & if we do not use the gifts they bring, they carry them as silently away" (*JMN* 10:61; used in "Works and Days," *CW* 7:85, as Oliver Wendell Holmes noted [pp. 312–313], in favorably comparing the poetic to the prose version). The notion of a "distant friendly party" conveys something of Aunt Mary's humor, but it begins also to draw attention to a conceptual division between the eternal and temporal aspects of the question—particularly whether we deal with days in time, as exemplary of what Emerson called "succession," or whether, instead, we deal *through* days with what is beyond time. This distinction was closer to the fore in a journal entry two years later:

> How difficult to deal erect with the Days! Each of these events
> which they bring,—this Concord thieving, the muster, the ripening
> of plums, the shingling of the barn, all throw dust in your eyes, &
> distract your attention. He is a strong man who can look them in
> the eye, see through this superficial juggle, feel their identity &
> keep his own; know surely that one will be like another to the end
> of the world, nor permit bridal or funeral, earthquake or church,
> election or revolution to draw him from his task. (*JMN* 11:154; cf.
> *JMN* 7:29)

So it is not wrong to be suspicious of the miscellaneous gifts that the "endless file" of days provides: the great enabling gift to which the soul is entitled—the gift beyond suspicion or hypocrisy—is, and indeed must be, singular and out of time, not plural or in time. Emerson once represented this possibility mythologically, effectively placing it out of time by framing it as a dream:

> I dreamed that I floated at will in the great Ether, and I saw this
> world floating also not far off, but diminished to the size of an ap-
> ple. Then an angel took it in his hand & brought it to me and said
> "This must thou eat." And I ate the world. (*JMN* 7:525; cf. Richard-
> son, p. 342: "This is Emerson's global Eucharist")

The world-apple represents the soul's entitlement, which is foregone in every tragic lapsing settlement for less. The gift of days may be petty decoys into time, where sight of the real is proportionately lost. It is a possibility recurrently considered in the world's transcendental mythologies, as, for example, in the "Hymn of the Pearl" from the apocryphal *Acts of the Apostle Thomas*: "They mixed me drink with their cunning and gave me to taste of their meat. I forgot that I was a king's son, and served their king. I forgot the Pearl for which my parents had sent me. Through the heaviness of their nourishment I sank into deep slumber" (quoted in Jonas, p. 69).

DAYS

Daughters of Time, the hypocritic Days,
Muffled and dumb, like barefoot dervishes,
And marching single in an endless file,
Bring diadems and fagots in their hands.
To each they offer gifts after his will,   5
Bread, kingdoms, stars, or sky that holds them all.
I, in my pleached garden, watched the pomp,
Forgot my morning wishes, hastily
Took a few herbs and apples, and the Day
Turned and departed silent. I, too late,   10
Under her solemn fillet saw the scorn.

1851 || 1857

THE CHARTIST'S COMPLAINT

Written in the late winter or early spring of 1851, at roughly the same time as "Days" and as a companion to it, "The Chartist's Complaint" was published, along with "Days," in the first issue of the *Atlantic Monthly*, in November 1857. They occupied consecutive pages in *May-Day*, but of the two only "Days" survived to appear in *Selected Poems* (1876).

In 1848, during his trip to England, Emerson had some firsthand experience of the democratic, mostly working-class reformers known as "Chartists." The name derived from their advocacy of the six points of the so-called People's Charter: annual parliaments, universal male suffrage, abolition of property requirements for members of the House of Commons, secret ballot, equally sized electoral districts, and salaries for members of Parliament. Both Emerson and Thomas Carlyle (who had written on the Chartist movement as early as 1840) sympathized with Britain's oppressed laboring class, but they differed sharply on the actions to be taken. Carlyle insisted that the aristocracy do its duty by the poor and govern more forcibly; Emerson supposed that a laissez-faire economic policy was more in the American democratic vein. Indeed, like many of his countrymen, Emerson believed that the revolutions of 1848 were evidence that American-style democracy would, by a historical necessity, prevail against monarchical and aristocratic models. In *English Traits* (1856), he wrote: "The English dislike the American structure of society, whilst yet trade, mills, public education, and chartism are doing what they can to create in England the same social condition" (*CW* 5:85; see also the chapter on "Chartism and Revolution" in Richardson, pp. 451–456).

But English politics are scarcely visible in the poem, which prefers to take a more universal look at the inequities of class and the differences that wealth or poverty makes for the experience of nature and days. A sense of brutal unfairness coexists with an oblique feeling of personal guilt. On the day of the grand Chartist demonstration in London, April 10, 1848, Emerson was present as workers rioted and the Duke of Wellington defended the city. The next day, as he would later learn, there was a devastating fire at "a rich man's wood and lake," when the Irish-built Fitchburg Railroad set the bucolic Walden woods ablaze (*L* 4:109–110).

THE CHARTIST'S COMPLAINT

Day! hast thou two faces,
Making one place two places?
One, by humble farmer seen,

Chill and wet, unlighted, mean,
Useful only, triste and damp,   5
Serving for a laborer's lamp?
Have the same mists another side,
To be the appanage of pride,
Gracing the rich man's wood and lake,
His park where amber mornings break,   10
And treacherously bright to show
His planted isle where roses glow?
O Day! and is your mightiness
A sycophant to smug success?
Will the sweet sky and ocean broad   15
Be fine accomplices to fraud?
O Sun! I curse thy cruel ray:
Back, back to chaos, harlot Day!

1851 || 1857

THE TITMOUSE

The titmouse, or black-capped chickadee, is a small, energetic bird commonly encountered in the woods around Concord and, at least in Emerson's day, more likely to show a friendly confidence in human beings than a fear of them. That was part of the point of the anecdote that Thoreau had included in *Walden* (1854) about his friend the Canadian woodchopper Alek Therien: "as he sat on a log to eat his dinner the chickadees would sometimes come round and alight on his arm and peck at the potato in his fingers; and he said that he 'liked to have the little *fellers* about him'" (p. 146). Emerson read the passage when the book first came out, but he also discussed it with the dying Thoreau late in the winter of 1862. Shortly after Thoreau's death on May 6, Emerson, reading through his friend's journals, came upon the entry on which the *Walden* anecdote was based (*JMN* 15:283). By then "the antidote to fear" in the face of death had been well worked out and "The Titmouse" written—a poem that R. A. Yoder has aptly called Emerson's "indirect tribute to Thoreau" (p. 157).

The poem was nearly finished by mid-February, according to a statement by Emerson in a letter of the 19th (*L* 9:71). Therefore, a journal passage dated March 3 could not have been the principal source, as Edward supposed (*W* 9:482). Still, it may have supplied—or rehearsed—some of the details:

> The snow still lies even with the tops of the walls across the Walden road, and, this afternoon, I waded through the woods to my grove. A chickadee came out to greet me, flew about me within reach of my hands, perched on the nearest bough, flew down into the snow, rested there two seconds, then up again, just over my head, & busied himself on the dead bark. I whistled to him through my teeth, and, (I think, in response,) he began at once to whistle. I promised him crumbs, & must not go again to these woods without them. I suppose the best food to carry would be the meat of shagbarks or castille nuts. Thoreau tells me that they are very sociable with wood-choppers, & will take crumbs from their hands. (*JMN* 15:241)

Edward was clearly miffed that Matthew Arnold should have singled out "The Titmouse" as a characteristic failure in the lecture he gave in Boston in 1883, the year after Emerson's death. "One never quite arrives at learning what the titmouse actually did for him at all," Arnold complained, "though one feels a strong interest and desire to learn it; but one is reduced to guessing, and cannot be quite sure that after all one has guessed right" (p. 158). Edward thought the Englishman's critical befuddlement strange, saying that "the American reader will hardly find the poem so obscure" (*W* 9:483), but in fact Arnold's disparagement of Emerson as poet adversely affected his reputation—and that of this poem—for a long time. It was not until 1974, when a stronger and more sympathetic reader, Hyatt Waggoner, identified "The Titmouse" as one of the best of Emerson's later poems, that it began to attract serious critical attention (see Waggoner, *Emerson as Poet*, pp. 109, 136; Yoder, p. 159).

THE TITMOUSE

You shall not be overbold
When you deal with arctic cold,
As late I found my lukewarm blood
Chilled wading in the snow-choked wood.
How should I fight? my foeman fine   5
Has million arms to one of mine:
East, west, for aid I looked in vain,
East, west, north, south, are his domain.
Miles off, three dangerous miles, is home;
Must borrow his winds who there would come.   10
Up and away for life! be fleet!—
The frost-king ties my fumbling feet,
Sings in my ears, my hands are stones,
Curdles the blood to the marble bones,
Tugs at the heart-strings, numbs the sense,   15
And hems in life with narrowing fence.
Well, in this broad bed lie and sleep,
The punctual stars will vigil keep,
Embalmed by purifying cold,
The winds shall sing their dead-march old,   20
The snow is no ignoble shroud,
The moon thy mourner, and the cloud.

    Softly,—but this way fate was pointing,
'Twas coming fast to such anointing,
When piped a tiny voice hard by,   25
Gay and polite, a cheerful cry,
Chic-chic-a-dee-dee! saucy note
Out of sound heart and merry throat,
As if it said, 'Good day, good sir!
Fine afternoon, old passenger!   30
Happy to meet you in these places,
Where January brings few faces.'

This poet, though he live apart,
Moved by his hospitable heart,
Sped, when I passed his sylvan fort,   35
To do the honors of his court,
As fits a feathered lord of land;
Flew near, with soft wing grazed my hand,
Hopped on the bough, then, darting low,
Prints his small impress on the snow,   40
Shows feats of his gymnastic play,
Head downward, clinging to the spray.

Here was this atom in full breath,
Hurling defiance at vast death;
This scrap of valor just for play   45
Fronts the north-wind in waistcoat gray,
As if to shame my weak behavior;
I greeted loud my little saviour,
'You pet! what dost here? and what for?
In these woods, thy small Labrador,   50
At this pinch, wee San Salvador!
What fire burns in that little chest,
So frolic, stout, and self-possest?
Henceforth I wear no stripe but thine;
Ashes and jet all hues outshine.   55
Why are not diamonds black and gray,
To ape thy dare-devil array?
And I affirm, the spacious North
Exists to draw thy virtue forth.
I think no virtue goes with size;   60
The reason of all cowardice
Is, that men are overgrown,
And, to be valiant, must come down
To the titmouse dimension.'

'Tis good will makes intelligence,   65
And I began to catch the sense
Of my bird's song: 'Live out of doors
In the great woods, on prairie floors.
I dine in the sun; when he sinks in the sea,
I too have a hole in a hollow tree;   70

And I like less when summer beats
With stifling beams in these retreats,
Than noontide twilights which snow makes
With tempest of the blinding flakes.
For well the soul, if stout within, 75
Can arm impregnably the skin;
And polar frost my frame defied,
Made of the air that blows outside.'

  With glad remembrance of my debt,
I homeward turn; farewell, my pet! 80
When here again thy pilgrim comes,
He shall bring store of seeds and crumbs.
Doubt not, so long as earth has bread,
Thou first and foremost shalt be fed;
The Providence that is most large 85
Takes hearts like thine in special charge,
Helps who for their own need are strong,
And the sky doats on cheerful song.
Henceforth I prize thy wiry chant
O'er all that mass and minster vaunt; 90
For men mis-hear thy call in spring,
As 't would accost some frivolous wing,
Crying out of the hazel copse, *Phe—be!*
And, in winter, *Chic-a-dee-dee!*
I think old Cæsar must have heard 95
In northern Gaul my dauntless bird,
And, echoed in some frosty wold,
Borrowed thy battle-numbers bold.
And I will write the annals new,
And thank thee for a better clew, 100
I, who dreamed not when I came here
To find the antidote of fear,
Now hear thee say in Roman key,
Pæan! Veni, vidi, vici.

1862 || 1862

SEA-SHORE

On July 31 and August 1, 1855, Emerson visited the Unitarian minister and Transcendental Club member Dr. Cyrus A. Bartol at his cottage in Pigeon Cove, Massachusetts, at the tip of Cape Ann (*L* 4:524, 8:447). He must have enjoyed the sea-baths on the rocky shore, the cool ocean breezes, the winds through the immense westward depths of pine forest, the tower atop Bartol's cottage, and the private observatory next door. The following summer he brought his family and stayed a week:

> 23 July [1856]. Returned from Pigeon Cove, where we have made acquaintance with the sea, for seven days. 'Tis a noble friendly power, and seemed to say to me, "Why so late & slow to come to me? Am I not here always, thy proper summer home? Is not my voice thy needful music; my breath, thy healthful climate in the heats; my touch, thy cure? Was ever building like my terraces? Was ever couch so magnificent as mine? Lie down on my warm ledges and learn that a very little hut is all you need. I have made thy architecture superfluous, and it is paltry beside mine. Here are twenty Romes & Ninevehs & Karnacs in ruins together, obelisk & pyramid and Giants' Causeway here they all are prostrate or half piled." And behold the sea, the opaline, plentiful & strong, yet beautiful as the rose or the rainbow, full of food, nourisher of men, purger of the world, creating a sweet climate, and, in its unchangeable ebb & flow, and in its beauty at a few furlongs, giving a hint of that which changes not, & is perfect. (*JMN* 14:100–101)

Though Emerson casts himself as a latter-day Pilgrim (l. 2), he arrives at the rock-bound coast of New England from the land side, in comfort, in search of yet more comfort, not a reenactor of Puritan settlement, but as a pioneer of the American summer vacation. Pigeon Cove began to attract attention in the early 1840s when the family of the elder Richard Henry Dana stayed there. Before long it became a fashionable resort, counting among its summer residents James Freeman Clarke, Thomas Wentworth Higginson, Ezra Stiles Gannett, Edwin Percy Whipple, Junius Brutus Booth, and James T. Fields. It was said that "Gentlemen, whether with or without families, came to Pigeon Cove . . . for rest and quiet and healthful pastimes; for ocean-view and seaside ramble; for good air from over the brine, and healing whiffs from the balsamic pines; and for all the pure and sweet pleasures which can be had where rural and marine attractions and charms are so singularly and happily brought together" (Leonard, p. 45).

Edward notes that his father, surprised that his journal entry was so nearly a poem already, read it as such to the family on their return to Concord (*W*

9:484–485). The first draft thus dates to late July 1856, though the poem was not put into final form until 1864, when it was offered for publication in *The Boatswain's Whistle*, a circular that appeared daily during the National Sailor's Fair in November of that year. The fair and the circular both served as fund-raisers for a hospital for sailors wounded during the Civil War. That project was headed by Julia Ward Howe, while Emerson's poem was directly solicited by Howe's advisor and assistant, the literary critic Edwin P. Whipple, late of Pigeon Cove.

SEA-SHORE

I heard or seemed to hear the chiding Sea
Say, Pilgrim, why so late and slow to come?
Am I not always here, thy summer home?
Is not my voice thy music, morn and eve?
My breath thy healthful climate in the heats,   5
My touch thy antidote, my bay thy bath?
Was ever building like my terraces?
Was ever couch magnificent as mine?
Lie on the warm rock-ledges, and there learn
A little hut suffices like a town.   10
I make your sculptured architecture vain,
Vain beside mine. I drive my wedges home,
And carve the coastwise mountain into caves.
Lo! here is Rome, and Nineveh, and Thebes,
Karnak, and Pyramid, and Giant's Stairs,   15
Half piled or prostrate; and my newest slab
Older than all thy race.

          Behold the Sea,
The opaline, the plentiful and strong,
Yet beautiful as is the rose in June,
Fresh as the trickling rainbow of July;   20
Sea full of food, the nourisher of kinds,
Purger of earth, and medicine of men;
Creating a sweet climate by my breath,
Washing out harms and griefs from memory,
And, in my mathematic ebb and flow,   25

Giving a hint of that which changes not.
Rich are the sea-gods:—who gives gifts but they?
They grope the sea for pearls, but more than pearls:
They pluck Force thence, and give it to the wise.
For every wave is wealth to Dædalus,   30
Wealth to the cunning artist who can work
This matchless strength. Where shall he find, O waves!
A load your Atlas shoulders cannot lift?

    I with my hammer pounding evermore
The rocky coast, smite Andes into dust,   35
Strewing my bed, and, in another age,
Rebuild a continent of better men.
Then I unbar the doors: my paths lead out
The exodus of nations: I disperse
Men to all shores that front the hoary main.   40

    I too have arts and sorceries;
Illusion dwells forever with the wave.
I know what spells are laid. Leave me to deal
With credulous and imaginative man;
For, though he scoop my water in his palm,   45
A few rods off he deems it gems and clouds.
Planting strange fruits and sunshine on the shore,
I make some coast alluring, some lone isle,
To distant men, who must go there, or die.

1856 || 1864

SONG OF NATURE

The earliest hint of this poem—in a sense its germ—is the detached phrase "the sportive sun" (l. 3), rejected from a draft of "The Humble-Bee" in 1837 (*PN*, p. 136) and copied into another journal in 1845 (*JMN* 9:292). There and in several later locations, where it is joined by other fragments on Spring, it seemed destined for inclusion in "May-Day," or in another poem, never finished, posthumously published under the title "Cosmos" (*W* 9:366–367; *PN*, p. 970). Ultimately, however, the "sportive sun" resisted these different purposes or gatherings and—as if with a gravitational force of its own—progressively organized a separate development, culminating in "Song of Nature," a work that has been called "the crown of Emerson's subjective evolutionary humanism" (Strauch, "The Sources," p. 300). Published in the *Atlantic Monthly* in January 1860, almost simultaneously with Charles Darwin's *On the Origin of Species,* Emerson's poem offers a theory of—that is to say, a way of thinking about—the ameliorating force of Nature and of the relation between persistent physical change and eternal spiritual constancy.

The erotic or generative connotation of the term "sportive" would be labeled archaic by the *OED* or even obsolete by later dictionaries, but it was a meaning perennially evoked in poetic representations of the sun, and here emphasized in the mating of the "sportive sun" with the swelling, female "gibbous moon." But the special fitness of the word may lie in the crypto-Darwinian meaning, which the *OED* supplies in its application to plants: "liable to sport or vary unusually from the true type"—which is to say, to develop by free accidents of mutation. In his important and subtle essay on the poem, Carl F. Strauch insisted that the phrase was "Emerson's own" ("The Sources," p. 320), yet he provided a convincing source in a work that Emerson is known to have read, the *Miscellaneous Essays* of Henry T. Colebrooke (1837). At one point Colebrooke quotes an ancient philosopher: "The parent of all beings produced all states of existence, for he generates and preserves all creatures: therefore is he called the generator. Because he shines and sports, because he loves and irradiates, therefore is he called resplendent or divine. . . . We meditate on light, which, existing in our minds, continually governs our intellects in the pursuits of virtue, wealth, love, and beatitude" (1:128; quoted in Strauch, "The Sources," p. 324). Emerson's science had more in common with such poetic, pagan formulations than with the modern forms of empiricism because he was fundamentally attuned to the interdependence of the observer and the showy old Not-Me of outward Nature. The "sportive sun" is the generative force in Nature, but Emerson has turned the venerable argument from design on its head by insisting that Nature's meanings are not a function of authorship, but lay, as it were, on the other side, with the adequate audience (the tarrying man-child of l. 37) whom all its splendid forms predict.

SONG OF NATURE

Mine are the night and morning,
The pits of air, the gulf of space,
The sportive sun, the gibbous moon,
The innumerable days.

I hide in the solar glory,   5
I am dumb in the pealing song,
I rest on the pitch of the torrent,
In slumber I am strong.

No numbers have counted my tallies,
No tribes my house can fill,   10
I sit by the shining Fount of Life,
And pour the deluge still;

And ever by delicate powers
Gathering along the centuries
From race on race the rarest flowers,   15
My wreath shall nothing miss.

And many a thousand summers
My apples ripened well,
And light from meliorating stars
With firmer glory fell.   20

I wrote the past in characters
Of rock and fire the scroll,
The building in the coral sea,
The planting of the coal.

And thefts from satellites and rings   25
And broken stars I drew,
And out of spent and aged things
I formed the world anew;

What time the gods kept carnival,
Tricked out in star and flower,   30
And in cramp elf and saurian forms
They swathed their too much power.

Time and Thought were my surveyors,
They laid their courses well,
They boiled the sea, and baked the layers   35
Of granite, marl, and shell.

But he, the man-child glorious,—
Where tarries he the while?
The rainbow shines his harbinger,
The sunset gleams his smile.   40

My boreal lights leap upward,
Forthright my planets roll,
And still the man-child is not born,
The summit of the whole.

Must time and tide forever run?   45
Will never my winds go sleep in the west?
Will never my wheels which whirl the sun
And satellites have rest?

Too much of donning and doffing,
Too slow the rainbow fades,   50
I weary of my robe of snow,
My leaves and my cascades;

I tire of globes and races,
Too long the game is played;
What without him is summer's pomp,   55
Or winter's frozen shade?

I travail in pain for him,
My creatures travail and wait;
His couriers come by squadrons,
He comes not to the gate.   60

Twice I have moulded an image,
And thrice outstretched my hand,
Made one of day, and one of night,
And one of the salt-sea-sand.

One in a Judæan manger,   65
And one by Avon stream,

One over against the mouth of the Nile,
And one in the Academe.

I moulded kings and saviours,
And bards o'er kings to rule;—   70
But fell the starry influence short,
The cup was never full.

Yet whirl the glowing wheels once more,
And mix the bowl again;
Seethe, Fate! the ancient elements,   75
Heat, cold, wet, dry, and peace, and pain.

Let war and trade and creeds and song
Blend, ripen race on race,
The sunburnt world a man shall breed
Of all the zones and countless days.   80

No ray is dimmed, no atom worn,
My oldest force is good as new,
And the fresh rose on yonder thorn
Gives back the bending heavens in dew.

1859 || 1860

TWO RIVERS

The central conceit of this poem—that a natural fact (Concord's Musketaquid River) can and does present itself as the symbol of a spiritual fact (the flow of spirit or divinity through the world)—concisely illustrates a foundational principle of Transcendentalist doctrine, as Emerson had announced it in the early manifesto *Nature* (*CW* 1:17). It is the same that Emerson captured in a pair of lines in "Woodnotes II" in his reference to "the primal mind / That flows in streams, that breathes in wind" (ll. 293–294). Such imagery has an especially rich and resonant history in the Judeo-Christian tradition, as Edward Emerson intimated in pointing out the relevance of the remarks of Jesus to the Samaritan woman in the fourth chapter of John (*W* 9:488). There Jesus says, "If thou knewest the gift of God, and who it is that saith to thee, Give me to drink; thou wouldest have asked of him, and he would have given thee living water" (John 4:10). Referring then to the water she had come to draw from Jacob's well, Jesus says, "Whosoever drinketh of this water shall thirst again: But whosoever drinketh of the water that I shall give him shall never thirst; but the water that I shall give him shall be in him a well of water springing up into everlasting life" (4:13–14; cf. l. 18 below). This metaphoric structure, in which water under the sign of spirit is played off against water as an element of the natural world, was held in common by orthodox and Gnostic writers alike in the early church but seems to have been especially emphasized by the latter. One begins to get a sense of the resonances of the motif in the so-called *Excerpts of Theodotus,* a Gnostic or Montanist text from the second century:

> Now regeneration is by water and spirit, as was all creation: "For the Spirit of God moved on the abyss." And for this reason the Saviour was baptized, though not Himself needing to be so, in order that He might consecrate the whole water for those who were being regenerated. Thus it is not the body only, but the soul, that we cleanse. It is accordingly a sign of the sanctifying of our invisible part, and of the straining off from the new and spiritual creation of the unclean spirits that have got mixed up with the soul.
>
> "The water above the heaven." [Cf. Gen. 1:7–8.] Since baptism is performed by water and the Spirit as a protection against the twofold fire,—that which lays hold of what is visible, and that which lays hold of what is invisible; and of necessity, there being an immaterial element of water and a material, is it a protection against the twofold fire. And the earthly water cleanses the body; but the heavenly water, by reason of its being immaterial and invisible, is an emblem of the Holy Spirit, who is the purifier of what is invisible, as the water of the Spirit, as the other of the body. (*Ante-Nicene Fathers,* 8:44)

In orthodox texts from the same period, the language has already lost much of its metaphorical quality: in the early second-century *Didache,* for example, it is directed that baptism be done in "running water" (i.e., "living" water or water infused with spirit), though if that is not available "ordinary water" will do (*Didache,* pp. 230–231).

Hans Jonas quotes from a Gnostic (Mandaean) creation myth:

> They brought living water and poured it into the turbid water; they brought shining light and cast it into the dense darkness. They brought the refreshing wind and cast it into the scorching wind. They brought the living fire and cast it into the devouring fire. They brought the soul, the pure Mana, and cast it into the worthless body. (pp. 58–59)

Jonas further points out that the heretical Mandaeans, who especially venerated John the Baptist, insisted more pointedly than the orthodox that their central rite of baptism could be performed only in flowing streams ("all of which the Mandaeans called 'Jordans'"), because only flowing water was divine (pp. 97–98). It is not too much to say that the Gnostics above all other groups asserted the metaphoric or "poetic" uses of water, some trace of which continues to inform its profounder meanings in modern religious and spiritual contexts.

TWO RIVERS

Thy summer voice, Musketaquit,
Repeats the music of the rain;
But sweeter rivers pulsing flit
Through thee, as thou through Concord Plain.

Thou in thy narrow banks art pent: 5
The stream I love unbounded goes
Through flood and sea and firmament;
Through light, through life, it forward flows.

I see the inundation sweet,
I hear the spending of the stream   10
Through years, through men, through nature fleet,
Through love and thought, through power and dream.

Musketaquit, a goblin strong,
Of shard and flint makes jewels gay;

They lose their grief who hear his song,   15
And where he winds is the day of day.

So forth and brighter fares my stream,—
Who drink it shall not thirst again;
No darkness stains its equal gleam,
And ages drop in it like rain.   20

1856–57 ‖ 1858

WALDEINSAMKEIT

Emerson wrote the first draft of "Waldeinsamkeit," or "woodland solitude," in August 1857, during a brief visit (the first of many) to Naushon Island, between New Bedford and Martha's Vineyard. The island, seven miles long, wooded, stocked with deer, and accessible by yacht, was the recently purchased private estate of Emerson's friend John Murray Forbes, railroad tycoon and fellow Saturday Club member (*L* 5:80–81; Forbes, 1:16–27). The prose germ of the poem seems to have been written on Naushon:

> I do not count the hours I spend in the woods, though I forget my affairs there & my books. And, when there, I wander hither & thither; any bird, any plant, any spring, detains me. I do not hurry homewards for I think all affairs may be postponed to this walking. And it is for this idleness that all my businesses exist. (*JMN* 14:145)

The poem received contributions from memories of other walks nearer home. By January or February 1858, Emerson submitted "Waldeinsamkeit" to James Russell Lowell for publication in the *Atlantic Monthly*, though it did not appear until October (*CW* 9:463–464).

WALDEINSAMKEIT

I do not count the hours I spend
In wandering by the sea;
The forest is my loyal friend,
Like God it useth me.

In plains that room for shadows make   5
Of skirting hills to lie,
Bound in by streams which give and take
Their colors from the sky;

Or on the mountain-crest sublime,
Or down the oaken glade,   10
O what have I to do with time?
For this the day was made.

Cities of mortals woe-begone
Fantastic care derides,
But in the serious landscape lone   15
Stern benefit abides.

Sheen will tarnish, honey cloy,
And merry is only a mask of sad,
But, sober on a fund of joy,
The woods at heart are glad.   20

There the great Planter plants
Of fruitful worlds the grain,
And with a million spells enchants
The souls that walk in pain.

Still on the seeds of all he made   25
The rose of beauty burns;
Through times that wear, and forms that fade,
Immortal youth returns.

The black ducks mounting from the lake,
The pigeon in the pines,   30
The bittern's boom, a desert make
Which no false art refines.

Down in yon watery nook,
Where bearded mists divide,
The gray old gods that Chaos knew,   35
The sires of Nature, hide.

Aloft, in secret veins of air,
Blows the sweet breath of song,
O, few to scale those uplands dare,
Though they to all belong!   40

See thou bring not to field or stone
The fancies found in books;
Leave authors' eyes, and fetch your own,
To brave the landscape's looks.

Oblivion here thy wisdom is,   45
Thy thrift, the sleep of cares;
For a proud idleness like this
Crowns all thy mean affairs.

1857 || 1858

TERMINUS

The history of this poem is complex and in many respects indeterminate. Edward Emerson fostered the idea that it had been composed in 1866—that is to say, in his father's sixty-third year (*Emerson in Concord*, p. 183; cf. *W* 9:489–490). Certainly it was in December of that year that he first heard his father read the poem. A late but undated signed copy carrying the title "Climacteric" (*PN*, pp. 702–703) further supports the 1866 dating, and indeed for a long time there was no reason to question Edward's conclusion. In 1950, however, Carl Strauch advanced a plausibly supported argument that the first draft was written in 1850 or 1851 ("The Date of Emerson's *Terminus*"). Certain evidence overlooked by Strauch might suggest an even earlier date: in the spring of 1846, for example, around the time of his forty-third birthday, Emerson wrote in his journal: "I grow old, I accept conditions;—thus far—no farther; to learn that we are not the first born, but the latest born; that we have no wings; that the sins of our predecessors are on us like a mountain of obstruction" (*JMN* 9:363). A year later he wrote to his brother William, ironically insisting that, like the profligate Falstaff, he meant "to live within bounds. And I am taking in sail; and shall break out of slavery, if I can" (*L* 3:390). The earliest attempt at versifying the ideas of "Terminus" occurs in poetry notebook X:

> As the bird trims himself to the gale
> So I trim myself to the tempest of time
> And I shall find something pleasant in my last throb that
>   I am getting out of mean politics. (*PN*, p. 222)

This abortive beginning, stripped of the reference to politics, became lines 33–34 of the finished poem. Strauch supposed that the expression of disgust with politics might have been prompted by the Compromise of 1850, the included Fugitive Slave Bill, and Daniel Webster's defection in support of both. And yet, in fact, that crisis energized Emerson's antislavery commitment, propelling him into politics; the satisfaction of "getting out" (or as he said in 1847 "break[ing] out of slavery") more likely belongs to 1846 or 1847 and the period following the writing of the "Ode to Channing."

TERMINUS

It is time to be old,
To take in sail:—
The god of bounds,
Who sets to seas a shore,
Came to me in his fatal rounds,   5

And said: 'No more!
No farther shoot
Thy broad ambitious branches, and thy root.
Fancy departs: no more invent,
Contract thy firmament   10
To compass of a tent.
There's not enough for this and that,
Make thy option which of two;
Economize the failing river,
Not the less revere the Giver,   15
Leave the many and hold the few.
Timely wise accept the terms,
Soften the fall with wary foot;
A little while
Still plan and smile,   20
And, fault of novel germs,
Mature the unfallen fruit.
Curse, if thou wilt, thy sires,
Bad husbands of their fires,
Who, when they gave thee breath,   25
Failed to bequeath
The needful sinew stark as once,
The Baresark marrow to thy bones,
But left a legacy of ebbing veins,
Inconstant heat and nerveless reins,—   30
Amid the Muses, left thee deaf and dumb,
Amid the gladiators, halt and numb.'

   As the bird trims her to the gale,
I trim myself to the storm of time,
I man the rudder, reef the sail,   35
Obey the voice at eve obeyed at prime:
'Lowly faithful, banish fear,
Right onward drive unharmed;
The port, well worth the cruise, is near,
And every wave is charmed.'   40

1846–1851? || 1867

THE PAST

The meaning of this poem is arguably affected by its placement in *May-Day* between "Terminus" and a poem not included in this selection, "In Memoriam. E. B. E.," Emerson's elegy for his brother Edward Bliss Emerson, who died in 1834.

THE PAST

The debt is paid,
The verdict said,
The Furies laid,
The plague is stayed,
All fortunes made;   5
Turn the key and bolt the door,
Sweet is death forevermore.
Nor haughty hope, nor swart chagrin,
Nor murdering hate, can enter in.
All is now secure and fast;   10
Not the gods can shake the Past;
Flies-to the adamantine door
Bolted down forevermore.
None can re-enter there,—
No thief so politic,   15
No Satan with a royal trick
Steal in by window, chink, or hole,
To bind or unbind, add what lacked,
Insert a leaf, or forge a name,
New-face or finish what is packed,   20
Alter or mend eternal Fact.

1863? || 1867

S. H.

Samuel Hoar, known as Squire Hoar (1778–1856), was one of the most distinguished and accomplished Concordians of his day, a leader of the Massachusetts bar, and active in Federalist and Whig politics before founding the state Free Soil Party in 1848, and, with Emerson, the state Republican Party in 1854. In 1844 he had been appointed by the governor of Massachusetts to investigate the treatment of the state's black sailors, who were being routinely incarcerated in South Carolina ports and sold into slavery if they could not pay the cost of their own detention. He and his daughter Elizabeth (who was to have married Emerson's brother Charles) were forcibly ejected from Charleston by a pro-slavery mob. When Squire Hoar died in 1856, Emerson published two brief memorial sketches, including, at the end of the second, the quatrain below (*CW* 10:376–384).

The first draft of the poem occurs among journal entries for October 1852, suggesting that Emerson may have been moved to write it by the death of Hoar's great professional colleague and frequent courtroom opponent Daniel Webster. It was Webster's dramatic endorsement of the Fugitive Slave Law in 1850 that cost him the respect of Hoar and Emerson both, who were thereby driven deeper into antislavery politics.

S. H.

With beams December planets dart
His cold eye truth and conduct scanned,
July was in his sunny heart,
October in his liberal hand.

1852 || 1857

A. H.

The subject of this quatrain is Ann Sturgis Hooper (1813–1884), elder sister of Caroline Sturgis Tappan and wife of Samuel Hooper, wealthy Boston importer and Republican politician. A letter from Emerson to Caroline of April 27, 1855, on the occasion of her departure for Europe, alludes to a recent visit to Mrs. Hooper, "who received me with great kindness. Her manners & beauty will serve to vindicate America to you in England & Italy, and, whilst she stays at home, I shall reckon securely on your return.

> Far capitals & marble courts her eye seemed still to see,
> Minstrels, & dames, & highborn men, the princeliest that be" (*L* 8:430).

The quatrain's second distich was the first written, as the notebook drafts reveal (*JMN* 13:407, 419–420).

A. H.

High was her heart, and yet was well inclined,
Her manners made of bounty well refined;
Far capitals, and marble courts, her eye still seemed to see,
Minstrels, and kings, and high-born dames, and of the best
    that be.

1855? || 1867

"SUUM CUIQUE"

The couplet seems to offer a bit of prudential advice and certainly has in its background the Yankee's instinctive thrift and horror of debt. But as metaphor this shortest of Emerson's poems extends its meaning very widely, when one considers (as Emerson did) that debt is another name for imbalance. "Always pay" (*JMN* 5:476, 7:144–145, 12:290) was the theme of the essay "Compensation" (*CW* 2:55–73), where the larger meanings of debt are discussed, as well as of the lecture on "Duty" (*EL* 3:138–150), where its moral implications are laid out. While the idea was long in contemplation, the couplet itself was the work of the late fall of 1859, at which time it seems to have precipitated out of thinking about the genuine heroism and bravery of the dutiful, obligation-minded John Brown (*JMN* 14:324–325, 331).

"SUUM CUIQUE"

Wilt thou seal up the avenues of ill?
Pay every debt, as if God wrote the bill.

1859 ‖ 1867

ARTIST

The title of this quatrain offers little support for the otherwise plausible hypothesis that Emerson had Thoreau in mind. In 1847, when the first draft was composed, Thoreau left his cabin at Walden to board at "Bush," as the Emerson house was known. At the same time, Emerson left for a lecture tour in England.

ARTIST

Quit the hut, frequent the palace,
Reck not what the people say;
For still, where'er the trees grow biggest,
Huntsmen find the easiest way.

1847–1852 || 1860

POET

Written in April 1855 (*JMN* 13:410–412), the quatrain remained unpublished until *May-Day* (1867). Ten manuscript drafts or fair copies have been noted.

POET

Ever the Poet *from* the land
Steers his bark, and trims his sail;
Right out to sea his courses stand,
New worlds to find in pinnace frail.

1855 ‖ 1867

POET

Edward Emerson quoted this poem in a note (*W* 6:415) to illustrate an observation in "Beauty" from *The Conduct of Life:* "In rhetoric, this art of omission is a chief secret of power, and, in general, it is proof of high culture, to say the greatest matters in the simplest way" (*CW* 6:157).

POET

To clothe the fiery thought
In simple word succeeds,
For still the craft of genius is
To mask a king in weeds.

1847 || 1860

GARDENER

In July 1840, through weeks of hottest weather—into the mid-90s, when "the dogstar raged" and withered crops (*JMN* 7:384)—Emerson proposed to be, himself, "coolness & shade." On July 28 he wrote to Samuel Gray Ward, saying that "in the sleep of the great heats there was nothing for me but to read the Vedas, the bible of the tropics, which I find I come back upon every three or four years. It is sublime as heat & night and a breathless ocean. . . . It is of no use to put away the book: if I trust myself in the woods or in a boat upon the pond Nature makes a Bramin of me presently: Eternal necessity, eternal compensation, unfathomable power unbroken silence,—this is her creed. Peace, she saith to me, and purity & absolute abandonment—these penances expiate all sin & bring you to the beatitude of the 'Eight Gods'" (*L* 7:398). At this time and in this mood he wrote in his journal:

> Go to the forest if God has made thee a poet and make thy life clean & fragrant as thy office.
>
> > True Bramin in the morning meadows wet
> > Expound the Vedas in the violet
>
> Thy love must be thy art. Thy words must spring from love, and every thought be touched with love. Only such words fly & endure. There are two ways of speaking—One, when a man makes his discourse plausible & round by considering how it sounds to him who hears it, and the other mode when his own heart loves & so infuses grace into all that drops from him. Only this is living beauty. Nature also must teach thee rhetoric. She can teach thee not only to speak truth, but to speak it truly. (*JMN* 7:386)

Emerson completed the quatrain in September 1849 (*JMN* 11:158).

GARDENER

True Bramin, in the morning meadows wet,
Expound the Vedas of the violet,
Or, hid in vines, peeping through many a loop,
See the plum redden, and the beurré stoop.

1840, 1849 || 1860

FORESTER

There is no evidence for dating this poem more precisely than to the period 1847–1860. Still, in 1853, when Emerson was writing a number of these quatrains, there is a journal entry about Henry Thoreau passing without permission, quietly and unobserved, through his neighbors' woods and pastures (*JMN* 13:187). After Thoreau's death in 1862, Bronson Alcott published a eulogy in the *Atlantic Monthly* entitled "Forester."

FORESTER

He took the color of his vest
From rabbit's coat or grouse's breast;
For, as the wood-kinds lurk and hide,
So walks the woodman, unespied.

1853? ‖ 1860

NORTHMAN

In 1853 Emerson was much occupied with researches in English history in preparation for writing *English Traits.* In June of that year he was reading Augustin Thierry's *History of the Conquest of England by the Normans* (London, 1841), in which, on p. 21, he found the paraphrase of a Viking song: "The force of the storm is a help to the arm of our rowers; the hurricane is in our service; it carries us the way we would go" (*JMN* 13:172). The idea and language may have caught Emerson's attention because of a similarity with passages he had noticed and quoted earlier: a line from Samuel Butler's *Hudibras,* for example—"We only row we're steered by fate" (*JMN* 5:33)—or the observation by Edward Gibbon that "The winds & waves are always on the side of the ablest navigators" (*JMN* 5:108). Robert D. Richardson shrewdly connects this poem with Emerson's inspection, on June 14, of Donald McKay's immense new clipper ship, the *Great Republic,* then under construction at the shipyard in East Boston (p. 516; cf. *JMN* 13:183). In fact, Emerson had withdrawn Thierry's book from the Boston Athenaeum just the day before (von Frank, *An Emerson Chronology,* p. 285). The source was versified a little more than a year later (*JMN* 13:356, 360–361).

NORTHMAN

The gale that wrecked you on the sand,
It helped my rowers to row;
The storm is my best galley hand,
And drives me where I go.

1854 || 1860

FROM ALCUIN

When Alcuin (735–804) was asked by Pepin, father of Charlemagne, to provide a definition of the sea, the English monk replied that it was "*Le chemin des audacieux, la frontière de la terre, l'hôtellerie des fleuves, la source des pluies*" (Baron, p. 340). According to a journal passage entered shortly before June 14, 1853, "Alcuin called the Sea, the road of the bold; the frontier of the land; the hostelry of the rivers; & the source of the rains." His versification followed immediately (*JMN* 13:180).

FROM ALCUIN

The sea is the road of the bold,
Frontier of the wheat-sown plains,
The pit wherein the streams are rolled,
And fountain of the rains.

1853 ‖ 1860

EXCELSIOR

This quatrain, originally lacking a title, was composed in the spring of 1838 (*JMN* 5:483). To a revised version produced no earlier than 1857, Emerson gave the title "Excelsior, *a song of degrees*" (*PN*, pp. 512–513). Given the immense popularity at that time of Henry Wadsworth Longfellow's rather silly poem "Excelsior" (meaning "higher") and the fact that beginning in 1857 with the founding of the Saturday Club the two poets were much more in each other's company, the allusion was likely deliberate. As different as these two performances are, they manage to convey their authors' respective views of the Transcendental project—parodically in Longfellow's case, sympathetically in Emerson's. For Longfellow, the fault of an idealistic philosophy is that it draws one away from the warmth of the "real" or social world into a cold and airless abstraction, mistakenly conceived by the idealist as a "higher" or better realm. If one reads Emerson's "Excelsior" as an offered reply, one sees that the ascending structure so familiar in Emerson's work enables a movement from prose (ll. 1–2) to poetry (ll. 3–4), with aesthetic rewards that deny Longfellow's presumption of an ultimate (and fatal) disconnection from humanity. In Emerson's quatrain the end of the ascending movement is a gracefully acknowledged reciprocal movement downward.

EXCELSIOR

Over his head were the maple buds,
And over the tree was the moon,
And over the moon were the starry studs,
That drop from the angels' shoon.

1838 || 1867

HOROSCOPE

Edward Emerson supposed that this quatrain was a translation, since the first draft occurs in notebook Orientalist (*TN* 2:50). Islam, as Emerson noted, had much to say on the subject of fate, but "Horoscope" was an original composition.

HOROSCOPE

Ere he was born, the stars of fate
Plotted to make him rich and great:
When from the womb the babe was loosed,
The gate of gifts behind him closed.

1847–1850? || 1867

CLIMACTERIC

The situation of the first drafts points to composition in 1847, which would seem too soon for complaints about old age. (Emerson was forty-four.) The "grand climacteric" traditionally refers to one's sixty-third year and signifies the onset of genuine old age, but "climacteric," without the modifier, can refer to any critical period, turning point, or climax in life. The complaint here, however, is that the grief that ages us—as, for example, the death of a son— brings with it no epochal revelations, no life-altering changes, no advance- ment. We do not "turn the leaf."

CLIMACTERIC

I am not wiser for my age,
Nor skilful by my grief;
Life loiters at the book's first page,—
Ah! could we turn the leaf.

1847 || 1860

HERI, CRAS, HODIE

The title derives from an anecdote drawn from *The Memoirs of Samuel Pepys:* John Bridgeman, bishop of Chester (1577–1652), having bought an estate previously owned first by the Lever family, then by the Ashton family, had four shields installed in the window of the great hall, representing the arms of the Levers ("Olim" ["Once"]), the Ashtons ("Heri" ["Yesterday"]), the Bridgemans ("Hodie" ["Today"]), and an empty shield ("Cras nescio cujus" ["I don't know whose"]). See *JMN* 13:361.

HERI, CRAS, HODIE

Shines the last age, the next with hope is seen,
Today slinks poorly off unmarked between:
Future or Past no richer secret folds,
O friendless Present! than thy bosom holds.

1855 || 1860

PERICLES

The source of this quatrain is the reply of Pericles when asked to swear falsely on behalf of a friend; as Emerson set it down in an 1826 notebook, "'I'm your friend,' said Pericles, 'as far as the altar'" (*JMN* 6:34)—or, in Plutarch's once familiar phrase, "amicus usque ad aras" (*Moralia,* 528c). In a brief essay on the history of the phrase, G. L. Hendrickson pointed out that the Latin form—and the word "aras" in particular—introduced an ambiguity not present in the original Greek, so that from the seventeenth century on it was increasingly taken to mean that Pericles was pledging friendship even to the grave. But Hendrickson noted that touching the altar was the equivalent, in Attic courts, of the modern Judeo-Christian practice of swearing on the Bible. The sanction against perjury, in other words, was religious, and Pericles was asserting that friendship could not overset a higher or transcendental responsibility to the truth (pp. 395–397).

PERICLES

Well and wisely said the Greek,
Be thou faithful, but not fond;
To the altar's foot thy fellow seek,
The Furies wait beyond.

1843 ‖ 1867

CASELLA

Casella (d. 1299), a Florentine composer and friend of Dante, sings of love at Dante's request in the second canto of the *Purgatorio.* Emerson mentions Casella's performance in a journal entry of September 25, 1838, adding that "a song of love that gave us to know & own the natural & the heavenly or divine—that were indeed uplifting music" (*JMN* 7:86; cf. *JMN* 10:70, where Casella is offered as a model of the "expressive person"). In July 1846, Emerson wrote, "Metre of the Poet again, is his science of love. Does he know that lore? Never was poet who was not tremulous with love-lore" (*JMN* 9:442). The quatrain was composed toward the end of 1857 (*JMN* 14:188).

Emerson would also have known of Casella from Milton's reference in his sonnet "To My Friend, Mr Henry Lawes, on His Airs": "*Dante* shall give Fame leave to set thee higher / Than his *Casella,* whom he woo'd to sing, / Met in the milder shades of Purgatory." Here Milton is particularly praising Lawes for his extraordinary sensitivity in setting words to music.

CASELLA

Test of the poet is knowledge of love,
For Eros is older than Saturn or Jove;
Never was poet, of late or of yore,
Who was not tremulous with love-lore.

1857 || 1867

HAFIZ

No source has been located for this poem, which would appear to be an original work by Emerson, written in 1855, in the manner of Hafiz.

HAFIZ

Her passions the shy violet
From Hafiz never hides;
Love-longings of the raptured bird
The bird to him confides.

1855 || 1867

NATURE IN LEASTS

Lines 1 and 2 of this quatrain were written ten years before lines 3 and 4 (*JMN* 8:241, 13:101). The two halves independently illustrate the principle named in the title ("Natura in minimis," in the first printing). The phrase comes from Marcello Malpighi, a seventeenth-century pioneer in medical and anatomical microscopy, in his work on the silkworm, *De Bombyce* (1669), p. 1: "Cum enim tota in minimis existat natura, si alicubi, magis equidem in *insectorum* moleculis id deprehendi par fuerit." Emerson did not read Malpighi, but he found the sentence quoted by Emanuel Swedenborg in "The Way to a Knowledge of the Soul," published in an English translation by James John Garth Wilkinson, *Posthumous Tracts* . . . (London 1847), pp. 4–5. Wilkinson provided Malpighi's Latin in a footnote and translated the gist of it: "Nature exists in totality in the smallest objects." Emerson read this in 1848 and referred to the principle as the "Doctrine of leasts" (*JMN* 11:17). In *Representative Men* (1850) he discussed its importance to Swedenborg's thought (*CW* 4:59, 64–65, 195–196).

NATURE IN LEASTS

As sings the pine-tree in the wind,
So sings in the wind a sprig of the pine;
Her strength and soul has laughing France
Shed in each drop of wine.

1852 || 1860

ἈΔΑΚΡΥΝ ΝΕΜΟΝΤΑΙ ΑΙΩΝΑ

The title is from Pindar, *Olympian Odes,* II, lines 66–67: "[All who were wont to rejoice in keeping their oaths,] share a life that knoweth no tears." Emerson used this phrase as the epigraph to his own notebook X, the principal poetry notebook of the 1840s (*PN,* p. 110), and also of his 1843 notebook Trees (*JMN* 8:519). Elsewhere (notebook S Salvage) it served as the heading for a passage elucidating the meaning it had for Emerson:

> Genius is good natured. . . . It is always gentle. Hence the safety we feel, whenever genius is entrusted with political or ecclesiastical power. There is no fanaticism as long as there is the creative muse. Genius is a charter of freedom, and as long as I hear one graceful modulation of wit, I know the genial soul, & do not smell fagots. The Bunyan, the Boehmen is nearer far to Montaigne & Rabelais, than to Bloody Mary & Becket & the Inquisition. Scaliger said, "Never was a man a poet, or a lover of the works of poets, who had not his heart in the right place." They are not tainted by the worst company. Genius hath an immunity from the worst times, & drawing its life from that which is out of time & place, is serene & glad amid bigots & juntoes. (*TN* 3:80)

As in the "Ode, Inscribed to W. H. Channing," written at the same time, Emerson pleads the case for the serenity and geniality of the poet as against the contentious didacticism of the reformer.

ἈΔΑΚΡΤΝ ΝΕΜΟΝΤΑΙ ΑΙΩΝΑ

'A new commandment,' said the smiling Muse,
'I give my darling son, Thou shalt not preach';—
Luther, Fox, Behmen, Swedenborg, grew pale,
And, on the instant, rosier clouds upbore
Hafiz and Shakspeare with their shining choirs.   5

1846 || 1867

SONG OF SEID NIMETOLLAH OF KUHISTAN

Arthur John Arberry, in his *Classical Persian Literature,* says that "the Ni'mat-Allāhī order of dervishes, active to this day in parts of Persia, derives its name from Shāh Nūr al-Dīn Muhammad Ni'mat Allāh Vāli, . . . a renowned poet and a powerful saint who was born at Aleppo in 1330. . . . When twenty-four years of age he made the pilgrimage to Mecca and there came under the influence of the Sūfī teacher and biographer 'Abd Allāh al-Yāfi'ī, whose khalifa he eventually became" (p. 412). Seid Nimat Allāh (or Nimetollah) wrote treatises on points of Sufi doctrine but is best known for his *Diwan,* a collection of lyric poems. In the poem below, Emerson translates one of the "Mystische Gaselle" from the German of Joseph von Hammer-Purgstall in *Geschichte der schönen Redekünste Persiens* (Vienna, 1818), p. 223, and quoted in full at *CW* 9:575–576.

The headnote that Emerson appended to his translation oddly slights the mystical content of the dance, stressing instead the appearance of the performance, its orbital character, and the dervish's relation to his sheik. But the poem makes clear that the purpose is not to compliment any human being but to achieve an ecstatic transcendence of ego-awareness such that one's own rapt loving, wholly yielded to, can combine with God's love, "all difference" (l. 26) expiring in the act. The various orders of dervishes all emphasized universal love as the pathway to God (the theme especially of the first stanza). As Sufis, they were essentially Gnostic in their search for truth or divine wisdom (the theme of the second stanza). The third stanza stresses the Sufi independence from tradition and dogma in a manner common also to Gnostics and Transcendentalists. This privileging of meaning over reverence for textual authority is an important key to the poetics of mysticism in its many forms. The coda of Emerson's translation dramatically represents the transcendence that the dance—and the reexpression of the dance as poem—had set out to achieve.

SONG OF SEID NIMETOLLAH OF KUHISTAN

[Among the religious customs of the dervishes is an astronomical dance, in which the dervish imitates the movements of the heavenly bodies, by spinning on his own axis, whilst at the same time he revolves round the Sheikh in the centre, representing the sun; and, as he spins, he sings the Song of Seid Nimetollah of Kuhistan.]

Spin the ball! I reel, I burn,
Nor head from foot can I discern,
Nor my heart from love of mine,

Nor the wine-cup from the wine.
All my doing, all my leaving,   5
Reaches not to my perceiving;
Lost in whirling spheres I rove,
And know only that I love.

I am seeker of the stone,
Living gem of Solomon;   10
From the shore of souls arrived,
In the sea of sense I dived;
But what is land, or what is wave,
To me who only jewels crave?
Love is the air-fed fire intense,   15
And my heart the frankincense;
As the rich aloes flames, I glow,

Yet the censer cannot know.
I'm all-knowing, yet unknowing;
Stand not, pause not, in my going.   20

Ask not me, as Muftis can,
To recite the Alcoran;
Well I love the meaning sweet,—
I tread the book beneath my feet.

Lo! the God's love blazes higher,   25
Till all difference expire.
What are Moslems? what are Giaours?
All are Love's, and all are ours.
I embrace the true believers,
But I reck not of deceivers.   30
Firm to Heaven my bosom clings,
Heedless of inferior things;
Down on earth there, underfoot,
What men chatter know I not.

1853? || 1858

FROM

Selected Poems

(1876)

CUPIDO

Emerson vacillated in his choice of title between the Greek and Roman names, Eros and Cupido (see *PN,* p. 583). At one time he thought of making this brief poem an introduction to "The Initial Love."

CUPIDO

The solid, solid universe
Is pervious to Love;
With bandaged eyes he never errs,
Around, below, above.
His blinding light   5
He flingeth white
On God's and Satan's brood,
And reconciles
By mystic wiles
The evil and the good.   10

1843 || 1876

Uncollected Poems

SILENCE

On July 19, 1840, Margaret Fuller, as editor of the *Dial*, asked Emerson to supply a brief poem to be used as filler in an upcoming issue. He obliged with "Silence." It is tempting to see the poem as a comment on their relationship, which had lately been somewhat flirtatious on Fuller's side. Thomas Wentworth Higginson later remarked that when first published, "the little verse was regarded as rather grotesque, and it will never, perhaps, be placed among his happier efforts" (p. 159). Indeed, it was not reprinted in *Poems* (1847). The objection is likely to the wording in line 3 (see note).

SILENCE

They put their finger on their lip,—
   The Powers above;
The seas their islands clip,
The moons in Ocean dip,—
   They love but name not love.   5

1840 || 1840

GRACE

This poem is an imitation of George Herbert's sonnet "Sinne," which Emerson found quoted in Samuel Taylor Coleridge's *Aids to Reflection* (p. 256):

> Lord! with what care hast thou begirt us round!
> Parents first season us. Then schoolmasters
> Deliver us to laws. They send us bound
> To rules of reason. Holy messengers;
> Pulpits and Sundays; sorrow dogging sin;
> Afflictions *sorted;* anguish of all sizes;
> Fine nets and stratagems to catch us in!
> Bibles laid open; millions of surprises;
> Blessings beforehand; ties of gratefulness;
> The sound of glory ringing in our ears:
> Without, our shame; within, our consciences;
> Angels and grace; eternal hopes and fears!
> Yet all these fences, and their whole array,
> One cunning BOSOM SIN blows quite away.

In January 1830, Emerson quoted the poem to his congregation at Boston's Second Church, asking rhetorically if it did not effectively summarize "the history of the world":

> This would be disheartening indeed to all lovers of virtue, to all who hope well for man; this gloomy experience casts a shade over all the future and is only to be resisted by the consoling fact of a few glorious exceptions and by that strong hope that dwells in the bottom of the Soul (that spark that lives among the ashes of the past) that amendment is never late, (that with God all things are possible), the conviction that power is never wanting to us when we will be true to ourselves. (*CS* 2:126)

The considerable fascination of Emerson's "Grace" has always consisted in its seeming denial of the poet's core doctrine of self-reliance, and yet here he makes his source an occasion for preaching truth to self and not for conforming the criminal to law. "Grace" is clearly the fruit of Emerson's pastoral career and might be said to capture the moment when the antinomian remembers that the force and effect of the other side—the side of discipline and of moral legalism—must be recognized as well.

Emerson published the poem anonymously in the *Dial* in 1842 but never collected or reprinted it. A decade later he was surprised to find that William Henry Channing had chosen it as epigraph to his section of the *Memoirs of*

Margaret Fuller Ossoli and had ascribed it to George Herbert. Emerson noticed this flattering mistake as he read proofs during his coauthor's absence. In the end he let the poem stand but struck out Herbert's name, which did not appear in the American edition (*L* 8:294–295).

GRACE

How much, preventing God, how much I owe
To the defences thou hast round me set!
Example, custom, fear, occasion slow,—
These scorned bondmen were my parapet.
I dare not peep over this parapet   5
To gauge with glance the roaring gulf below,
The depths of sin to which I had descended,
Had not these me against myself defended.

1832? || 1842

NATURE

Although Emerson never collected this motto, it is probably his best known, both because it came to be attached as epigraph to the most important of his early publications, *Nature,* in its 1849 second edition, and because it was eventually regarded—after the publication of *On the Origin of Species* in 1859—as a singular anticipation of Darwinian evolution. In its 1836 first edition, *Nature* had as its motto a paraphrase drawn from Plotinus: "Nature is but an image or imitation of wisdom, the last thing of the soul; nature being a thing which doth only do, but not know" (*CW* 1:1, 247). Between 1836 and 1849 Emerson had developed a practice of supplying his essays with poetic epigraphs of his own composition, so this substitution, the single most important revision in the 1849 text of *Nature,* may not imply any substantial dissatisfaction with the original.

In later years, when the "evolutionary" character of the poem became a subject of comment, it seemed obvious that the substitution had been prompted by the insight into scientific matters that Emerson gained in his 1847–48 trip to England. But, in fact, the ascent of the "worm," or serpent, draws mainly on the fanciful theories of the German scientist Lorenz Oken, of the Scottish surgeon and anatomist John Hunter (for the idea that Emerson called "arrested and progressive development"), and of a "poetic anatomist of our own day," the German-American John Bernhard Stallo, whose *General Principles of the Philosophy of Nature* Emerson began to read in May 1849 (Richardson, p. 467). It was Oken, as explained by Stallo, who taught "that a snake, being a horizontal line, and man, being an erect line, constitute a right angle, and between the lines of this mystical quadrant all animated beings find their place" (*CW* 4:61, and the note at 196–197). The idea that nature is an organized aspiration after consciousness, a means of arriving at the human capacity for *knowing,* in fact repeats the major implication of the original epigraph from Plotinus (see also *W* 1:403–405)

NATURE

A subtle chain of countless rings
The next unto the farthest brings;
The eye reads omens where it goes,
And speaks all languages the rose;
And, striving to be man, the worm   5
Mounts through all the spires of form.

APPENDIX
The Ellen Poems, 1828–1831

Emerson's first wife, Ellen Louisa Tucker (1811–1831), was the daughter of Beza-leel and Margaret Tucker. Following Bezaleel's death in 1820, Ellen's mother married Colonel William Austin Kent, who organized the first Unitarian church in Concord, New Hampshire. Newly licensed to preach but not as yet settled, Emerson was asked to supply the pulpit at Concord on successive Sundays at the end of 1827. He first saw Ellen, then sixteen years old, on Christmas Day of that year. They were engaged the following December and married at the Kent mansion on September 30, 1829. The couple then settled into rented quarters in Chardon Street, Boston, Emerson having been ordained at the prestigious Second Church the previous March.

Throughout this period, and indeed for the rest of her short life, Ellen suf-fered from acute tuberculosis, a condition that had already claimed two of El-len's siblings and from which Emerson himself had only recently recovered. This fatal shadow hung over the pair, lending a special depth and urgency to their emotional life. They communicated, often and characteristically, in po-etry. When they traveled together they would maintain a playful account in verse of what they had seen (*JMN* 3:159–162); when they were apart, as when Ellen's illness required southern travel, Emerson wrote poetic laments about their separation, three of which he later published. Their life seems almost to have been conducted in poetry, on Emerson's part of a kind—intimate, impas-sioned, unstudied—that he had not written before, but that now fell into the very rhythms and diction of Ellen's own poems. It was during this period that Emerson first came to think of himself as a poet, and certainly the brief, in-tensely sustained turn to themes of love and death (central, he would discover, to the work of poetry in general) contributed greatly to the maturity of his writer's voice, evident as early as 1834.

What follows is the first selection ever made of the poems and poetic fragments that Emerson addressed to his wife, from the period of their courtship and marriage, and concluding with the anguish of bereavement following Ellen's death on the morning of February 8, 1831.

I.

All that thy virgin soul can ask be thine
Beautiful Ellen   Let this prayer be mine
The first devotion that my soul has paid
To mortal grace it pays to thee fair maid
I am enamoured of thy loveliness   5
Lovesick with thy sweet beauty which shall bless
With its glad light my path of life around
Which now is joyless where thou art not found
Now am I stricken with the sympathy
That binds the whole world in electric tie   10
I hail love's birth within my hermit breast
And welcome the bright ordinance to be blest
I was a hermit whom the lone Muse cheers,
I sped apart my solitary years,
I found no joy in woman's meaning eye   15
When Fashion's merry mob were dancing by;
Yet had I read the law all laws above,
—Great Nature hath ordained the heart to love—
Yet had I heard that in this mortal state
To every mind exists its natural mate,   20
That God at first did marry soul to soul
Tho' lands divide & seas between them roll.
Then eagerly I searched each circle round
I panted for my mate, but no mate found
I saw bright eyes, fair forms, complexions fine,   25
But not a single soul that spoke to mine.
At last the star broke thro' the hiding cloud,
At last I found thee in the silken crowd
I found thee, Ellen, born to love & shine,
And I who found am blessed to call thee mine.   30

December 1828 || *JMN* 2:410–411

II.

And do I waste my time
Scribbling of love to my beautiful queen
And is it idle to talk in prose & rhyme
Of one who at midnight & morning's prime
In daylight is fancied, in visions seen?   5
And do I forget the burning crown
That Glory should weave of light for me—

ca. May 1829 || *OFL*, p. 25

III.

I've found the dainty malice out
Of Ellen's hypocritic eye
She's wound her gipsy nets about

I thought it was no harm to watch
The features of an artless maid   5

1829 || *JMN* 3:151

IV.

TO EVA

"To Eva" was published in the *Dial*, July 1840. In form it is a Spanish sestet, or sextilla.

TO EVA

O fair and stately maid, whose eyes
Were kindled in the upper skies
    At the same torch that lighted mine;
For so I must interpret still
Thy sweet dominion o'er my will,   5
    A sympathy divine.

Ah! let me blameless gaze upon
Features that seem at heart my own;
   Nor fear those watchful sentinels,
Who charm the more their glance forbids,   10
Chaste-glowing, underneath their lids,
   With fire that draws while it repels.

                                1829 || 1840

V.

The seventh line originally read "Her soul like mine is unconfined."

Though her eye seek other forms
And a glad delight below
Yet the love the world that warms
Bids for me her bosom glow

She must love me till she find   5
Another heart as large & true
Her soul is frank as the Ocean wind
And the world has only two

If Nature hold another heart
That knows a purer flame than we   10
I too therein would challenge part
And learn of love a new degree

                         1829[?] || *PN*, p. 69

VI.

Emerson wrote this and the next poem in Pepperell, Massachusetts, while stopping briefly during an excursion to Springfield with Ellen, her mother, and her sister.

Dear Ellen, many a golden year
May ripe, then dim, thy beauty's bloom
But never shall the hour appear

In sunny joy, in sorrow's gloom,
When aught shall hinder me from telling   5
My ardent love, all loves excelling.

The spot is not in the rounded earth,
In cities vast, in islands lone,
Where I will not proclaim thy worth,
And glory that thou art mine own;   10
Will you, nill you, I'll say I love thee,
Be the moon of June or of March above thee.

And when this porcelain clay of thine
Is laid beneath the cold earth's flowers,
And close beside reposes mine,   15
Prey to the sun & air & showers,
I'll find thy soul in the upper sphere,
And say I love thee in Paradise here.

September 11, 1829 || *PN*, p. 10

VII.

Emerson begins to experiment with the quatrain form and hymn stanza, influenced by Ellen's verse (see *OFL*, pp. 147–168) and by the hymns he selected each Sunday for the worship service. "Beauty" (l. 18) was one of Emerson's affectionate names for Ellen (*JMN* 3:146). This poem was also written at Pepperell.

I call her beautiful;—she says
Go to; your words are idle;
My lips began to speak her praise,
My lips she tried to bridle.
But, Ellen, I must tell you this,   5
Your prohibition wasted is,
Unless among your things you find
A little jail to hold the mind;
If you should dazzle out mine eyes,
As dimmer suns sometimes have done,   10

My sleepless ears, those judges wise,
Would say, Tis the *voice* of the Peerless one.
And if your witchery decree
That my five senses closed should be,
The little image in my soul   15
Is Ellen out of Ellen's controul,
And whilst I live in the Universe
I will say 'tis my beauty, for better, for worse.

September 11, 1829 || *PN*, pp. 10–11

VIII.

And Ellen, when the greybeard years
Have brought us to life's Evening hour
And all the crowded Past appears
A tiny scene of sun & shower.———

Then, if I read the page aright   5
Where Hope the soothsayer reads our lot,
Thyself shalt own the page was bright[.]
Well that we loved   wo had we not.

When Mirth is dumb & Flattery's fled   10
And thy mute music's dearest tone
When all but Love itself is dead,
And all but deathless Reason gone

February 1830 || *JMN* 3:181–182

IX.

In the spring of 1830 Ellen's health took a turn for the worse, and on
March 9 she and Waldo and Ellen's sister Margaret departed for Phila-
delphia in search of warmer weather. By the time they got to New York,
Ellen, now "very weak," was coughing up blood (*L* 1:296). Emerson
saw to it that she was comfortably situated in Philadelphia, where she
would be joined by her mother and "troops of friends" (*L* 1:299; Pom-
mer, p. 40). At the end of the month Emerson returned to Boston alone.
The ensuing six weeks' separation would be the longest of their mar-
riage.

I am alone. Sad is my solitude.
O thou sweet daughter of God, my angel wife,
Why dost thou leave me thus in the great stranger world
Without one sign or token, one remembrancer
Sent o'er the weary lands that sunder us   5
To say I greet thee with a beating heart.
Does thy heart beat with mine? does thy blue eye
Ever look northward with desire, O do thy prayers
Remember me when thou hallowest thy maker's name,
Remember him   10
Who never failed to grace his orison
With thy dear name, believes it acceptable
And prays,   that he may pray for thee—

ca. April 1830 || *OFL*, p. 127

X.

TO ELLEN,

AT THE SOUTH

Like "To Eva," this poem was published in the *Dial* (January 1843) and
collected in *Poems* (1847). Line 11 recalls the couple's trip to the Shaker
community at Canterbury, New Hampshire, in August 1829. Early in
April 1830, Emerson reported to his brother Edward, "There is little nat-
ural beauty I think in the environs of Phil—the little wildflowers look as
if Dame Quaker rather than Dame Nature had arranged them and
hardly condescend to nodd [sic] to Zephyrus as he passes by" (*OFL*,
p. 128).

The green grass is bowing,
    The morning wind is in it;
'Tis a tune worth thy knowing,
    Though it change every minute.

'Tis a tune of the spring;   5
    Every year plays it over
To the robin on the wing,
    And to the pausing lover.

O'er ten thousand thousand acres
    Goes light the nimble zephyr;   10
The Flowers—tiny sect of Shakers—
    Worship him ever.

Hark to the winning sound!
    They summon thee, dearest,—
Saying, 'We have dressed for thee the ground,   15
    Nor yet thou appearest.

'O hasten; 'tis our time,
    Ere yet the red Summer
Scorch our delicate prime,
    Loved of bee,—the tawny hummer.   20

'O pride of thy race!
    Sad, in sooth, it were to ours,
If our brief tribe miss thy face,
    We poor New England flowers.

'Fairest, choose the fairest members   25
    Of our lithe society;
June's glories and September's
    Show our love and piety.

'Thou shalt command us all,—
    April's cowslip, summer's clover,   30
To the gentian in the fall,
    Blue-eyed pet of blue-eyed lover.

'O come, then, quickly come!
    We are budding, we are blowing;
And the wind that we perfume   35
    Sings a tune that's worth the knowing.'

April 1830 || 1843

XI.

THINE EYES STILL SHINED

Thine eyes still shined for me, though far
    I lonely roved the land or sea:
As I behold yon evening star,
    Which yet beholds not me.

This morn I climbed the misty hill,   5
    And roamed the pastures through;
How danced thy form before my path
    Amidst the deep-eyed dew!

When the redbird spread his sable wing,
    And showed his side of flame;   10
When the rosebud ripened to the rose,
    In both I read thy name.

April 1830 || 1846

XII.

And though he dearly prized the bards of fame
His sweetest poem was one maiden's name

ca. April–May 1830 || *PN*, p. 61; *TN* 3:345

XIII.

The following was written a week after Ellen died. This poem and the next occupy consecutive pages in the journal.

Dost thou not hear me Ellen
Is thy ear deaf to me
Is thy radiant eye
Dark that it cannot see

In yonder ground thy limbs are laid   5
Under the snow

And earth has no spot so dear above
As that below

And there I know the heart is still
And the eye is shut & the ear is dull   10

But the spirit that dwelt in mine
The spirit wherein mine dwelt
The soul of Ellen the thought divine
From God, that came—for all that felt

Does it not know me now   15
Does it not share my thought
Is it prisoned from Waldo's prayer
Is its glowing love forgot

February 15, 1831 || *JMN* 3:228

XIV.

Teach me I am forgotten by the dead
And that the dead is by herself forgot   20
And I no longer would keep terms with me.
I would not murder, steal, or fornicate,
Nor with ambition break the peace of towns
But I would bury my ambition
The hope & action of my sovereign soul
In miserable ruin. Not a hope
Should ever make a holiday for me
I would not be the fool of accident
I would not have a project seek an end
That needed aught
Beyond the handful of my present means
The sun of Duty drop from his firmament
To be a rushlight for each petty end
I would not harm my fellow men
On this low argument, *'twould harm myself*

February 15[?], 1831 || *JMN* 3:228–229

XV.

What from this barren being do we reap
And what shall hinder the wise
From lying down to sleep in the earth
The innocent child is dead
The blushing cheek of youth is cold   5
Genius hath untimely fled
Nor hath the world a face
To fill thy vacant place
O radiant daughter of light & love
Too rich in the graces that dwell above   10
To be lent long to the sinful earth
God had garnished with thy birth.
Thou wert pure as they are not
Who dwell upon this murky spot
And every thing that's fair below.   15

February 1831 || *JMN* 3:232

XVI.

Ellen's death was a decisive challenge to Emerson's conventionally Christian view of the afterlife. Their communion, in which love and language had certainly made them one, was broken in ways that Emerson struggled to understand.

Shalt thou go to thy grave unsung
Shall no flower be plucked for thee
Shall no rites be paid no death bell rung
When the desire of all eyes is gone
'Tis well for we   5
Are on the outside of that world
Wherein thou enterest fair & free
And all the rites we pay
Are symbols bodily
Gropings in the dark   10
Around the door
Thou art gone in to God

Thou walkest in heaven's day
Thou talkest with the seraphim
The select sons of truth   15
Thou addest a verse to their hymn
And curious speculation occupies
Thy radiant eyes
Every thought fresh wonders brings
On his planetary wings   20
And every thought is a chapel where
Thou perfumest heaven with prayer
And the eldest born of Godhead say
What star beams new on us today
And yet thou hast a bond on earth   25
Which thou wilt keep in heaven
The nearer to the throne thou goest
The more place it will have in thy holy breast.

February 1831 || *JMN* 3:232–233

XVII.

Dust unto dust! and shall no more be said
Ellen for thee, and shall a common fate
Blend thy last hour with the last hours of all?
Of thee my wife, my undefiled, my dear?
The muse thy living beauty could inspire   5
Shall spare one verse to strew thy urn
Or be forever silent. Ellen is dead
She who outshone all beauty yet knew not
That she was beautiful, she who was fair
After another mould than flesh & blood.   10
Her beauty was of God—The maker's hand
Yet rested on his work,
And cast an atmosphere of sanctity
Around her steps that pleased old age & youth.
Yea that not won the eye, but did persuade   15
The soul by realizing human hopes,
Teaching that faith & love were not a dream,
Teaching that purity had yet a shrine,

And that the innocent & affectionate thoughts
That harbour in the bosom of a child   20
Might live embodied in a riper form,
And dwell with wisdom never bought by sin.
Blessed, sweet singer, were the ears that heard
To her, the eye that saw, bare witness.
The holy light of her eye did prophesy   25
The impatient heaven that called her hence.

February 1831 || *JMN* 3:235

XVIII.

The following appears to be an Easter meditation. The Latin phrase means "Welcome, day of salvation!"

Salve dies Salutis————The holy day is come to the sad wanderer from a sad home And he sends up his sighs, for other cause for other vanities than he mourned yesterday; o rather let him now repress Heart's anguish & sin's distress And in his soul this solemn morn Let the son of God be born. Howbeit high God who made the heart, And made the object of its love, So that death cannot make them part but I below love her above Clothed her in grace with this intent, And filled our souls with mutual fires That we should outlive his firmament And still relume these dear desires—He never meant his Sabbath day should fright the heart's yearnings away but by the light the gospel shed And o'er creation's face outspread—the Resurrection of the dead

April 3, 1831 [?] || *JMN* 3:234

XIX.

Emerson wrote these lines in the Berkshires, near Williamstown, Massachusetts, during a trip with his brother Charles to Burlington, Vermont.

Why fear to die
And let thy body lie
Under the flowers of June

Thy body food
For the groundworm's brood   5
And thy grave smiled on by the visiting moon

Amid great Nature's halls,
Girt in by mountain walls,
And washed with waterfalls,
It would please me to die,   10
Where every wind that sweeps my tomb
Goes loaded with a free perfume,
Dealt out with a God's charity.

I should like to lie in sweets,
A hill's leaves for winding sheets,   15
And the searching sun to see
That I'm laid with decency
And the commissioned wind to sing
His mighty Psalm from fall to spring
And annual tunes commemorate   20
Of nature's child the common fate.

June 1, 1831 || *PN,* pp. 36–37

XX.

The days pass over me,
And I am still the same;
The aroma of my life is gone
With the flower with which it came.

ca. June 20, 1831 || *PN,* p. 47

XXI.

All the great & good,
And all the fair,
As if in a disdainful mood,
Forsake the world, & to the grave repair.

Is there a sage   5
Needed to curb the unruly times;—

He hastes to quit the stage,
And blushing leaves his country to its crimes.

Is there an angel drest
In weeds of mortal beauty, whom high Heaven   10
With all sweet perfections doth invest;—
It hastes to take what it hath given.

And, as the delicate snow
Which latest fell, the thieving wind first takes
So thou, dear wife, must go,   15
As frail, as spotless, as those new fallen flakes.

Let me not fear to die,
But let me live so well,
As to win this mark of death from on high,
That I with God, & thee, dear heart, may dwell.   20

July 6, 1831 || *PN*, pp. 14–15

XXII.

   Leave me, Fear! thy throbs are base,
Trembling for the body's sake.
Come, Love! who dost the spirit raise,
Because for others thou dost wake.
O it is beautiful in death   5
To hide the shame of human nature's end
In sweet & wary serving of a friend.
Love is true Glory's field, where the last breath
Expires in troops of honorable cares.
   The wound of Fate the hero cannot feel   10
Smit with the heavenlier smart of social zeal.
It draws immortal day
In soot & ashes of our clay.
It is the virtue that enchants it.
It is the face of God that haunts it.   15

1831 || *PN*, p. 342

XXIII.

Where art thou
Thou beautiful dream
Whom every grace & every joy
Clothed in sunbeams dearest best,
Whom every fleeting hour in new graces drest   5
And every wondering eye that saw thee blest

Where art thou now
Sad I miss thy beaming brow
I miss thy radiant eye
The joyful noon of my life is past   10
My sun is set my moon is gone
Each star of hope sunk one by one
And in this cold damp silent eve of life
I walk alone, oh Ellen, oh my wife.

One by one those graces come   15
Day by day to memory's eye
Which thou worest as a robe
And I live over thy history
Thy thots were wove in beauty
Wisdom drest in dewbright flowers;   20
And sad & sportive hours
Had swelled alike the potent melody

1831 || MH MS Am 1280.235(39)

XXIV.

She never comes to me
She promised me a thousand times
That she would dearly dearly love me
That in sickness & in health
Others present others absent   5
Whilst air was round & heaven above me
She would be present as my life
My holy gentle tender wife

She promised in my secret ear
When none by God & I could hear   10
That she would cleave to me forever
There was one will between us
There was one heart within us
And God upon his children smiled
As we the hours with love beguiled   15

And now I am alone
Unheard I moan
She never comes to me
Sits never by my side
I never hear her voice   20
She comes not even to my dreams
O Ellen

And comes she not
Ask thy heart, Waldo.
Doth she break her word   25
Doth not her love embrace thee yet
Even from the Spirits' land?

September 19, 1831 || *JMN* 3:285–286

XXV.

What avails it me
That I have many friends
If when my walking ends
I come back to a lonely house

What boots it that I dwell   5
In a city free & rich & old
If the long streets never hold
The only form I love

What avails it I have bread
Raiment & books & leisure   10
Access to wisdom & to pleasure
If Ellen still is dead

In my chamber she is not
From my parlour joy is gone
Round the house I roam & groan   15
The glory of my house is fled

What avails it me
That I have many thoughts
That the nimble brain can run
Through all lands that see the sun   20
Hath a record of each race
That have had a dwelling place

If only I have right of seeing
In this wilderness of being
And from the vision glorious   25
Must come back to my lonely house

December 1831 || MH MS Am 1280.235(91)

NOTES

THE SPHINX

9 Emerson's first readers would have heard in the term "man-child" an allusion to Revelation 12:5, where that mystical figure is born to "the woman clothed with the sun"; i.e., is the offspring of Christ and the Church and destined to "rule all the nations."

12 In Greek mythology Dædalus was a gifted artificer, creating with such cunning and intricacy as to rival nature; he was also the architect of the Labyrinth of Minos on Crete, which concealed the Minotaur.

77 Lethe: The river of forgetfulness, which the dead crossed on their way to Hades.

107 Rue, myrrh, and cummin are aromatic substances used for medicinal purposes. Arthur E. Bestor identified Emerson's source as Edmund Spenser's *Muiopotmos, or the Fate of the Butterflie* (l. 188): "Ranke smelling Rue, and Cummin good for eyes."

128 Monadnoc, a mountain in southern New Hampshire: see Emerson's poem of that title.

EACH AND ALL

1 Cf. Emerson's 1834 reminiscence of something he saw in Italy the year before: "The shepherd or the beggar in his red cloak little knows what charm he gives to the whole landscape that charms you on the mountain top . . . & I no more the part my individuality plays in the All" (*JMN* 4:345–346). Clown: a peasant, or rustic.

5–8 Based on an anecdote of Napoleon's Italian campaign from Louis A. F. de Bourienne, *Private Memoirs of Napoleon Bonaparte* (1830), 2:33–34 (see *JMN* 9:135), or from John Kidd, *On the Adaptation of External Nature to the Physical Condition of Man* (1833), p. 143.

12 "The river flowed brimful & I philosophised upon this composite collective beauty which refuses to be analysed. Nothing is beautiful alone. Nothing but is beautiful in the Whole" (*JMN* 5:26; March 28, 1835).

19–28 "I remember when I was a boy going upon the beach & being charmed with the colors & forms of the shells. I picked up many & put them in my pocket. When I got home I could find nothing that I gathered—nothing but some dry ugly mussel & snail shells. Thence I learned that Composition was more important than the beauty of individual forms to effect. On the shore they lay wet & social by the sea & under the sky" (*JMN* 4:292; May 16, 1834 [cf. *EL* 1:73–74]).

29–36 These lines were probably added in 1837 or 1838, after the poem was otherwise finished. They appear to be based on a journal entry of April 12, 1837: "In life all finding is not that thing we sought, but something else. The lover on being accepted, misses the wildest charm of the maid he dared not hope to call his own. The husband loses the wife in the cares of the household" (*JMN* 5:297).

THE PROBLEM

10 Phidias (ca. 480–430 BCE), Greek sculptor, responsible for the statue of Jove in the temple at Elis, one of the seven wonders of the ancient world, and for much of the Parthenon (see l. 33). On April 11, 1839, Emerson wrote, "That is the best part of each [artist] which he does not know, that which flowed out of his constitution, & not from what he called his talents. . . . Phidias it is not but the work of Man in that early Hellenic World that I would know. The name & circumstance of Phidias, however convenient for history, embarrasses merely when we come to the highest criticism. We are to see that which Man was tending to do in a given period & was hindered or . . . modified in doing by the interfering volitions of Phidias, of Dante, of Shakspear, the Organ whereby Man at the moment wrought" (*JMN* 7:185; cf. "Compensation," *CW* 2:63).

12 Seat of the oracle of Apollo near Mount Parnassus in Greece.

19 Michelangelo Buonarroti was the principal architect of the cathedral of Saint Peter at the Vatican in Rome.

32 "Love & fear laid the stones in their own order": said by Emerson of the great European cathedrals (*JMN* 5:196; September 20, 1836).

44 The Andes are a mountain range in South America, Ararat a mountainous region in Turkey, where, according to Genesis 8:4, Noah's ark came to rest.

51–54 As described in Acts 2, the Holy Ghost on the day of Pentecost imparted his Spirit to the Apostles in tongues of flame and facilitated prophecy by making them intelligible to all despite the diversity of the auditors' native languages.

55–56 Reference to Moses' breaking of the tablets on which the Ten Commandments had been inscribed: see Exodus 32:19.

65 Saint John (ca. 347–407), archbishop of Constantinople, called Chrysostom (or "Golden Mouth") for his eloquence. Saint Augustine, bishop of Hippo (354–430), author of the *Confessions* and *Meditations*.

68 Jeremy Taylor (1613–1667), chaplain to Archbishop William Laud, became

himself bishop of Down and Connor after the restoration of the monarchy in 1660. "I have thought him a Christian Plato; so rich & great was his philosophy" (*JMN* 6:68).

THE VISIT

27 Saturn is the Roman name for the Greek god Kronos, or time. To be saturnine, or under the astrological influence of Saturn, is to be glum and taciturn.

URIEL

1–4 In the creation myth as given in the apocryphal 2 Enoch, God speaks of the interval after the seven days ("which revolve in the form of seven thousand"): "At the beginning of the eighth thousand I appointed an uncounted time, an infinity, unmeasured by years, months, weeks, days, or hours" (Barnstone, p. 6).

5 Uriel (meaning the fire of God and associated with the sun), together with Michael, Gabriel, and Raphael, comprised the four principal archangels. Of these Uriel is the only one not mentioned in the canonical books of the Bible, appearing instead in such apocryphal works as Enoch and 2 Esdras. In the latter he appears to the prophet Esdras (Ezra) as a Sphinx-like riddler. Popular veneration of Uriel was suppressed by the medieval pope Zachary and the Renaissance pope Clement III, who banned the angel's images because of his role in heretical narratives that identified John the Baptist as the Messiah. Milton made Uriel an important figure in Book III of *Paradise Lost,* describing him as "The sharpest-sighted Spirit of all in Heav'n" (l. 691).

7 The seven daughters of Atlas were set into the heavens as stars by Jove, known thereafter as a star-cluster in the constellation Taurus.

8 A variant spelling of Saadi, one of Emerson's favorite Sufi poets: here, perhaps, taken as a name for himself.

21 "There is no line that does not return; I suppose the mathematicians will tell us that . . . straight lines are lines with long curves, but that there is no straight line in nature" (*JMN* 8:339; February 1843); cf. "Extremes meet: there is no straight line" (*JMN* 8:397; May 1843).

27 With the phrase "stern old war-gods" Emerson characterizes the militant defenders of religious orthodoxy, and principally his most outraged critic, Andrews Norton (1786–1853), who had retired as Harvard's Dexter Professor of Sacred Literature in 1830, but who still protected the Divinity School from young heretics.

39–40 "Every partial soul must make periods of ascents from, and descents into generation, and . . . this must be unceasing through an infinite time" (*The Six Books of Proclus,* trans. Thomas Taylor, 2 vols. [London, 1816], 2:438).

41–42 Cf. Milton, "Il Penseroso": "Hail divinest Melancholy, / Whose visage is too bright / To hit the sense of human sight" (ll. 12–14).

ALPHONSO OF CASTILE

26 Pan: the goatish god of the woodland, of pastoral nature and mountaintops; a figure of enlivening power, given to ambushes. "I love the wood god. I love the mighty PAN" (*JMN* 5:179). See also the note to "Woodnotes II," line 331.

MITHRIDATES

7 Cantharids (more properly cantharides) are a species of beetle, or Spanish Fly, crushed and used as a poison or as an aphrodisiac.

17 Hydrocyanic acid, from which the toxic salt cyanide (potassium cyanide) is made.

18–19 The tropical upas tree *(antiaris toxicaria)* is notoriously poisonous ("upas" is the Javanese word for "poison"). It provides a habitat for bats, which spread the seeds of the tree.

HAMATREYA

1 Names of the first settlers of Concord, Massachusetts, who arrived at the town site in 1635. Peter Bulkeley (pronounced Buckley), who as minister led the company, was Emerson's lineal ancestor. Emerson spoke of Concord's early history in his 1835 *Historical Discourse . . . on the Second Centennial Anniversary of the . . . Town* (*CW* 10:17–54).

5 "The Hindoo said, You are enveloped in the deceptions of matter. You call *'me'* that which is not yourself, and you call *'mine'* that which is flowing away from you. These illusions are the two branches of the tree of ignorance" (*LL* 2:267).

8 Flags are aquatic plants, like cattails or reeds, with blade-like leaves.

17–18 An 1852 journal entry makes the anti-imperialist implication clear: "The farmer said, he should like to have all the land that joined his own. Bonaparte who had the same appetite, endeavoured to make the Mediterranean a French lake. The Russian czar Alexander was more expansive, & wished to call the Pacific *My ocean*. . . . But if he got the earth for his cowpasture & the sea for his fishpond, he would be a pauper still. He only is rich who owns the day" (*JMN* 13:90).

25–26 Emerson had a more definite sense of his fleeting hold on the Concord landscape: "When I must leave land, house, & Lidian, / Of all my planted trees & shade / Will none but funeral firs & cypresses / Follow their shortlived lord" (*TN* 3:355).

THE RHODORA

7 The scarlet tanager migrates in May to its breeding grounds in the northeast United States. Because it habitually forages high in the trees, it is said often to go unobserved.

10 Cf. Thomas Gray, "Elegy in a Country Churchyard" (1751): "Full many a flower is born to blush unseen, / And waste its sweetness on the desert air" (ll. 55–56), and Edward Young, "Satire V" from *The Love of Fame* (1728): "In distant wilds, by human eyes unseen, / She rears her flowers, and spreads her velvet green; / Pure gurgling rills the lonely desert trace, / And waste their music on the savage race" (ll. 230–233).

11–12 One of the first important deployments in Emerson of imagery relating to eyes and eyesight, signaling a new attention to the role of the observer, this passage was likely influenced by the Cambridge Platonist Ralph Cudworth: "The eye, whose structure and fabric consisting of many parts (humours and membranes), is so artificially [i.e., artfully] composed, no reasonable person . . . can think otherwise of it, but that it was made out of design for the use of seeing; and did not happen accidentally to be so made, and then the use of seeing follow. . . . [E]yes were made for the sake of seeing, and ears for the sake of hearing" (3:284).

THE HUMBLE-BEE

2 Climate.

3 During the antebellum period sufferers from tuberculosis often sought relief in traveling to Puerto Rico. Among these were Emerson's brothers Charles and Edward; Edward died there in 1834. When "The Humble-Bee" was written, Emerson's own health was precarious, and he thought of making a similar trip (*L* 2:83).

38 "Syrian peace" may refer to the Hebrew Bible's representation of Canaan (or Syria) as "a land of milk and honey," or perhaps to the enervating climate of the extensive Syrian Desert.

48 Emerson recorded Thoreau's opinion that "the adderstongue arethusa smells exactly like a snake" (*TN* 1:56).

BERRYING

2 The phrase, from Deuteronomy 32:10, was appropriated by New England's Puritan settlers to convey their antagonistic sense of nature in the New World.

7 Perhaps a recollection of Keats, *Endymion,* II, lines 412–413: "the ivy mesh, / Shading its Ethiop berries."

10 According to Puritan (Calvinist) doctrine, only a fraction of mankind would be among the "elect": those who experienced saving grace, a free, unmerited, and arbitrary gift of God.

THE SNOW-STORM

1–9 John Greenleaf Whittier chose these lines as the epigraph for his popular *Snow-Bound* (1866).

18 The fine white marble from the isle of Paros, favored by Greek and Roman sculptors.

WOODNOTES II

13–48 Struck through in Emerson's correction copy and omitted in *Selected Poems* (1876). Waggoner, *Emerson as Poet,* p. 76, argued that this excision of the most irregular lines weakened the poem.

52 A scrip is a bag, originally a pilgrim's knapsack; a canister is a metal container, sometimes used to store communion wafers before consecration.

85–86 Emerson boasts of the commercial and cultural leadership of New England and of the advantages it brings to other regions of the country.

161 In an early journal Emerson slightly misquoted a line from *The Excursion* by William Wordsworth: "To hear the mighty stream of Tendency" (*JMN* 3:80). In his note at this point (*W* 9:422–423), Edward Emerson alludes to his father's interest in the nebular hypothesis, first enunciated by the Swedish scientist and theologian Emanuel Swedenborg (1688–1772), and subsequently developed by Pierre-Simon Laplace (1749–1827), the French scientist associated with the field of celestial mechanics.

162 The *OED* cites no use of the term "star-dust" before 1844.

167–170 "Metamorphosis is nature. The foetus does not more strive to be man than yonder bur of light we call a nebula tends to be a ring, a comet, a solid globe, a sun, & the parent of new stars" (*JMN* 7:428; used in "The Method of Nature," *CW* 1:126).

197–198 Emerson's awkward syntactical inversion obscures the meaning, which is that the universe understands the pine tree's incantations or "runes" (cf. l. 222). Emerson uses the same trope in "Monadnoc" at line 260.

200 See Acts 2:1–6.

222 In 1850 Emerson wrote: "I praised the rhymes of sun & shade, man & maid, in my Woodnotes. But how far that can be carried! inasmuch as every substance is only the reflection or rhyme of some truth" (*JMN* 11:271).

296 "The great Pan of old, who was clothed in a leopard skin to signify the beautiful variety of things, and the firmament, his coat of stars,—was but the representative of thee, O rich and various Man! thou palace of sight and sound, carrying in thy senses the morning and the night and the unfathomable galaxy; in thy brain, the geometry of the City of God; in thy heart, the bower of love and the realms of right and wrong" ("Method of Nature," *CW* 1:127).

331ff According to Bacon's account in *The Wisdom of the Ancients,* Pan represents "universal nature" (p. 248). Further, "that Pan is the second messenger of the gods after Mercury is plainly a divine allegory; since, next to the word of God, the image of the universe itself is the masterpiece of divine wisdom" (p. 255). See also Anderson.

372 Metest: measure.

379 Spar: any of several lustrous minerals, such as feldspar.

MONADNOC

19 Oreads: the mountain nymphs of Greek mythology.

95–97 The opposition of the Welsh bards to the English king Edward I, together with their connection to Mount Snowdon, the highest peak in Great Britain, is described in "The Bard: A Pindaric Ode" by Thomas Gray (1757). The topic is also treated by Felicia Hemans in "Chant of the Bards before Their Massacre by Edward I" (1822), and by Henry Gilpin in *The Massacre of the Bards* (1839). Rob Roy, title character of Walter Scott's popular 1817 novel, was a Highland chieftain, outlaw, and Jacobite. Gjevgj Kastrioti Scanderbeg (1405–1486), called "the Dragon of Albania," took up arms against the Ottomans. William Tell, of the Canton of Uri, fought against the Habsburg Empire in the fourteenth century, in a conflict that led to the Swiss Confederation.

118–124 The critical depiction of the locals probably derives from Emerson's 1839 trip to the White Mountains of northern New Hampshire (see *L* 2:220), rather than from his 1846 trip to Monadnoc in the south.

219 The constellation Lyra dominated by the bright star Vega.

228 For Pan, see note to "Woodnotes II," line 331.

255–256 John Tyndall, the eminent nineteenth-century British physicist, was fond of quoting these, along with many other lines of Emerson's poetry, to illustrate his scientific observations and arguments. See *L* 10:16–18, and Haugrud.

269 Mount Zion, on which the Temple at Jerusalem is located; Mount Meru, the center of the world in Hindu and Buddhist lore, home of Brahma.

316–318 "When he [the poet] spoke of the stars, he should be innocent of what he said; for it seemed that the stars, as they rolled over him, mirrored themselves in his mind as in a deep well, & it was their image & not his thought that you saw" (*JMN* 9:27; 1843). In 1845 Emerson described to Caroline Sturgis the effect of looking out from the summit of Mount Wachusett: "At once all is changed, & all assumes a planetary air, & I begin to see the shining of it, when a little further withdrawn, like Mars & Jupiter" (*L* 8:18).

320 Specular: affording an extensive view.

322 Plumule: down feather.

362–367 Monadnoc's unusually low tree line was artificially created when, early in the century, sheepherders fired the mountaintop in an effort to eradicate wolves. The summit burned for three weeks. Thoreau learned these facts in 1852 (*Journal,* 5:339). Emerson seems not to have known the story when he wrote the poem, though he alluded to it in his 1861 lecture "Boston" (*W* 12:191).

367 Ceres: goddess of agriculture.

369–370 In a journal entry of June 27, 1846, Emerson invoked the symbolic character of Monadnoc, calling it a "grand expressor of the present tense; of permanence" (*JMN* 9:432–433; see the discussion of this passage in *CW* 9:lviii–lx, and cf. ll. 413–414 below).

ODE, INSCRIBED TO W. H. CHANNING

3–6 In 1844, the year of his first major antislavery address, Emerson wrote in his journal, "I do not & can not forsake my vocation for abolitionism" (*JMN* 9:64n).

7–9 "What satire on government can equal the severity of censure conveyed in the word *politic,* which now for ages has signified cunning, intimating that the State is a trick?" ("Politics," *CW* 3:122).

10–11 "At times the whole world seems to be in conspiracy to importune you with emphatic trifles. Friend, client, child, sickness, fear, want, charity, all knock at once at thy closet door and say,—'Come out unto us.' But keep thy state; come not into their confusion" ("Self-Reliance," *CW* 2:41).

15 The blindworm, native to Europe and west Asia, looks like a snake but is actually a lizard.

21–22 Contoocook: a river in New Hampshire. Agiochook: Algonquin name for Mount Washington.

24 "In New Hampshire the dignity of the landscape made more obvious the meanness of the tavern-haunting men" (*JMN* 7:236; September 1839). Since the "Ode" was written at Mount Monadnoc in June 1846 (as the manuscript attests), Emerson probably had in mind his unfavorable impressions of people he had met elsewhere in the state on previous occasions. It has been suggested that the poem's geography involves a veiled allusion to New Hampshire native Daniel Webster (1782–1852), notorious by 1850 for supporting the Fugitive Slave Bill. However, in 1845–46, Webster, as senator from Massachusetts, was opposing Texas annexation and the Mexican War, just as Emerson was. It is more likely, then, as Len Gougeon has suggested ("The Anti-Slavery Background," p. 76), that Emerson's disapproving reference is to the state's Democratic, proslavery electorate rather than to any particular politician.

31 In certain ancient fables, crocodiles were said to shed tears, either to lure humans to their death or while devouring them.

41 The monument at Bunker Hill, commemorating an important early battle in the Revolutionary War, is visible from Boston Bay, then the hub of Northern commercial shipping.

45 Neat: cattle.

50–51 "If a man live in the saddle the saddle somehow will come to live in him" (*JMN* 7:102).

52–54 "Things have their laws, as well as men" ("Politics," *CW* 3:120).

57 This idea was familiar to the New England Puritans. See, for instance, Urian Oakes's *Seasonable Discourse* (Cambridge, Mass., 1682): "Man is dethroned, and become a servant and slave to those things that were made to serve him, and he puts those things in his heart, that God hath put under his feet" (p. 27). Cf. Matthew 6:20–21 and Luke 12:33–34.

58 Emerson grudgingly reconciled himself to the new railroad that snaked through Walden woods: it "was very odious to me when it began, but it is hard to resist the joy of all one's neighbours, and I must be contented to be carted like a chattel in the cars & be glad to see the forest fall. This rushing on your journey is plainly a capital invention for our spacious America, but it is more dignified & manlike to walk barefoot" (*CEC*, p. 355).

77 Issues: i.e., outcomes.

77–85 Emerson's views on race generally aligned with his proto-Darwinian thoughts on natural selection, as was the case with several other thinkers of this period (see Walls, chap. 5). Several years after writing the "Ode," Emerson reworked these lines in a quatrain he never published ("With the key of the secret," *W* 9:357; *PN*, p. 972). He was prompted to do so by a coinciding remark of Karl Marx's that he found in the New York *Tribune* on March 22, 1853: "The classes and the races too weak to master the new conditions of life must give way" (*JMN* 13:127). As Walls and Gougeon point out, Emerson's position is more precisely indicated in the caveat that ultimately it is the weakness and not the race that "must give way."

86–87 Samson's encounter with the lion at Timnah is narrated in Judges 14:5–9.

90 Russia occupied and partitioned Poland in the late eighteenth century, while as recently as 1830 a popular uprising had been decisively quelled. In the New York *Tribune* of December 1, 1845, Margaret Fuller reported on a gathering to commemorate the fifteenth anniversary of the revolt, attended by Felix Paul Wierzbicki, whose own series of articles in *The American Whig Review* in 1846 may likewise have influenced Emerson (see *CW* 9:152–153). "Nature is always gainer, & reckons surely on our sympathy. The Russians eat up the Poles. What then? when the last Polander is gone, the Russians are men, are ourselves, & the Pole is forgotten in our identification with Russian parties. A philosopher is no philosopher unless he takes lively part with the thief who picks his pocket and with the bully that insults or strikes him" (*JMN* 9:383; cf. *CW* 9:153).

ASTRÆA

2 Quartered: divided a heraldic shield (in a coat of arms) into four equal parts to show lineage.

6 More correctly, cap-à-pie, meaning armed head to foot.

18 Cf. Mark 8:27, where Jesus asks his disciples, "Whom do men say that I am?"

ÉTIENNE DE LA BOÉCE

21–22 John S. Harrison explained the couplet in terms of the philosophy of Plotinus, who, in "On Suicide," said of the mystic devotee that "he will be ignorant of the manner in which he sees it [the One]; but the vision filling the eyes with light, will prevent him from seeing anything else, since the light itself will be the object of his vision." Harrison comments, "It is an experience in which the traveler, or the soul of the devotee, the errand, or the vision of the One, and the road, or the light from the One, are one" (pp. 162–163). The couplet was a late addition to the poem, belonging to the stage of its final revision in 1846 (*CW* 9:157–158).

COMPENSATION

7 The "silent throngs" are presumably the audience at the Second Church in their Sabbath sedateness, imagined as boisterous street demonstrators during the week.

8 In 1837 Margaret Fuller had a manuscript copy of the poem that read in the last line "their turn has come" (*CW* 9:162; *PN*, pp. 762–763).

FORBEARANCE

2 I.e., any wild rose found in the woods; "wood-rose" was not, in 1842, the name of any particular variety.

3 Pulse is a porridge of peas or beans; humble fare.

THE PARK

9 This line is associated with the first draft of the poem "Manners," written in August 1841 (see below and *JMN* 7:510–511). It seems there to have arisen from a journal entry made two months earlier, on June 6: "The chief is the chief all the world over, & not his hat or shoes, his land, his title or his purse. He who knows the most,—he who knows what sweets & virtues are in the ground beneath him, the waters before him, the plants around him, the heavens above him,—he is the enchanter, he is the rich & the royal man" (*JMN* 7:454). This passage is immediately followed by an appreciation of the park-like satisfactions of nature, revealed to him by Thoreau during an evening's boating on the Concord River.

FORERUNNERS

4 A leaguer is an encampment of besieging forces. The word survives as metaphor in the term "beleaguered."

GIVE ALL TO LOVE

18 Mean: middling, common, or mediocre in character. The modern sense of "cruel" had not yet arisen, according to the *OED*.

43–49 Used as an epigraph to Rudyard Kipling's story "Children of the Zodiac," which itself interprets the entire poem.

48–49 "The beloved is the half-god, and the god is love itself directed toward impersonal ideals" (Yoder, p. 128).

INITIAL, DÆMONIC, AND CELESTIAL LOVE

1 The motif of the "hue and cry after Cupid" was first developed by Moschus around 150 BCE in his first Idyll, "The Runaway Love." Important later treatments include Edmund Spenser, *The Faerie Queene*, III, vi, and Ben Jonson, *The Hue and Cry after Cupid* (1608), as well as the "Cupid's Conflict" by Henry More, mentioned in the headnote.

39ff. Strauch ("Emerson's Adaptation of Myth," p. 57) connects these lines with an 1838 journal entry: "Eyes are bold as lions [—] roving, running, leaping here & there; far, near; they wait for no introduction, they ask not leave of age or rank. They respect neither poverty nor riches[,] neither learning nor power nor virtue nor Sex but intrude & pierce & come again & go through & through you in a moment of time. . . . The power of eyes to charm down insanity or ferocity in beasts is a power behind the eye[;] it must be a victory first achieved in the will before it can be signified in the eye" (*JMN* 7:52). See also the note to line 65.

50 In its entry for "tort," the *OED* condemns "tortest" as "an erroneous variant of tautest," yet in its entry for "taut," it cites this line, without objection, to illustrate a variant spelling. In either form the word is associated with nautical contexts.

65 Clairvoyance: the paranormal ability of remote seeing. This is the earliest recorded American use of the term, according to the *OED*. In the 1840s clairvoyance was associated with mesmerism, one of the "occult sciences."

108 A Pundit is a Hindu scholar, originally one who advised British colonial officials on points of Indian law.

122 Sovran: The *OED* identifies this form as John Milton's spelling of "sovereign" and its use as "chiefly poetic."

232 The *OED*, defining "fringent" as "Exercising friction," cites no example of its application but this by Emerson. Before the *OED* was published, Gamaliel Bradford, Jr., condemned Emerson's use of the term as, probably, "a fault of style, though the dictionary gives me no clue to what it means" ("Emerson," *New Princeton Review* 5 [March 1888]: 151). In fact, Emerson's brief description of meteors is more accurate than the scientists of his day could have supplied: the old view of the Scottish geologist James Hutton (1726–1797) that meteors were the product of lunar volcanoes enjoyed diminished support, though by 1845 astronomers had advanced few better ideas. See John Robie Eastman, *The Progress of Meteoric Astronomy in America* (Washington, D.C., 1890), p. 282.

MERLIN I

32 Aye: always.

49 Sybarites: persons given to pleasure and luxury; from the legendary volup-
tuousness of Sybaris, an ancient Greek city in southern Italy.

58 The Welsh bards were especially connected with the ideal of peace or recon-
ciliation: see Adkins, "Emerson and the Bardic Tradition," and Cameron,
"The Potent Song in Emerson's Merlin Poems," for Emerson's likely sources.

70–77 In a journal entry Emerson described and celebrated these "open hours," or
moments of clear insight: "But suddenly in any place, in the street, in the
chamber, will the heavens open, and the regions of wisdom be uncovered,
as if to show how thin the veil, how null the circumstances. As quickly, a
Lethean stream washes through us and bereaves us of ourselves" (*JMN* 5:275;
cf. Cameron, "The Potent Song," p. 28).

MERLIN II

5 Antipode: a relatively rare term, evidently a back-formation from the more
common Antipodes, meaning the direct opposite position on the globe. As
the *OED* notes, the Greek etymology ("opposing foot") offers an image of
soles of feet pressing diametrically down from opposite sides of the planet,
one set in daylight, the other in night (cf. l. 52 below). Emerson's use of the
singular form of the noun suggests as well a simpler left/right opposition.

6 The allusion is to Johann Wolfgang von Goethe's *Farbenlehre*, or *Theory of
Colors*, (1810), which treated colors as variant combinations of light and dark-
ness and asserted that each color had in itself an opposite. The reference to
leaves and cotyledons in lines 10–11 is also a reference to Goethe, who "sug-
gested the leading idea of modern Botany, that a leaf or the eye of a leaf is the
unit of botany" (*JMN* 5:191; *EL* 2:24; *CW* 4:159).

13–15 An echo, perhaps, of Margaret Fuller's observation in *Woman in the
Nineteenth Century* that "Male and female represent the two sides of the great
radical dualism. But, in fact, they are perpetually passing into one another.
Fluid hardens to solid, solid rushes to fluid. There is no wholly masculine
man, no purely feminine woman" ([New York, 1845], p. 103).

24–25 Cf. "Thy thoughts come in bands / Sisters hand in hand," unused lines from
an early draft of "Saadi" (*JMN* 7:480).

39 Counting: i.e., accounting, as in the keeping of ledgers by merchants' clerks.

41 Nemesis: Greek goddess of retributive justice.

49 Sisters: in Greek mythology the three Fates, who spin, measure, and cut the
thread of life.

50–53 Based on lines 57–60 of "Providence" by the English poet George
Herbert (1593–1633): "How finely dost thou times and seasons spin, / And
make a twist checkered with night and day! / Which as it lengthens winds,

and winds us in, / As bowls go on, but turning all the way" (quoted in *JMN* 9:94). Emerson's line 50 is in fact taken from his unpublished poem "Water" (1841), where it appears as line 10 (see *PN*, p. 960).

BACCHUS

4 The Andes are a mountain range in western South America; the Cape, or Cape Horn, is the continent's southernmost tip.

9 Respectively, the river of the dead and the dark underground, which, in Greek myth, departed souls cross into Hades. According to Hesiod's *Theogony*, Erebus, a personification of primordial darkness, was the son of Chaos (see l. 39).

12–13 Elements of the rite of communion.

24–25 Cf. "Hafiz," lines 3–4, and "Nature," line 4, below.

29–30 Emerson suggests that the currents of the South Atlantic are affected by tides and currents in the South Pacific, or "South Sea."

32 In the course of an excellent discussion of this poem, R. A. Yoder offers an important generalization: "To doctrinal transubstantiation Emerson opposed the natural law of transformation, so that the metaphor of dissolution and circulation assumes an essential role in almost every one of his poetic encounters" (p. 101).

39–40 Separately, metonyms for past and future, origin and destiny; together, a metonym for the interval of evolution. According to Hesiod, Chaos was the first of the deities, presiding over the formless void before creation. Cf. "*Chaos and old Night*" (Milton, *Paradise Lost,* I, 543).

41–42 Cf. "Woodnotes II," lines 337–338, and its context there.

43–44 A promise of resurrection to accompany the communion imagery.

45–50 Bernard J. Paris (pp. 150–151) pointed out a relevant passage in "Circles": "In my daily work I incline to repeat my old steps, and do not believe in remedial force, in the power of change and reform. But some Petrarch or Ariosto, filled with the new wine of his imagination, writes me an ode, or a brisk romance, full of daring thought and action. He smites and arouses me with his shrill tones, breaks up my whole chain of habits, and I open my eye on my own possibilities. He claps wings to the sides of all the solid old lumber of the world, and I am capable once more of choosing a straight path in theory and practice" (*CW* 2:185).

47 As Saundra Morris suggests (Porte and Morris, p. 453, n. 9), the restorative "joyful juice" of Bacchus, is contrasted, over the course of this and the next strophe, with the amnesiac effects of Lethe (along with Erebus, another river of the Greek underworld) and the similarly stupefying experience of the lotus plant, as described in Book IX of Homer's *Odyssey* or in Alfred Tennyson's "The Lotos-Eaters" (1833).

62–63 Allusions to processes of art restoration: when stone or metal plates in lithography or engraving become worn from repeated pressings, they have to be recut to restore sharpness in the images. The metaphor is reflected in the image of original or divine engraving that occupies the poem's concluding lines.

67 For the Pleiades, see the note to "Uriel," line 7.

GHASELLE: FROM THE PERSIAN OF HAFIZ

Title Emerson described the ghaselle (or ghazal) as a "shorter ode [which] requires that the poet insert his name in the last stanza" (*CW* 8:135).

9 A Muslim ascetic, the fakir typically expresses faith and devotion through acts of self-denial and physical endurance. Addressed in line 1 as a "hermit wise," he appears as a figure of "austere" justice and legalistic religious views.

13 Kiosk: a garden pavilion, the term deriving from the Persian word for palace. William R. Alger, a friend of Emerson's, refers to "the kiosks of Shiraz" in *The Poetry of the Orient* (Boston, 1865), p. 13.

15–16 I.e., the freedom of Hafiz from conventional morality declares his antinomianism or opposition to law and legalism: "Nothing stops him; he makes the dare-God and dare-devil experiment; he is not to be scared by a name or a religion" (*TN* 2:119).

20 Hafiz was born and died in the city of Shiraz.

25–26 "Talk not to me of mosques or of dervishes; God is my witness, I am where he dwells" (*TN* 2:120).

XENOPHANES

2 Plants native to China and Europe, respectively.

BLIGHT

4 Simples: medicinal plants, as instanced in lines 5–7.

14–17 Edward's note at *W* 9:450 calls attention to a passage in "The Poet": "He [the poet] uses forms according to the life, and not according to the form. This is true science. The poet alone knows astronomy, chemistry, vegetation, and animation, for he does not stop at these facts, but employs them as signs" (*CW* 3:13).

19–20 "Can you believe it, the little town is full of Irish ready to cut a railroad through Walden Woods this very month?" (Emerson to Caroline Sturgis on the construction of the Fitchburg Railroad, May 3, 1843; *L* 7:540).

22 "Natural History is now little but a nomenclature" ("The Naturalist," *EL* 1:79, from a section of the lecture that is virtually an abstract of the sixth essay on "Method" in *The Friend,* by Samuel Taylor Coleridge: "What is BOTANY at the present hour? Little more than an enormous nomenclature" [1:469]. The whole of Emerson's 1833 lecture provides an interesting gloss on "Blight"). Cf. "Beauty," *Conduct of Life, CW* 6:150: "Our botany is all names, not powers:

poets and romancers talk of herbs of grace and healing: but what does the botanist know of the virtues of his weeds?"

27 Reference is not to the religious denomination, but to seers and promoters of unity. In 1846 Emerson referred to Johannes Kepler as a "unitarian of the united world" (*JMN* 9:360), presumably because he, along with Galileo, had shown that physical laws operative on earth hold as well throughout the universe (see Walls, p. 42).

52 Reference may be in part to the death of Emerson's son Waldo little more than a year earlier; and yet he would also have had in mind the death of the brilliant Charles Stearns Wheeler (1816–1843), news of which he conveyed to Margaret Fuller on July 11, even as the poem was being written (*L* 3:182–183).

MUSKETAQUID

Title In his "Historical Discourse at Concord" (1835), Emerson noted that "Musketaquid" in the language of the local Massachusetts Indians meant "Grassy Brook" (*CW* 10:19). He derived this information from Lemuel Shattuck, who cited authorities in his *History of the Town of Concord* (1835) to argue that the word meant "grassy brook" when applied to the river and "grass-ground" when applied to the great meadows adjacent (p. 5). This was close to Thoreau's understanding also, as evidenced by the first sentence of his *Week on the Concord and Merrimack Rivers* (1849), though years later he learned from Indian guides that the word actually meant "Dead Stream" or "Dead-water" (*The Maine Woods*, ed. Joseph J. Moldenhauer [Princeton, 1974], pp. 142, 169).

7 Emerson discussed the "Lords of Life" in his 1844 essay "Experience" and in its poetic motto (*CW* 3:25–49, 9:482–483).

24–25 "The Cliff/Has thousand faces in a thousand hours" (*JMN* 8:458; September 1842). The "Cliff" was a hill near Walden Pond, used by the locals as a picnic ground: see "Woodnotes II," line 251.

26–31 Thoreau used these lines as the epigraph to the introductory chapter of his *Week on the Concord and Merrimack Rivers.*

33–51 Emerson celebrated the transformation of the landscape by the work and talent of Yankee farmers: "The Deity," he said on one occasion, "wants his earth gardened, so in addition to frost & heat & wet, which do not work fast enough[,] he perfects the disintegrating pick or spade to the uttermost, & sends the ears of corn & the potato vines *in human shape*, & they cultivate these, break up the rock, the bog, & the sandhill, & terrace & ditch & dress & adorn them" (*JMN* 10:111; cf. *JMN* 10:101).

DIRGE

29–32 Edward identifies this flower as the lespedeza, "which, in after years, Mr. Emerson seldom passed without a tender word for it to his children" (*W* 9:452).

51 When Charles died, his estate was valued at $886, including $300 as the esti-
mated value of an organ, clearly his one extravagant possession (*L* 2:42, 58).

THRENODY

1–8 "It seems as if I ought to call upon the winds to describe my boy, my fast re-
ceding boy, a child of so large & generous a nature that I cannot paint him by
specialties, as I might another" (*JMN* 8:165; cf. *JMN* 8:166 n. 62, January 30,
1842).

15 Hyacinthus was a beautiful child beloved of Apollo but accidentally killed by
him, from whose blood the grieving Apollo caused the fragrant hyacinth to
grow.

59 Waldo, along with the children of several neighbors, attended school in a
small building near the home of Samuel Hoar on Main Street (for Hoar, see
the poem "S. H." below), kept by Mary Russell of Plymouth, whom Emerson
had brought to Concord for this purpose in the summers of 1840 and 1841
(Ellen T. Emerson, p. 78; *L* 2:402; *JMN* 8:165).

62 The "babe" would have been Ellen T. Emerson, born in 1839, Emerson's sec-
ond child.

100–101 "He gave up his little innocent breath like a bird" (*JMN* 8:164).

106–109 "Every tramper that ever tramped is abroad but the little feet are still"
(*JMN* 8:164).

165 Emerson may be recalling a bit of mythopoesis by Charles Emerson in a letter
to Ralph Waldo of October 29, 1834, concerning the recent death of their
brother Edward: "When he was born into rational thought & affection, he
lifted up his eyes, & a bright circle of stars bent their aspect on him & he said in
his heart, These will watch over me even to the end—But star after star shoots
from its place & sets untimely, & he feels alone, & the new constellations wear
not such eyes of love to him" (quoted in Bosco and Myerson, p. 147).

177–178 Emerson held this paradox in common with Thoreau, who on March 2
wrote to Lidian's sister, Lucy Brown, "As for Waldo, he died as the mist rises
from the brook, which the sun will soon dart his rays through. Do not the
flowers die every autumn? He had not even taken root here. I was not startled
to hear that he was dead:—it seemed the most natural event that could hap-
pen. His fine organization demanded it, and nature gently yielded its request.
It would have been strange if he had lived" (*Correspondence*, p. 63).

214 "The babe cheers me with his hearty & protracted laugh which sounds to me
like thunder in the woods" (*JMN* 5:371; August 20, 1837).

289 Cf. line 175, the last line of the first half of the poem.

CONCORD HYMN

Title For the complicated history of the poem's title, see *CW* 9:305–308.

7–8 The modest wooden bridge had been replaced at least twice before 1837.

10 Votive: Signifying a vow or pledge.

MAY-DAY

5 Cf. Thoreau: "The marsh marigold—catha palustris improperly called cowslip" (*Journal*, 3:236).

8 The balm of Gilead tree is a variety of poplar; its resinous leaf buds were harvested in early spring for medicinal purposes.

12 "The air is full of whistlings" (*JMN* 9:169; 1844–45).

21–22 "Apr. 5, [1856] Walden fired a cannonade yesterday of a hundred guns, but not in honor of the birth of Napoleon" (*JMN* 14:62; versified in 1861: see *JMN* 15:124). Edward cites this journal passage (*W* 9:457) but supposes that it refers to a literal cannonading by the Concord Artillery Company—and yet the reference is surely to the breaking up of the ice on Walden Pond (cf. ll. 149–155, below).

27–35 These lines were written in the spring of 1863: see *JMN* 15:341. In line 29 Emerson puns on Nestor, the aged counselor or guide in the Homeric poems—and creatures that build nests.

49 Felloes are the curved elements that, joined at the end of the spokes, form the rim of a wooden wheel. Emerson originally wrote "spondyls," but these, the joints between the felloes, cannot be grasped. In the next line Emerson substituted "orbs" for "tires": in the metaphoric context of wooden wheels, tires would refer to the iron band affixed to the outside of the rim.

55–67 "Spring. Why complain of the cold slow spring? the bluebirds don't complain, the blackbirds make the maples ring with social cheer & jubilee, the robins know the snow must go & sparrows with prophetic eye that these bare osiers yet will hide their future nests in the pride of their foliage. And you alone with all your six feet of experience are the fool of the cold of the present moment, & cannot see the southing of the sun" (*JMN* 15:249–250; April 1862).

67 Emerson's astronomy is at fault here: he should say "northing," as Edward noticed (*W* 9:548).

85–86 "How all magnifies New England & Massachusetts! A. said, her ice burns more than others' fire" (*JMN* 15:406).

94 The line occurs by itself on a journal page inscribed in 1863 (*JMN* 15:308).

97 The allusion is at once to the "Sweet Auburn" of Oliver Goldsmith's popular "Deserted Village" (1770) and to a wooded area in Cambridge, Massachusetts, which Emerson knew from his Harvard days before it was developed into Mount Auburn Cemetery, dedicated in 1831.

98–103 Evidently these lines derive from the same journal entry (March 3, 1862) that describes Emerson's encounter with the titmouse in snow-choked Walden woods (see *JMN* 15:241, and "The Titmouse").

110–112 "Winter builds / Sudden cathedrals in the wilds" occurs as a detached fragment (*JMN* 9:169), perhaps written in 1844 or 1845, recalling the early poem "The Snow-Storm."

117 Brakes: thickets.

126–127 "The delight in the first days of spring, the 'wish to journeys make,' seems to be a reminiscence of Adam's Paradise, & the longing to return thither" (*JMN* 15:319; 1863; cf. ll. 137–142, below).

128–131 Linnet: a small European songbird of the finch family that migrates north to England in the spring. During the Victorian period there was a fad for capturing linnets and keeping them in cages.

132–136 Edward Emerson associates these lines with his father's visit to the Cincinnati winery of Nicholas Longworth (*W* 9:457). He was accompanied on this visit by Moncure Conway, who recalled it in his *Autobiography*, mentioning the master-vintner's caution about the tendency of bottles to burst in the spring: "We find out about them when the vines in the vintage begin to flower; then the wine ferments and some bottles break" (1:283–284). Conway's estimate of the date of this visit seems confused: probably it occurred in 1857.

137–142 These lines were written in 1863 (see *JMN* 15:318–319).

164–173 These lines were written in 1859 (*JMN* 14:245 and 336).

196 Fells: hides or coats of fur.

205 Water-line plans are design schematics for the hulls of ships, based on a series of lines parallel to the line of flotation. See the *OED*, which cites this verse by Emerson.

209 The horn of plenty (cornucopia), a never-depleted source of nourishment, is associated with Jove. See also "The Adirondacs," line 155.

211–216 An allusion to the pagan festival of the first of May, a topic that Emerson developed further in an unpublished poem, "May-Day [Invitation]" (see *PN*, pp. 856–857).

278–279 "How gladly, after three months sliding on snow, our feet find the ground again!" (*JMN* 9:150; March 15, 1845 [versified at *JMN* 9:169]).

297–300 These lines were written in 1854 (*JMN* 13:318, 411, 491–492).

307–316 A journal passage of 1848 seems to recall Emerson's son Waldo: "The earth takes the part of her children so quickly & adopts our thoughts, affections, & quarrels. The schoolboy finds every step of the ground on his way to school acquainted with his quarrel, & smartly expressing it. The ground knows so well his top & ball, the air itself is full of hoop-time, ball-time, swimming, sled, & skates. So ductile is the world. The rapt prophet finds it not less facile & intelligent. 'Tis Pentecost all, the rose speaks all languages" (*JMN* 11:61–62). This entry is the source also of the poetic motto to the 1849 edition of *Nature* (see "Nature" below), which is repeated in "May-Day," lines 321–322, 315–316, 323–324.

331 Wight: valorous.

376 Byre: barn. Meadow-pipes: a weed also known as Common Horsetail, *Equisetum arvense*.

465–479 In 1866 Emerson recorded an anecdote from his brother-in-law, Dr.

Charles T. Jackson (1805–1880), who had conducted a geological survey in Michigan twenty years earlier: "Dr. Jackson said, he was at Pulpit rock, Lake Superior, when he heard music, like rhythmical organ or vocal chanting, & believed it to come from some singers. But going on a little further, it ceased; in another direction, heard it again; by & by perceived that it was the beating of the waves on the shore deprived of its harshness by the atmosphere" (*JMN* 16:46). The draft of these verses in poetry notebook KL[A] (*PN*, p. 575) is cross-referenced by Emerson to a passage in notebook S (Salvage): "'Tis because Nature is an instrument so thoroughly musical, that the most aukward hand cannot draw a discord from it. A devil struck the chords in defiance, & his spite was punished by a sweeter melody than the angels made" (*TN* 3:126).

480–603 Evidence from the manuscripts shows that these lines were independently conceived, taking off from an 1861 journal entry about the Æolian Harp (see the discussion at *CW* 9:312). Their excision and separate publication under the title "The Harp" in the 1876 *Selected Poems* might therefore represent a return to an original intention, while at the same time effecting a reduction in the bulk of "May-Day." Edward Emerson attributed to his father this decision to excise (*W* 9:460–461), but the evidence is inconclusive.

517–519 A small Æolian harp, or "wind-harp" (so called for Æolus, Greek god of the winds) hung in the window of Emerson's study, while a much larger one was set in the branches of his front-yard tree (*W* 9:483; *CW* 9:584). The idea of an instrument "played" by nature apart from all human agency was very attractive to romantic poets, including Samuel Taylor Coleridge and Henry Thoreau. In his essay on "The Tragic," Emerson wrote that "melancholy cleaves to the English mind in both hemispheres as closely as to the strings of an Æolian harp" (*CW* 10:334).

526 "Waldo asks if the strings of the harp open when he touches them" (*JMN* 7:520; October 1840).

532–535 See Sir Thomas Malory, *The Byrth, Lyf, and Actes of King Arthur . . . and Le Morte Darthur,* introduction and notes by Robert Southey, 2 vols. (London, 1817), 1:xlvi–xlviii. Emerson borrowed these volumes from the Boston Athenaeum in 1860 (Cameron, *Ralph Waldo Emerson's Reading,* pp. 32, 89) and quoted the passage about Merlin's imprisonment in "Poetry and Imagination" (*CW* 8:34–35). See also the note by B. J. Whiting.

560 "Scott, crowned bard of generous boys" occurs as a detached line in journal ML, dating to 1865 (*TN* 3:328).

570 Harlot flies: fireflies.

578 Delphian: an allusion to the oracle of Apollo at Delphi.

597 Elysium in Greek mythology is the happy abode of the blessed after death.

652 Types: examples or symbols, especially as pointing to or indicating a future fulfillment, as in the system of scriptural interpretation known as typology.

THE ADIRONDACS

1–4 The references to Chaucer *(The Canterbury Tales)* and Boccaccio *(The Decameron)* signal Emerson's storytelling motive and its development through particular "characters." In fact, Emerson wrote profiles in verse of his fellow campers, though he never published them (see *PN*, pp. 722–725).

10 Actually, there were eight guides, since Stillman served as guide to Agassiz, absenting himself frequently, however, to spend time with Emerson. The guides' names are given in Emerson's notebook WA (*TN* 1:277).

14–15 Taháwus, said to mean "cloudsplitter" or "he splits the sky" in some unspecified Indian language, was more likely invented by New York writer Charles Fenno Hoffman to replace the prosaic "Mt. Marcy" (named for Senator William L. Marcy) as the name of the state's tallest peak. "Seward" was named for William Henry Seward, another New York senator, later Lincoln's secretary of state.

26 Stillman believed that the Raquette River had been named for "one of the first of the Jesuit explorers of the northern states, Père Raquette" (p. 268). But this explorer is unknown to history, and the fact that his name is French for "snowshoe" casts further doubt on the identification.

29 The name has since been standardized as Follansby. Early accounts say that a certain Captain Follansbee, an English expatriate, set up as a hermit at this location around 1820.

34 This landfall, later named Agassiz Bay, is actually on the west side of Follansbee. Emerson and his party entered the lake from the north and rowed due south. An entry in notebook WA may acknowledge Emerson's tendency to confuse directions: "It soon comes out in the woods whether you know where the north is" (*TN* 1:275).

39 Weatherfend: The *OED* credits Shakespeare for this word, remarking that it remains a poetic locution.

41 Sovran: The *OED* identifies this form as John Milton's spelling of "sovereign" and its use as "chiefly poetic."

42–43 Stillman corrected Emerson's catalogue: "There is no oak, linden, or poplar in these forests. He had passed them in the Ausable valley on his way up and probably forgot their exact habitat" (p. 274). Indeed Emerson knew better, having made a notation on the spot: "The pond is totally virgin soil without a clearing in any point, & covered with primitive woods, rock-maple, beech, spruce, white cedar, arbor vitae" (*JMN* 13:56).

44–45 In notebook WA Emerson identified the five-leaved, three-leaved, and two-leaved varieties as, respectively, *Pinus strobus, Pinus rigida,* and *Pinus resinosa* (*TN* 1:274).

50–53 "As water is poured out lavishly to fill all the hollows of those mountains, making an endless chain of lakes, so is beauty poured out profusely everywhere. The stars peeped through our maple boughs which oerhung like cloud our camping fire and old decaying trunks the forest floor lit with phosphoric crumbs" (*TN* 1:276). Cf. lines 152–155, below.

56 One of Emerson's rare puns, depicting his fellow campers, accurately enough, as Saxon Sioux. See *CW* 9:359 for the popularity of punning among this group.

86–87 "On the top of a large white pine in a bay was an osprey's nest around which the ospreys were screaming, 5 or 6. We thought there were young birds in it, & sent [William] Preston to the top. This looked like an adventure. The tree must be 150 ft. high at least; 60 ft. clean straight stem, without a single branch &, as Lowell & I measured it . . . 14 ft 6 inches in girth. Preston took advantage of a hemlock close by it & climbed till he got on the branches, then went to the top of the pine & found the nest empty, though the great birds wheeled & screamed about him." The next morning Lowell returned to the scene alone and duplicated Preston's feat (*JMN* 13:34, 56).

100–101 "Our party when assembled in costume were a remarkable set, considering who they were, and I think any one of them would have been convicted of piracy on very slight evidence, especially Mr. Emerson" (Ebenezer Rockwood Hoar, quoted in Storey and Emerson, p. 148).

103 To "catch a crab" in rowing is to have the water catch and push the oar rather than vice versa, as normally: a sign of incompetence in the activity.

104 Sallow: a variety of willow wood. Cf. *TN* 1:276: "The saugh knows the basketmaker's thumb, and the oar knows the guide's." At *JMN* 7:407, "The saugh kens the basketmaker's thumb" is identified as a Scottish proverb.

110–127 Emerson describes two styles of deer hunting, "hounding" and "jacking." In the former the hunter waited in his boat while a guide took a dog into the woods to drive the deer out. The deer was to be shot in the water. In jacking, the hunter in his boat at night sat behind a light (or "jack") with a forward-pointing shade. With the light shining shoreward over the bow, leaving the hunter in darkness, any deer feeding on lily pads in the shallows could be closely approached. Emerson's one experience with jacking failed because his night vision was impossibly poor: "I was to aim at a square mist. I knew not whether it were a rock or a bush. Stillman fired & shot the deer" (*TN* 1:275). He had better luck in daylight, both in target practice with "some dozens of ale-bottles" (an activity Thoreau judged "rather Cockneyish") and in bagging a "peetweet," or spotted sandpiper, for Agassiz to dissect (Thoreau, *The Journals*, 11:119–120).

119 "The tall white pines, which when full grown rise from one hundred and fifty to two hundred feet, towering nearly half their height above the mass of deciduous trees, and beyond the protection which the solid forest gives against the dominant west winds, acquire a leaning to the east; and as they grew in long lines along the shores, or followed the rocky ridges up the mountain

sides, they seemed to be gigantic human beings moving in procession to the east. I had the year before painted a picture of the subject, and Emerson had been struck by it at the [Boston] Athenaeum exhibition; and when we were established in camp, almost the first things he asked to see was the 'procession of the pines'; and our last evening on the lake was spent together watching the glow dying out behind a noble line of the marching pines on the shore of Follansbee Water" (Stillman, p. 283).

135–136 The legend of the "Great Carbuncle," a treasure guarded in the wilderness by evil spirits, was long current in the region of the White Mountains. It was the basis for "The Great Carbuncle," a short story by Nathaniel Hawthorne, who claimed to have encountered the legend in James Sullivan's *History of the District of Maine* (1795), but who seems also to have heard it from Ethan Allen Crawford, the storytelling innkeeper at the Notch of the White Mountains. A similar tale is told in chapter 19 of Walter Scott's *The Pirate* (1821), which locates the gem in the mountains of Hoy Island in the Orkneys. These sources are discussed by Haskell (pp. 533–535) and Doubleday (pp. 145–151).

136 The two doctors were Agassiz, founder of Harvard's Museum of Comparative Zoology, and Jeffries Wyman, first curator of Harvard's Peabody Museum.

145–148 The whip-scirpus is the common bulrush (*Scirpus validus*); polygonum is a genus in the buckwheat family, some species of which produce small pink flowers (e.g., *Polygonum pennsylvanicum*, or pink smartweed); Hypnum is a widespread genus of moss, and hydnum is a kind of fungus, including the hedgehog mushroom *(Hydnum repandum)*, common throughout North America. "On the gorge of the Ausable River [at Keeseville] was the harebell. Campanula rotundifolia" (*TN* 1:276).

152–155 See the note to lines 50–53.

155 An allusion to the cornucopia: see "May-Day," line 209.

164–167 This "planning" led to the formation of the Adirondack Club, comprised of shareholders in the purchase of an immense tract of wilderness—some 22,500 acres, including Ampersand Pond—that Stillman acquired at an Albany sheriff's sale for $600 in back taxes. The intention of the club was to ward off development and keep the wilderness pristine while ensuring access for themselves and their children. In the summer of 1859, Samuel Gray Ward, his son, and Edward Emerson were among those who came to the first annual on-site meeting, but plans foundered thereafter. Emerson himself continued to pay assessments until 1862, but the Civil War killed the project, and the land reverted to state ownership. Stillman's celebrated painting of the encampment—later purchased by Judge Hoar and donated to the Concord Free Public Library—is entitled "The Philosophers' Camp," but when Edward Emerson reproduced it in *The Early Years of the Saturday Club,* he took the liberty of calling it "The Adirondack Club," contributing to a confusion between actual club members and the excursion party of 1858.

187 The Latin epithet "Pius," applied by Virgil to the hero Æneas, does not mean "pious"—at least not in the modern sense—but denotes the Roman virtue of pietas, implying faithfulness to duties and loyalty to friends, family, and the gods.

197 The Oreads were the fabled nymphs of the mountains, companions of Diana the huntress.

204 A reference to the system of watches set by the ancient Israelites between sunset and sunrise; although the phrase does not appear in the English Bible, it occurs frequently in poetry and hymns, including "'Twas in the watches of the night, I thought upon thy power" by Isaac Watts.

216–223 These lines versify two passages from the diaries, or "Almanacks," of Mary Moody Emerson: "The clouds are rich & dark,—air serene,—so like the soul of me, t'were me" and "Is sadness on me at retrospection?—or at prospect of darker years, like the cloud on which the purple iris dwells in beauty,—superior to its gaudy colors" (*PN*, p. 723).

233–246 According to Emerson's journal entry, he, Agassiz, and Woodman, together with their guides, set out on the morning of August 11 down the Raquette River for fourteen miles into "Big Tupper" Lake, then "6 miles to Jenkins's near the Falls of the Bog River" (*JMN* 13:56). While this is clearly the excursion Emerson memorializes, there is no mention of hearing about the transatlantic cable. News that the cable had been successfully laid between Ireland and Newfoundland was first announced in the New York *Herald* on August 5 in an article widely reprinted in the days following. The public excitement was quite as general as Emerson indicates. In a *Herald* article on August 6, for example, it was said that "no man can estimate the full importance of this event, which will be the starting point of the civilization of the latter half of the nineteenth century, as Fulton's first trip up the Hudson in the steamer Claremont was its starting point in the first half thereof" ("The Atlantic Cable—The World Revolution Begun," p. 4, cols. 2–3). In fact, the cable ceased to function within a month and service was not restored until 1866.

250 Hebrews 12:1.

282–283 On January 24, 1848, James Wilson Marshall, a carpenter, discovered gold at the sawmill he was building with John Sutter on the American River near Coloma, California. Agassiz conducted a number of important geological surveys in the United States following his arrival from Switzerland in 1846. His 1848 survey in Michigan did not discover the valuable Michigan copper deposits (these were already known), but in due course his son Alexander became wealthy by developing the Hecla and Calumet mines there. He was also involved in supervising mining activities for Emerson's friend, the railroad magnate John Murray Forbes.

333–346 A note on the manuscript of printer's copy shows that Emerson belatedly supplied the concluding lines on November 1, 1866, while *May-Day* was going to press (see *CW* 9:343).

BRAHMA

1–4 In notebook Orientalist Emerson copied a coinciding passage from *The Bhăgvăt-Gēētă*: "The man who believeth that it is the soul which killeth, & he who thinketh that the soul may be destroyed, are both alike deceived; for it neither killeth, nor is killed. It is not a thing which a man may say, it hath been, it is about to be, or is to be hereafter; for it is a thing without birth; it is ancient constant & eternal, & is not to be destroyed in this its mortal frame" (*TN* 2:131).

9 In his 1836 lecture "Humanity of Science," Emerson cited as a proverb "he counts without his host who leaves God out of the reckoning" (*EL* 2:30).

13 Edward identifies the "strong gods" as "Indra, god of the sky and wielder of the thunderbolt; Agni, the god of fire; and Yama, the god of death and judgment" (*W* 9:466), but compare Emerson's list at *JMN* 13:434: Indra (firmament), Agni (fire), Vritra (cloud), Maruts (winds), and Aswins (waters). He derived this list in May 1855 from H. H. Wilson, trans., *Rig-veda Sanhitá. A Collection of Ancient Hindú Hymns*, 4 vols. (London, 1850–1866), vols. 1–2.

FREEDOM

4 In "Poetry and Imagination" Emerson quoted the boast of an unnamed "Runic bard": "I know a song which I need only to sing when men have loaded me with bonds: when I sing it, my chains fall in pieces and I walk forth in liberty" (*CW* 8:33). This passage, in fuller form, is among the sources for Emerson's "Merlin's Song" as well.

22–23 Not present in the *Autographs* text, these lines appear in the poem as reprinted in *May-Day*.

ODE SUNG IN THE TOWN HALL

13–16 Interrupting the draft of the poem in notebook WO Liberty is a prose passage, evidently written out to facilitate composition of this stanza: "Saying to you men of this land I give a new law[:] Be strong through freedom. Make your duty your fate & see that you cling to it while you live" (*JMN* 14:427).

19–20 Len Gougeon (*Virtue's Hero*, pp. 243–244) plausibly associates this injunction with Emerson's impressions of abolitionist John Brown, whom he met for the first time in Concord just a few months earlier, on March 14.

25 In "Self-Reliance" Emerson had faulted the inconsistent philanthropy of a certain class of abolitionists: "Thy love afar is spite at home" (*CW* 2:30). Between 1865 and 1867 Emerson made three unsuccessful attempts to revise this stanza (see *TN* 3:328).

27–28 Emerson believed that trade and commerce had a significant liberalizing effect, though he may also be alluding to the fact that England and America at this time maintained naval squadrons off the coast of Africa to interdict the smuggling of slaves.

29 The "chain" combines the imagery of the slave's fetters and the projected transatlantic cable, which promised greatly to enlarge the sense of human community. See Cameron, "Emerson, Thoreau, and the Atlantic Cable."

BOSTON HYMN

5–6 In *The Letters of Alexander von Humboldt to Varnhagen von Ense,* trans. Friedrich Kapp (New York, 1860), p. 193, Emerson read the comment of a "wise Counsellor" to Philip II: "Should God once be tired of monarchies, he will give another form to the political world." Emerson jotted this down in his journal under the heading "God getting tired of Kings" (*JMN* 14:356; cf. *JMN* 15:338).

19–20 Evidently an allusion to Brackett's unveiling of the bust of John Brown.

40 Asserting the political equality of the hireling and "him that hires" belongs to the abolitionist argument that a (Southern) slave and a (Northern) worker employed at wages occupy radically different situations, from both a moral and an economic standpoint. The proslavery side to this argument was at its most emphatic at the time Emerson wrote, and it might be said to have reached a crescendo with Thomas Carlyle's notorious squib, "The American Iliad in a Nutshell," published in August 1863, which equated chattel slavery with "hiring for life." The statement drew angry rejoinders from several of the Transcendentalists.

50 "ICH DIEN, *I serve,* is a truly royal motto" (*CW* 10:403), identified in the lecture "Boston" as the "most noble motto" of the Prince of Wales (*W* 12:205; cf. *JMN* 13:98).

65–66 Emerson may be thinking of John Brown here, but in June 1854, he said of Thomas Wentworth Higginson, injured in the attempt to liberate fugitive slave Anthony Burns, then in federal custody, "It is only they who save others that can themselves be saved" (*L* 4:449).

75 The Comstock Lode was discovered in 1859 at Virginia City, in what was then Utah. By 1861 instreaming Californians had wrested the area from Mormon control, and Nevada Territory was created. The Comstock mines supplied the United States Mint in San Francisco; the one at Carson City, Nevada, did not begin operation until 1870.

78 The phrase "to sit in darkness" occurs several times in the Bible: see, e.g., Matthew 4:16 and Luke 1:79.

VOLUNTARIES

Title James T. Fields, to whom Emerson read a portion of the unfinished work in August 1863, suggested the title (Fields, pp. 84–85). According to the *OED,* the term had been used in the seventeenth century as a collective noun for volunteer soldiers; more recently it had come to refer to the somber organ solos heard in church, fit for a dirge or sacred things in general.

30 Northern politicians (Daniel Webster most notoriously) often declined to agitate the slavery question for fear that doing so might jeopardize the Union.

37 Van: vanguard.

39–42 In an 1862 journal entry Emerson wrote, "Wherever snow falls, man is free. Where the orange blooms, man is the foe of man" (*JMN* 15:178). And again, "Freedom does not love the hot zone. The snow-flakes are the right stars of our flag, & the Northern streamers the stripes" (*JMN* 15:246; cf. *JMN* 15:250).

109 The judicial image of God's "red right arm" originates with Horace and was probably best known to Emerson through Milton's adaptation of it in *Paradise Lost,* II, 174, and through Byron's translation of Horace, *Odes,* 3.3, though the crucial phrase "*rubente dextera*" actually occurs in *Odes,* 1.2.

126–127 "I have read in our old Norse bible of the Edda, that the God *Freye,* or *Freedom,* had a sword so good that it would itself strew a field with carnage, whenever the owner ordered it—Yet I think dwarves killed him once" (*PN,* p. 311).

128–129 Edward Emerson (*W* 9:470–471) points out this passage from *Representative Men:* "The word Fate or Destiny expresses the sense of mankind in all ages that the laws of the world do not always befriend, but often hurt and crush us. Fate in the shape of *Kinde* or Nature, grows over us like grass" (*CW* 4:100). The phrase "the castled steep" well describes the approach to Fort Wagner.

LOVE AND THOUGHT

2–3 Eros was one of the oldest gods, self-born, responsible for bringing order and harmony out of an original unformed Chaos: hence his association in later versions of the myth with Aphrodite, goddess of love and beauty. Although Emerson here reformulates the myth in making Eros a twin of "the Muse," the several Muses (three or nine in various accounts) were the daughters of Zeus, goddesses who inspired poetry, science, and the arts, the vehicles of knowledge. Thus in Emerson's view Love and Thought are the mutually indispensable components of poetry. See "Love" (*CW* 2:99–110, and Gougeon, *Emerson and Eros*).

THE ROMANY GIRL

5 In 1840 (*JMN* 7:536) and again in 1853 (*JMN* 13:268) Emerson quoted line 132 of "L'Apparition" by Hégésippe Moreau (1810–1838): "Pâles filles du Nord! vous n'êtes pas mes sœurs" (*Œuvres Complètes de Hégésippe Moreau* [Paris, 1890], p. 60).

13 The *Atlantic Monthly* text had "under the moon." At the time of first publica-
tion, Emerson rejected the suggestion of *Atlantic* editor James Russell Lowell
that "beneath the moon" would help with the rhythm, but he partly relented
ten years later, when, in the *May-Day* printing he changed it to "below" (see
L 8:532–533).

DAYS

1 The first line of the poem has a famously vexed textual history. For the poem's
first printing in the *Atlantic Monthly* (1857), the phrase was "Daughters of
Time," changed by an authorial mistake to "Damsels of Time" in the *May-
Day* printing (1867). See Strauch, "The Manuscript Relationships of Emerson's
'Days'" for the phrase "daughters of time" in poems by Edward Young and
Alfred Tennyson (pp. 199–200). Also, when Emerson submitted "Days" for
publication in the *Atlantic,* its editor, James Russell Lowell, objected to the
word "hypocritic," suggesting the more customary (but metrically problem-
atic) form "hypocritical" (*L* 8:533). For more on both these issues, see *CW*
9:428.

5 Possibly there is a recollection here of Saint Paul's discussion of the diversity
of spiritual gifts in 1 Corinthians 12:11: "But all these worketh that one and
selfsame Spirit, dividing to every man severally as he will."

7 The term "pleached" is explained in the headnote above. Holmes (p. 313)
noted appreciatively that the word was "an heir-loom from Queen Eliza-
beth's day." Emerson probably gave it a two-syllable pronunciation, to judge
from the accent over the final *e* in one manuscript and in the *Selected Poems*
text.

THE CHARTIST'S COMPLAINT

1 To one of the late manuscript drafts (*PN*, p. 110), Emerson gave the title
"Janus," in Roman mythology the two-faced god of doors and gates, sugges-
tive of a number of important polarities, such as past and future or war and
peace. To Horace he was "Father of the morning" (*Satires,* II, 6), in allusion to
his oversight of beginnings. Ovid, in *Fasti,* I, 101–114, claims that Janus origi-
nated with the primordial Chaos, from which he created and ordered the cos-
mos by dividing the four elements, fire, air, water, and earth. Proverbially, to
be "Janus-faced" is to be a hypocrite.

8 Appanage: a provision for the maintenance of the younger sons of royalty or
the aristocracy.

THE TITMOUSE

89 Emerson seems to have noticed that it was habitual with Thoreau to speak
of the chickadee's song as "wiry" (see, e.g., *Journal,* 5:112, 203, 421). In 1838
Emerson listed "the thin note of the titmouse & his bold ignoring of the

bystander" as among the things that poets had yet to record (*JMN* 5:469; cf. *JMN* 4:273).

104 Pæan: a hymn of praise, thanksgiving, or deliverance, originally addressed to Apollo in his guise as Pæan, physician to the gods. Later, in the Roman tradition, it was a song in celebration of a military victory. "*Veni, vidi, vici*" (I came, I saw, I conquered) is famously associated with Julius Caesar.

SEA-SHORE

8 Robert H. Woodward has pointed out that Emerson echoes lines 32–33 of "Thanatopsis" by William Cullen Bryant ("nor couldst thou wish / Couch more magnificent"). Various structural and prosodic features (the soothing address of Nature, the choice of blank verse) also recall Bryant. The opening lines of "Sea-Shore" may have been influenced as well by Emerson's quatrain "From Alcuin," composed at about the same time.

14–15 To get to Pigeon Cove one was obliged to follow the winding ocean road from Rockport two miles, past several granite quarries: these probably suggested the classic ruins mentioned in the prose source.

15 The "Giant's Stairs" (or "Causeway") refers to a volcanic formation on the coast of Northern Ireland consisting of thousands of hexagonal basalt columns. The "Giant," its putative builder, was the legendary Finn McCool.

27–33 At the end of the journal source quoted in the headnote, Emerson added a cross-reference to an earlier entry, dating from the summer of 1847: "On the seashore at Nantucket I saw the play of the Atlantic with the coast. Here was wealth[:] every wave reached a quarter of a mile along shore as it broke. There are no rich men, I said[,] to compare with these. Every wave is a fortune. One thinks of Etzlers [J. A. Etzler, author of *The Paradise within the Reach of All Men* (1833), proposed harnessing energy from wind and tides] and great projectors who will yet turn this immense waste strength to account and save the limbs of human slaves" (*JMN* 10:62).

47–49 Tennyson's dreamy "Lotos-Eaters" (1832) may have suggested this way of representing the allure of the shore. In July 1868, following a visit to the beach at Newport, Rhode Island, Emerson wrote in a scrap of verse that the waves "give my guest eternal afternoon" (*JMN* 16:104).

SONG OF NATURE

5 As Strauch points out ("The Sources," pp. 315–318), the stanza draws on two essays from Plutarch's *Morals,* "Why the Oracles Cease to Give Answers" and "Of Osiris, or Of the Ancient Religion and Philosophy of Egypt." The latter identifies Osiris as the god "who lies hidden in the Arms of the Sun."

17–20 Emerson was a considerable orchardist, selling upward of a hundred barrels of apples a year in addition to pears and other fruits. He was well acquainted with the theories of the Belgian horticulturalist Jean-Baptiste van Mons, principally through Andrew J. Downing, *Fruits and Fruit Trees of America,* the 1846 edition of which he owned. Improvements in apples and pears (coming to a "state of amelioration") were effected by the deliberate channeling of natural forces (Strauch, "The Sources," pp. 312–313; *JMN* 10:156).

25–28 In reading Sir David Brewster's *Memoirs of the Life . . . of Sir Isaac Newton* (1855), Emerson took note of the recent discovery of changes in the rings of Saturn and of "twenty-seven small planets" between Mars and Jupiter (the asteroid belt). See Strauch, "The Sources," pp. 313–314.

37 The "man-child" is related to similar figures in "The Sphinx" and in a letter of October 13, 1857, to Caroline Sturgis (*L* 5:86).

45–56 Strauch was the first to note the dependence of these stanzas on a passage from Mary Moody Emerson's Almanacks: "1834 x x x x x I forget what I meant to say—likely that Doctor [Ezra] Ripley would not live. But he has to return, and willingly. Ah! as I walked there [to the Old Manse] just now, so sad was wearied nature, that I felt her whisper, 'Even these leaves you used to think my better emblems—have lost their charm on me too, & I weary of my pilgrimage,—tired that I must again be clothed in the grandeurs of winter, and anon be bedizened in flowers & cascades. Oh if there be a Power superior to me, (& that there is, my own dread fetters proclaim,) when will he let my lights go out,—my tides cease to an eternal ebb,—my wheels which whirl this ceaseless rotation of suns & satellites stop the great chariot of their maker in mid career?" (quoted in Strauch, "The Sources," pp. 322–323).

65–68 The combination of allusions here, to Jesus, Shakespeare, Moses (probably), and Plato, may have seemed a too heterodox jumble: the stanza was suppressed in the *Atlantic Monthly* printing, though it is unclear by whom.

TWO RIVERS

5–8 In *Nature* (1836), Emerson had written, "The river, as it flows, resembles the air that flows over it; the air resembles the light which traverses it with more subtle currents; the light resembles the heat which rides with it through space" (*CW* 1:27). In an 1840 journal entry he wrote, "We see the river glide below us but we see not the river that glides over us & envelopes us in its floods" (*JMN* 7:499). In "The Over-Soul" (1841), he developed the proposition that "man is a stream whose source is hidden" by saying, "When I watch that flowing river, which, out of regions I see not, pours for a season its streams into me, I see that I am a pensioner; not a cause, but a surprised spectator of this ethereal water; that I desire and look up, and put myself in the attitude of reception, but from some alien energy the visions come" (*CW* 2:159–160).

19 "George Fox saw that there was 'an ocean of darkness and death but withal

an infinite ocean of light and love which flowed over that of darkness'"
("Montaigne," *Representative Men, CW* 4:103; cf. *EL* 1:171).

WALDEINSAMKEIT

1–2 Edward Emerson notes that his father was fond of quoting the adage "Allah
does not count the days spent in the chase" (*W* 9:489). It appears in *English
Traits* (*CW* 5:38), "Inspiration" (*CW* 8:156), and "Country Life (Concord)"
(*LL* 2:38) as well as in the journals (*JMN* 13:203).

13–14 Emerson alludes to the financial panic of 1857.

19–20 Jottings from a journal dating to the spring of 1845: "The wood is soberness
with a basis of joy / Sober with a fund of joy" (*JMN* 9:169).

26 "See how the roses burn! / Bring wine to quench the fire! / Alas! the flames
come up with us, / We perish with desire." The lines are Emerson's translation
from the *Diwan* of Hafiz and were first published in the 1858 essay "Persian
Poetry" (see *TN* 2:65; *CW* 8:129).

33–36 In September 1857, during a "valuable walk [with Thoreau] through
the savage fertile houseless land" at Ebba Hubbard's swamp near Concord,
Emerson "saw pigeons & marsh-hawks, &, ere we left it, the mists, which de-
note the haunt of the elder Gods, were rising" (*JMN* 14:162). See the note to
line 1 of "The Chartist's Complaint," above, regarding Ovid's description of
the role of Janus in the creation of the universe.

41–44 After a walk to Flint's Pond with Ellery Channing in August 1857, Emerson
wrote, "Reading is a languid pleasure and we must forget our books to see the
landscape's royal looks." This journal entry is immediately followed by the
first draft of these lines (*JMN* 14:161).

TERMINUS

1–2 "Take in your canvass or clear your decks before the gale comes" (*JMN* 7:496;
1840). In "Montaigne," Emerson gives a portrait of the skeptic: "He is the
Considerer, the prudent, taking in sail, counting stock, husbanding his
means, believing that a man has too many enemies, than that he can afford to
be his own foe" (*CW* 4:91).

12–13 "You must elect your work; you shall take what your brain can, and drop all
the rest. Only so, can that amount of vital force accumulate, which can make
the step from knowing to doing" ("Power," *The Conduct of Life, CW* 6:39).

23–32 In an 1847 journal entry Emerson wrote, "We have experience, reading, re-
latedness enough, o yes, & every other weapon, if only we had constitution
enough. But, as the doctor said in my boyhood,—'You have no stamina'"
(*JMN* 10:110). Cf. "Fate": "How shall a man escape from his ancestors, or draw
off from his veins the black drop which he drew from his father's or his moth-
er's life?" (*CW* 6:5). In 1859 he wrote, "Shall I blame my mother, whitest of
women, because she was not a gypsy, & gave me no swarthy ferocity? or my

father, because he came of a lettered race, & had no porter's shoulders?" (*JMN* 14:283).

36 It is important to Strauch's argument for an earlier date for "Terminus" that the first draft of this line is "The voice at noon obeyed <in> ↑at↓ prime" (*PN*, p. 224).

37–40 These lines were added late, likely in 1866.

S. H.

1 Franklin B. Sanborn (p. 65) reports a manuscript with a variant first line ("With beams that stars at Christmas dart"), noting that "the allusion to Christmas suggests the old-fashioned religion of this aged Christian, a true follower of Emerson's grandfather, Parson [Ezra] Ripley."

"SUUM CUIQUE"

Title A lawyer's phrase, as in Justinian: "Justicia suum cuique distribuit," or in Cicero: "Suum cuique tribuere," meaning, in either case, "to each his own." It may be thought of as a secular equivalent of the dictum of Jesus, "Render unto Cæsar the things that are Cæsar's, and to God the things that are God's" (Mark 12:17).

POET

4 Pinnace: A small boat equipped with oars and used as a tender on larger ships. The reference to "New worlds" suggests that Emerson may have had in mind the pinnace transported between decks on the *Mayflower,* which the Pilgrims used to explore Cape Cod and to land at Plymouth in 1620.

GARDENER

4 The beurré is a variety of pear, its name derived from the French word for butter. On July 24, 1847, Emerson wrote admiringly of the "Golden Buerre of Bilboa" that he had planted and that was just then sprouting in his orchard (*JMN* 10:118).

HOROSCOPE

3–4 In a journal entry from the spring of 1847, Emerson wrote, "When he comes forth from his mother's womb, the gate of gifts closes behind him" (*JMN* 10:34; used in "Fate," *CW* 6:6).

SONG OF SEID NIMETOLLAH OF KUHISTAN

10 The jewel or signet ring of Solomon was a favorite trope of Sufi poets, as explained by Emerson's friend William Rounseville Alger in *The Poetry of the East*: "Such were the incredible virtues of [Solomon's] little talisman, that the touch of it exorcised all evil spirits, commanded the instant presence and ser-

vices of the Genii, laid every secret bare, and gave its possessor almost unlimited powers of knowledge, dominion, and performance" (pp. 59–60). Since Solomon had been preeminently a symbol of wisdom (or gnosis), the loss of this jewel by its first possessor spawned dreams of its recovery. Cf. *JMN* 10:65–66.

17 Although the fragrant wood of the Asian tree *Aquilaria agallocha* is called "aloes," it properly, if awkwardly, takes a singular verb, which probably accounts for Emerson's 1860 revision, which he ultimately rejected: "Ah! I flame as aloes do."

21 Muftis: Islamic scholars.

27 Giaours: non-Muslims.

SILENCE

1–2 A journal entry for October 9, 1838, reads, "They put their finger on their lip—the Powers above,—" (*JMN* 7:98), referring to the controversy following Emerson's delivery of the Divinity School Address and the alarm of the Harvard authorities. Emerson here redeploys the lines in an entirely different context.

3 To clip is, simply, to embrace, though in Elizabethan poetic usage, as in the phrase "kiss and clip," a more specifically sexual embrace is implied.

GRACE

1 Emerson uses the word "preventing" in the old theological sense of prevenient or preventing grace. As the *OED* notes, the term does not imply restraint so much as the provision, before specific need arises, of spiritual strength ("to go before with spiritual guidance and help: said of God, or of his grace, anticipating human action or need"). In the Augustinian tradition, the corrupt human will is first opened to choosing good by *gratia præveniens* (Herbert's "blessings beforehand") and is thereafter, in the converted soul, enabled to cooperate with divinity *(gratia cooperans).*

4–5 The use of the word "parapet" in an identical rhyme connecting the two quatrains may owe something to Thomas Jefferson's description of the sublime effect of the "Natural bridge" in *Notes on the State of Virginia:* "Though the sides of this bridge are provided in some parts with a parapet of fixed rocks, yet few men have resolution to walk to them, and look over into the abyss. You involuntarily fall on your hands and feet, creep to the parapet and peep over it" (pp. 21–22). Emerson was reading Jefferson's works in March 1830 (*L* 1:297, 300).

NATURE

4 In December 1848, Emerson commented on how thoroughly nature sympathized with the various phases of human consciousness: "'Tis Pentecost all,

the rose speaks all languages[,] the sense of all affections" and is intelligible to all races (*JMN* 11:62; cf. "Bacchus," l. 25).

5–6 Emerson's first draft: "And willing to be God the worm / Flees through all the round [added variant: spire] of form" (*JMN* 9:163; possibly 1845).

1–6 The lines of the motto reappear in the 1867 text of "May-Day" as lines 321–322, 315–316, and 323–324, respectively.

WORKS CITED

Adkins, Nelson F. "Emerson and the Bardic Tradition." *PMLA* 63 (June 1948): 662–677.

Alcott, Amos Bronson. *The Journals of Bronson Alcott.* Edited by Odell Shepard. Boston: Little, Brown, 1938.

Alger, William Rounseville. *The Poetry of the East.* Boston: Wittemore, Niles, and Hall, 1856.

Anderson, John Q. "Emerson's 'Eternal Pan'—The Re-creation of a Myth." *American Transcendental Quarterly,* no. 25 (Winter 1975): 2–6. Reprinted in *Characteristics of Emerson, Transcendental Poet: A Symposium,* edited by Carl F. Strauch, pp. 2–6. Hartford, Conn.: Transcendental Books, 1975.

Ante-Nicene Fathers. Edited by Alexander Roberts, James Donaldson et al. 10 vols. 1885–1887. Peabody, Mass.: Hendrickson Publishers, 1994.

Arberry, Arthur John. *Classical Persian Literature.* New York: MacMillan, 1958.

Arnold, Matthew. "Emerson." In *Discourses in America,* pp. 138–207. London: Macmillan, 1885.

Bacon, Francis. *The Essays or Counsels Civil and Moral and Wisdom of the Ancients.* Edited by Basil Montagu. London: William Pickering, 1840.

Barnstone, Willis, ed. *The Other Bible.* San Francisco: HarperSanFrancisco, 1984.

Baron, A[uguste]. *Histoire Abrégée de la Littérature Française.* 2nd ed. Bruxelles: Librairie Universelles de Rozez, 1851.

Bestor, Arthur E. "Emerson's Adaptation of a Line from Spenser." *Modern Language Notes* 49 (April 1934): 265–267.

Bosco, Ronald A., and Joel Myerson. *The Emerson Brothers: A Fraternal Biography in Letters.* New York: Oxford University Press, 2004.

Cameron, Kenneth Walter. "Emerson, Thoreau, and the Atlantic Cable." *Emerson Society Quarterly* 26 (First Quarter 1962): 45–86.

———. "The Potent Song in Emerson's Merlin Poems." *Philological Quarterly* 32 (1953): 22–28.

———. *Ralph Waldo Emerson's Reading.* Raleigh, N.C.: Thistle Press, 1941.

Capper, Charles. *Margaret Fuller: An American Romantic Life.* 2 vols. New York: Oxford University Press, 1992–2007.

Carlyle, Thomas. *Sartor Resartus.* London: Saunders and Otley, 1838.

Cheney, Ednah Dow. "Memoir of Harriet Winslow Sewall." In *The Poems of Harriet Winslow Sewall.* Cambridge, Mass.: The Riverside Press, 1889.

Cole, Phyllis. *Mary Moody Emerson and the Origins of Transcendentalism: A Family History.* New York: Oxford University Press, 1998.

Colebrooke, Henry T. *Miscellaneous Essays.* 2 vols. London: Wm. H. Allen, 1837.

Coleridge, Samuel Taylor. *Aids to Reflection. With . . . notes by James Marsh.* Burlington, Vt.: Chauncey Goodrich, 1829.

———. "On the Grounds of Morals and Religion, and the Discipline of the Mind Requisite for a True Understanding of the Same." In *The Friend,* 1:464–471. Princeton: Princeton University Press, 1969.

Conway, Moncure D. *Autobiography: Memories and Experiences of Moncure Daniel Conway.* 2 vols. Boston: Houghton, Mifflin, 1904.

Cudworth, Ralph. *The True Intellectual System of the Universe* (1678). Edited by Thomas Birch. 4 vols. London: Richard Priestley, 1820.

Didache. In *Early Christian Writings,* translated by Maxwell Staniforth, pp. 223–237. London: Penguin, 1968.

Doubleday, Neal Frank. *Hawthorne's Early Tales: A Critical Study.* Durham, N.C.: Duke University Press, 1972.

Emerson, Edward. *Emerson in Concord: A Memoir Written for the "Social Circle" in Concord, Massachusetts.* Boston: Houghton, Mifflin, 1889.

Emerson, Ellen T. *The Life of Lidian Jackson Emerson.* Edited by Delores Bird Carpenter. Boston: Twayne, 1980.

Emerson, Mary Moody. *The Selected Letters of Mary Moody Emerson.* Edited by Nancy Craig Simmons. Athens: University of Georgia Press, 1993.

Emerson, William. *Diaries and Letters of William Emerson, 1743–1776.* Edited by Amelia Forbes Emerson. [Boston: Thomas Todd, 1972].

Fields, Annie. "Glimpses of Emerson." In *Authors and Friends,* pp. 65–106. Boston: Houghton, Mifflin, 1896.

Foote, Lorien. *Seeking the One Great Remedy: Francis George Shaw and Nineteenth-Century Reform.* Athens: Ohio University Press, 2003.

Forbes, John Murray. *Letters and Recollections of John Murray Forbes.* Edited by Sarah Forbes Hughes. 2 vols. Boston: Houghton, Mifflin, 1899.

Fuller, Margaret. "Menzel's View of Goethe." *Dial* 1 (January 1841): 340–347.

Goldstein, Bernard R. "The Blasphemy of Alfonso X: History or Myth?" In *Revolution and Continuity: Essays in the History and Philosophy of Early Modern Science,* edited by P. Barker and R. Ariew, pp. 143–153. Washington, D.C.: Catholic University of America Press, 1991.

Gougeon, Len. "The Anti-Slavery Background of Emerson's 'Ode Inscribed to W. H. Channing.'" In *Studies in the American Renaissance: 1985,* edited by Joel Myerson, pp. 63–77. Charlottesville: University Press of Virginia, 1985.

———. *Emerson & Eros: The Making of a Cultural Hero.* Albany: State University of New York Press, 2007.

———. *Virtue's Hero: Emerson, Antislavery, and Reform.* Athens: University of Georgia Press, 1990.

Harding, Walter. *The Days of Henry Thoreau.* New York: Knopf, 1965.

———. *Emerson's Library.* Charlottesville: University Press of Virginia, 1967.

Harrison, John S. *The Teachers of Emerson.* New York: Sturgis and Walton, 1910.

Haskell, Raymond I. "The Great Carbuncle." *New England Quarterly* 10 (1937): 533–535.

Haugrud, Raychal A. "Tyndall's Interest in Emerson." *American Literature* 41 (January 1970): 507–517.

Hendrickson, G. L. "Amici usque ad aras." *The Classical Journal* 45 (May 1950): 395–398.

Higginson, Thomas Wentworth. *Margaret Fuller Ossoli.* Boston: Houghton, Mifflin, 1884.

Hodder, Allan D. *Emerson's Rhetoric of Revelation.* University Park: Pennsylvania State University Press, 1989.

Holmes, Oliver Wendell. *Ralph Waldo Emerson.* Boston: Houghton, Mifflin, 1884.

[Howells, William Dean.] Review of *May-Day and Other Pieces. Atlantic Monthly* 20 (September 1867): 376–378.

Ives, Sidney, ed. *The Parkman Dexter Howe Library, Part II.* Gainesville: University of Florida Press, 1984.

James, Henry. "Emerson." In *Partial Portraits,* pp. 1–33. London: Macmillan, 1888.

Jarvis, Edward. *Traditions and Reminiscences of Concord, Massachusetts, 1779–1878.* Edited by Sarah Chapin. Amherst: University of Massachusetts Press, 1993.

Jefferson, Thomas. *Notes on the State of Virginia.* Boston: Wells & Lilly, 1829.

Jonas, Hans. *The Gnostic Religion.* 2nd ed. Boston: Little, Brown, 1963.

Leonard, Henry C. *Pigeon Cove and Vicinity.* Boston: F. A. Searle, 1873.

Longfellow, Henry Wadsworth. *The Letters of Henry Wadsworth Longfellow.* Edited by Andrew Hilen. 6 vols. Cambridge, Mass.: The Belknap Press of Harvard University Press, 1966–1982.

Matthiessen, F. O. *American Renaissance: Art and Expression in the Age of Emerson and Whitman.* New York: Oxford University Press, 1941.

Morris, Saundra. "Through a Thousand Voices: Emerson's Poetry and 'The Sphinx.'" In *Emerson's Prose and Poetry,* edited by Joel Porte and Saundra Morris, pp. 777–790. New York: W. W. Norton, 2001.

Murray, Meg McGavran. *Margaret Fuller: Wandering Pilgrim.* Athens: University of Georgia Press, 2008.

Murray, William H. H. *Adventures in the Wilderness; Or, Camp-Life in the Adirondacks.* Boston: Fields, Osgood, 1869.

Paris, Bernard J. "Emerson's 'Bacchus.'" *Modern Language Quarterly* 23 (June 1962): 150–159.

Parker, Theodore. "German Literature." *Dial* 1 (January 1841): 315–339.

Pommer, Henry F. *Emerson's First Marriage.* Carbondale: Southern Illinois University Press, 1967.

Porte, Joel, and Saundra Morris, eds. *Emerson's Prose and Poetry.* New York: W. W. Norton, 2001.

Porter, David. *Emerson and Literary Change.* Cambridge, Mass.: Harvard University Press, 1978.

Richardson, Robert D., Jr. *Emerson: The Mind on Fire.* Berkeley: University of California Press, 1995.

Robinson, James M., ed. *The Nag Hammadi Library in English.* 3rd ed. San Francisco: HarperCollins, 1990.

Sanborn, Franklin B. *The Personality of Emerson.* Boston: Charles E. Goodspeed, 1903.

Schneider, Paul. *The Adirondacks: A History of America's First Wilderness.* New York: Henry Holt, 1997.

Shattuck, Lemuel. *A History of the Town of Concord.* Boston: Russell, Odiorne; Concord: J. Stacy, 1835.

Smith, Gayle L. "The Language of Identity in Emerson's 'The Sphinx.'" *ESQ: A Journal of the American Renaissance* 29 (1983): 136–143.

Stillman, William J. "The Philosophers' Camp." In *The Old Rome and the New and Other Studies,* pp. 265–296. London: Grant Richards, 1897.

Storey, Moorfield, and Edward Waldo Emerson. *Ebenezer Rockwood Hoar: A Memoir.* Boston: Houghton, Mifflin, 1911.

Stowe, William. "Linnaean Poetics: Emerson, Cooper, Thoreau, and the Names of Plants." *ISLE: Interdisciplinary Studies in Literature and Environment* 17.3 (2010): 567–583.

Strauch, Carl F. "The Background of Emerson's 'Boston Hymn.'" *American Literature* 14 (March 1942): 36–47.

———. "The Date of Emerson's *Terminus.*" *PMLA* 65 (June 1950): 360–370.

———. "Emerson's Adaptation of Myth in 'The Initial Love.'" *American Transcendental Quarterly* 25 (Winter 1975): 51–65.

———. "The Manuscript Relationships of Emerson's 'Days.'" *Philological Quarterly* 29 (April 1950): 199–208.

———. "The Sources of Emerson's 'Song of Nature.'" *Harvard Library Bulletin* 9 (Autumn 1955): 300–334.

———. "The Year of Emerson's Poetic Maturity: 1834." *Philological Quarterly* 34 (October 1955): 353–377.

Thomas, Dwight, and David K. Jackson. *The Poe Log: A Documentary Life of Edgar Allan Poe,* 1809–1849. New York: G. K. Hall, 1987.

Thoreau, Henry David. *The Correspondence of Henry David Thoreau.* Edited by Walter Harding and Carl Bode. New York: New York University Press, 1958.

———. *Journal.* Edited by John C. Broderick et al. 8 vols. to date. Princeton: Princeton University Press, 1981–.

———. *The Journals.* Edited by Bradford Torrey and Francis H. Allen. 14 vols. Boston: Houghton, Mifflin, 1906.

———. *Walden.* Edited by J. Lyndon Shanley. Princeton: Princeton University Press, 1971.

von Frank, Albert J. *An Emerson Chronology.* New York: G. K. Hall, 1994.

Waggoner, Hyatt H. *Emerson as Poet.* Princeton: Princeton University Press, 1974.

Walls, Laura Dassow. *Emerson's Life in Science: The Culture of Truth.* Ithaca, N.Y.: Cornell University Press, 2003.

Whiting, B. J. "Emerson and Merlin's 'Dungeon Made of Air.'" *PMLA* 64 (June 1949): 598–599.

Woodward, Robert H. "Emerson's 'Seashore' and Bryant's Poetic Theory in Practice." *Emerson Society Quarterly* 19 (Second Quarter 1960): 21–22.

Yoder, R. A. *Emerson and the Orphic Poet in America.* Berkeley: University of California Press, 1978.

FURTHER READING

Anderson, John Q. *The Liberating Gods: Emerson on Poets and Poetry.* Coral Gables, Fla.: University of Miami Press, 1971.

Arms, George. "The Dramatic Movement in Emerson's 'Each and All.'" *English Language Notes* 1 (March 1964): 207–211.

Baym, Nina. "From Metaphysics to Metaphor: The Image of Water in Emerson and Thoreau." *Studies in Romanticism* 5 (Summer 1966): 231–243.

Benton, Joel. *Emerson as a Poet.* New York: M. L. Holbrook, 1883.

Blair, Walter, and Clarence Faust. "Emerson's Literary Method." *Modern Philology* 42 (November 1944): 79–95.

Blasing, Mutlu Konuk. *American Poetry: The Rhetoric of Its Forms.* New Haven: Yale University Press, 1987.

Bloom, Harold. "Bacchus and Merlin: The Dialectic of Romantic Poetry in America." *Southern Review* n.s. 7 (Winter 1971): 140–175. Reprinted in *Ringers in the Tower: Studies in the Romantic Tradition.* Chicago: University of Chicago Press, 1971.

Broderick, John C. "The Date and Source of Emerson's 'Grace.'" *Modern Language Notes* 73 (January 1958): 91–95.

Cameron, Kenneth Walter. "Early Background for Emerson's 'The Problem.'" *Emerson Society Quarterly* 27 (Second Quarter 1962): 37–46.

———. "Emerson, Thoreau, Parson Frost, and 'The Problem.'" *Emerson Society Quarterly* 6 (First Quarter 1957): 16.

Cowen, Michael H. "The Loving Proteus: Metamorphosis in Emerson's Poetry." In *Characteristics of Emerson, Transcendental Poet: A Symposium,* edited by Carl F. Strauch, pp. 11–22. Hartford, Conn.: Transcendental Books, 1975.

Elliott, G. R. "On Emerson's 'Grace' and 'Self-Reliance.'" *New England Quarterly* 2 (1929): 93–104.

Gelpi, Albert. "Emerson: The Paradox of Organic Form." In *Emerson: Prophecy, Metamorphosis and Influence,* edited by David Levin, pp. 149–170. New York: Columbia University Press, 1975.

Gordon, Jan B. "Emerson's 'The Snow-Storm' and an 1835 Journal." *Emerson Society Quarterly* 47 (Second Quarter 1967): 42–48.

Gross, Seymour L. "Emerson and Poetry." *South Atlantic Quarterly* 54 (January 1955): 82–94.

Hotson, C. P. "A Background for Emerson's Poem 'Grace.'" *New England Quarterly* 1 (April 1928): 124–132.

Kane, T. Paul. "The Stairway of Surprise: Form and Power in Emerson's Poetry." PhD diss., Yale University, 1990.

McEuen, Kathryn Anderson. "Emerson's Rhymes." *American Literature* 20 (March 1948): 31–42.

Miller, Norman. "Emerson's 'Each and All' Concept: A Reexamination." *New England Quarterly* 41 (September 1968): 381–392. Reprinted in *Critical Essays on Ralph Waldo Emerson,* edited by Robert E. Burkholder and Joel Myerson, pp. 346–354. Boston: G. K. Hall, 1983.

Morris, Saundra. "Whim upon the Lintel: Emerson's Poetry and a Politically Ethical Aesthetic." *Nineteenth-Century Prose* 40.2 (2014): 189–216.

Oliver, Egbert S. "Emerson's 'Days.'" *New England Quarterly* 19 (December 1946): 518–524.

Scheick, William J. "Emerson the Poet: A Twenty-Year Retrospective." *American Poetry* 1 (Spring 1984): 2–19.

Shea, Daniel B. "Emerson and the American Metamorphosis." In *Emerson: Prophecy, Metamorphosis and Influence,* edited by David Levin, pp. 29–56. New York: Columbia University Press, 1975.

Strauch, Carl F. "The Background and Meaning of the 'Ode Inscribed to W. H. Channing.'" *Emerson Society Quarterly* 42 (1st Quarter 1966): 4–14.

———. "Emerson and the Doctrine of Sympathy." *Studies in Romanticism* 6 (Spring 1967): 152–174. Reprinted in *Critical Essays on Ralph Waldo Emerson,* edited by Robert E. Burkholder and Joel Myerson, pp. 326–345. Boston: G. K. Hall, 1983.

———. "Hatred's Swift Repulsions." *Studies in Romanticism* 7 (Winter 1968): 65–103.

———. "The Mind's Voice: Emerson's Poetic Styles." *Emerson Society Quarterly* 60 (Summer 1970): 43–59.

Thomas, Joseph M. "Harnessing Proteus: Publishing the Canon of Emerson's Poetry." PhD diss., Rutgers University, 1994.

———. "Late Emerson: *Selected Poems* and the 'Emerson Factory.'" *ELH* 65 (1998): 971–994.

———. "Poverty and Power: Revisiting Emerson's Poetics." In *Emerson: Bicentennial Essays,* edited by Ronald A. Bosco and Joel Myerson, pp. 213–246. Boston: Massachusetts Historical Society, 2006.

———. "'The Property of My Own Book': Emerson and the Literary Marketplace." *New England Quarterly* 69 (September 1996): 406–425.

Van Anglen, Kevin. "Emerson, Milton, and the Fall of Uriel." *ESQ: A Journal of the American Renaissance* 30 (1984): 139–154.

von Frank, Albert J. "Emerson's Boyhood and Collegiate Verse: Unpublished and New Texts Edited from Manuscript." In *Studies in the American Renaissance, 1983,* edited by Joel Myerson, pp. 1–56. Charlottesville: University Press of Virginia, 1983.

Waggoner, Hyatt H. *American Poets from the Puritans to the Present.* Boston: Houghton, Mifflin, 1968.

Whitaker, Thomas. "The Riddle of Emerson's Sphinx." *American Literature* 27 (1955): 179–195.

Wright, Conrad. "Emerson, Barzillai Frost, and the Divinity School Address." *Harvard Theological Review* 49 (January 1956): 19–43.

Yoder, R. A. "Emerson's Dialectic." *Criticism* 11 (Fall 1969): 313–328. Reprinted in *Critical Essays on Ralph Waldo Emerson,* edited by Robert E. Burkholder and Joel Myerson, pp. 354–367. Boston: G. K. Hall, 1983.

Yohannan, J. D. "Emerson's Translations of Persian Poetry from German Sources." *American Literature* 14 (January 1943): 405–420.

———. "The Influence of Persian Poetry on Emerson's Work." *American Literature* 15 (March 1943): 25–41.

ACKNOWLEDGMENTS

Since the present volume is so much the stepchild of volume IX in the Harvard University Press edition of *The Collected Works of Ralph Waldo Emerson* (the 2011 Variorum *Poems*), I find I have the same friends and scholars to thank now as I did then. Principal among these is Thomas Wortham, at whose invitation I joined the edition and who labored with me to establish the texts. His many indispensable contributions, going back several decades, included locating and transcribing all of Emerson's loose poetry manuscripts, scattered as they had been among libraries in this country and abroad—a task that also made possible the editing of Emerson's *Poetry Notebooks* (1986). It was a privilege to have worked as coeditor on that project—my first major foray into editing—and to have learned so much in the course of it from Ralph Harry Orth, the veteran editor-in-chief of the *Journals and Miscellaneous Notebooks*. Harry (aka "the Chief") made it his mission to mentor a new generation of Emerson editors, and Ronald A. Bosco and I are among those with reason to acknowledge his help and good influence. In fact, Professor Orth, now deep into his Vermont retirement, remains a friend, as evidenced by his willingness to read through this current work with his still-sharp editor's eye, simply because I asked him to. As is his wont, he caught some errors; those that escaped his notice (there can't be many) must be charged to my account.

As the last general editor of the *Collected Works,* Ronald Bosco provided much support and encouragement over the several years of our preparation of volume IX and was a strong advocate of the plan to bring out selected editions of Emerson's prose and poetry in twin volumes for students and general readers. We are grateful to Harvard University Press, which sustained the *Collected Works* edition over many years, for taking this last, important step in making their definitive scholarly editions available in this way to serve the interests of a larger public. We are grateful to the Press as well for permission to quote from their editions of *The Collected Works of Ralph Waldo Emerson, The Journals and Miscellaneous Notebooks of Ralph Waldo Emerson,* and *One First Love,* edited by Edith W. Gregg.

Thanks, too, to the Ralph Waldo Emerson Memorial Association for permission to quote from copyrighted materials in *The Poetry Notebooks of Ralph Waldo Emerson,* and also for its permission to publish in the Appendix to the present volume two manuscript verse fragments, "Where art thou" (MS Am 1280.235[39]) and "What avails it me" (MS Am 1280.235[91]), Ralph Waldo Emerson Memorial Association deposit, Houghton Library, Harvard University.

Apart from these very specific occasions for gratitude and acknowledgment, I would like to express my sense of indebtedness to the wider circle of Emerson scholars, whose geniality and helpfulness were, over the course of a career, a perpetual refreshment and, as it seemed, a sustained and sustaining endorsement of our common subject. In this regard I would mention most especially Joel Myerson, Len Gougeon, Phyllis Cole, Wes Mott, David Robinson, Saundra Morris, Larry Buell, Sue Dunston, David W. Hill, Joe Thomas, Douglas Emory Wilson, and Barbara Packer. It is also a pleasure to find that new names continue to add themselves to this list, including, most recently, Mark Scott, a lively reader of Emerson's poetry and a poet himself.

CREDITS

Emerson poetry presented in this volume is collected and reprinted from the following sources by kind permission of the publishers and organizations.

THE COLLECTED WORKS OF RALPH WALDO EMERSON, VOLUME IX: THE POEMS, A VARIORUM EDITION, Historical Introduction, Textual Introduction, and Poem Headnotes by Albert J. von Frank; Text Established by Albert J. von Frank and Thomas Wortham, Cambridge, Mass.: The Belknap Press of Harvard University Press. Copyright © 2011 by the President and Fellows of Harvard College.

From Poems (1847)
From May-Day and Other Pieces (1867)
From Selected Poems (1876)
Uncollected Poems
Appendix: The Ellen Poems, 1828–1831
    IV. To Eva, 1829
    X. To Ellen, at the South, April 1830
    XI. Thine Eyes Still Shined, April 1830

EMERSON FAMILY PAPERS
Houghton Library, Harvard College Library, Harvard University

Appendix: The Ellen Poems, 1828–1831
    XXIII. Where art thou, 1831; *MH MS Am* 1280.235(39)
    XXV. What avails it me, December 1831; *MH MS Am* 1280.235(91)

THE JOURNALS AND MISCELLANEOUS NOTEBOOKS OF RALPH WALDO EMERSON, VOLUME II: 1822–1826, edited by William H. Gilman, Alfred R. Ferguson, and Merrell R. Davis, Cambridge, Mass.: The Belknap Press of Harvard University Press. Copyright © 1961 by the President and Fellows of Harvard College. Copyright © renewed 1989 by Margaret Reilly Gilman.

Appendix: The Ellen Poems, 1828–1831
    XII. *And though he dearly prized the bards of fame,* ca. April–May 1830;
        p. 345; *PN,* p. 61

INDEX OF TITLES
AND FIRST LINES